CORNERSTONES OF DECISION MAKING

Profiles of Enterprise ABM

Steve Player and Carol Cobble

This publication is designed to provide accurate and authoritative information in regard to the subject matter covered. It is sold with the understanding that the publisher is not engaged in rendering legal, accounting, or other professional service. If legal advice or other expert assistance is required, the services of a competent professional person should be sought. *From a Declaration of Principles jointly adopted by a committee of the American Bar Association and a committee of Publishers.*

10 9 8 7 6 5 4 3 2 1

Library of Congress Cataloging in Publication Data

Player, Steve, 1958–
    Cornerstones of decision making: profiles of enterprise ABM / Steve
    Player and Carol Cobble
        p. cm.
    Includes bibliographical references and index.
    ISBN 1-886939-29-2
    1. Activity-based costing. 2. Decision making. I. Cobble, Carol,
1958–   . II. Title.
HF5626.C6   1998
658.4'03--dc21   98-40951
                                                    CIP

Oakhill Press
3400 Willow Grove Court
Greensboro, NC 27410-8600
Printed in the United States of America

Dedication

We dedicate this book to our parents Bobby and Violet Player
and Bill and Betty Cobble. Any success we have achieved lies
in the foundation that they so generously provided for us.
They set the cornerstones that have guided our way.

Table of Contents

Part I

Part II

Case Studies

Part III

Appendices

Foreword

Since joining the American Productivity & Quality Center (APQC) in 1978, I have seen thousands of organizations improve dramatically. The variety of approaches for achieving improvement has been equally amazing. Many have worked while others have failed.

We at the APQC have been fortunate to have helped create many of the more lasting improvement efforts. These include founding the Malcolm Baldrige National Quality Award, which was first awarded in 1987.

In 1988, the APQC produced the first public training course for the new field of activity-based costing (ABC). The focus was directed toward:

- Implementing activity-based costing (ABC) in eight steps; and
- Establishing performance measurement systems that worked with total quality management (TQM).

In 1992, the APQC again took the forefront by creating the International Benchmarking Clearinghouse (IBC) as a resource for organizations that use benchmarking as a tool for breakthrough improvements. Today, more than 500 leading organizations from around the globe have joined and use the IBC.

IBC's ABM and benchmarking efforts converged in 1995 with the launch of a landmark study on the best practices for ABM. In collaboration with its research partner, the Consortium for Advanced Manufacturing—International, which includes both Arthur Andersen and Armstrong Laing, IBC has produced the most comprehensive work ever undertaken to evaluate the emerging field of ABM.

In 1997, Phase 2 of the ABM Best Practices Study was conducted in conjunction with Arthur Andersen. Phase 2 focused more deeply on three aspects of ABM systems–transfer of ownership, systems development, and reporting. A Phase 3 Study has recently been launched to examine how ABM supports revenue enhancement, activity-based budgeting, and measuring the results and benefits of an ABM system.

When ABM was first introduced, many people thought that it was a passing fancy that would not last. Yet the last ten years have seen the use of ABM grow and expand. Results from the Phase 2 Best Practices Study show that organizations of various kinds are implementing ABM in record numbers, and that they are moving much more aggressively toward enterprise-wide implementations. Over 40 percent of the best practices companies selected for Phase 2 site visits have implemented ABM enterprise-wide. By 1990, an estimated 110 ABM implementations were under way. By 1997, this number had skyrocketed to over 15,000 implementations.

Other key findings from the Phase 2 Study show that the trend among best practice companies also extends to other companies that use ABM. Organizations are beginning to aggressively replace traditional cost systems with activity-based systems. Pilot efforts are required less frequently, but when they are, the scope of the effort is usually much wider.

As the case studies chosen for this book show, ABM has spread from the back room to the boardroom. It is being used to improve companies around the globe. This book is a landmark work documenting how companies are implementing enterprise-wide ABM worldwide.

The APQC is very pleased to have been closely involved in the early beginnings of ABM. We also look forward to continuing to assist with research about ABM and in educating management and companies as a whole about ABM as we move into the 21st century.

Carla O'Dell
President
APQC

Acknowledgements

The authors would like to thank the clients of Armstrong Laing and Arthur Andersen who have permitted us to learn with them in their quest to implement enterprise-wide ABM. Their willingness to share ideas, tools, techniques, and experiences has greatly accelerated the learning process for us all.

In particular, we wish to thank the case study companies and the people who helped us in preparing their stories. These include:

American Seating: Thomas Bush

AscoForge Safe: Daniel Souloumiac

Blue Cross Blue Shield of North Carolina: Jim Emmons and John Friesen

Central and South West Corporation: Bryan Kaiser, Larry Connors, and Glenn Rosilier

CinCFleet: Mark Harrison and Brian Brader

Dana Commercial Credit Corporation: Brad Gillespie, Jim Beckham, Gerry Fuller, and Stan Rubini

DHL: Martin Holton and Joeri Weyenbergh

GTE Supply: Don Miller, Warren Rappleye, and Jenny Xu

John Deere Health Care, Inc.: Keith Wilson, Chuck Parsons, Craig Strajer, and Ross Lund

Portugal Telecom: Manuel Palma

Shiloh Industries, Inc.: Thom Weber

The Mutual Group: Andrew Beacom

Transco: Ian Brown, Mark McGill, Richard Cribb, Kanthi Ford, and Mike Walpole

Warner Lambert, S.A.: Wayne Elsom

We gratefully acknowledge the assistance and input of the Consortium for Advanced Manufacturing—International's (CAM-I) Cost Management System Program; in particular the Enterprise-wide ABM Interest Group; Tom Freeman, Program Manager of CAM-I; and Pete Zampino. We also wish to acknowledge the assistance and input of the American Productivity & Quality Center (APQC), in particular Laura DeVries, Lisa Higgins and Carla O'Dell.

We would also like to thank our colleagues around the globe who have generously given of their time, their experience, and their expertise to the completion of this book. As authors, our main function is to report their many achievements.

We would like to especially thank Tony Braniff, COO of Armstrong Laing Group-Americas, and Chuck Ketteman, Managing Partner of Arthur Andersen's Worldwide Business Consulting Practice. Without their continued leadership and support this project would not have been possible.

We also appreciate the contributions of Allen Brewer, Frederic Laluyaux, Grace Martin, Debby Robic, Mike Sherratt, Ellen Valentine, and Megan Wardlaw, from Armstrong Laing, and the contributions of Margarida Bajanco, Michelle Behrenwald, Nuno Belo, Jay Collins, Marieta Gundova, Randolf Holst, Rene Kiehn, Matt Kolb, Isabelle Lacombe, Chuck Marx, Marilyn Mayes, Mitch Max, Mamie Rogers, Paulo Salgado, and Scott Smith from Arthur Andersen.

In addition, we appreciate Paula Gould and Ed Helvey of Oakhill Press for their flexibility and persistence in helping us achieve our publishing deadlines. Also, Craig Hines of Pegasus, our designer, whose drive, dedication, and superior design skills turned our manuscript into this final product.

Thanks to Barry Brinker, our editor, for his diligent editing efforts and to Robin Baumgartner for her ongoing logistical support which helped to sustain us throughout the project.

Special thanks goes to Paige Dawson for coordinating the publication, expediting the text, and many other tasks too numerous to mention. Without her continued assistance and support this book might never have been completed.

Finally, we are especially grateful to those friends and family members whose support and encouragement kept us going. These special thanks go to Lydia, Dave, Emily, and Cole Player, Becky Carlisle, Bill Cobble, and Jeannie King.

Part I

1

Introduction

Do you have "solid information that empowers you to exercise leadership and wisdom in decision making?" That is what best-selling author Stephen R. Covey states activity-based management (ABM) can do for you. Covey states, "ABM gives you the operational guts to meet the leadership challenge and to see and seize your opportunities."[1]

Would you like a second opinion? Consider the advice of preeminent management authority Peter F. Drucker:

> Questions can only be answered by analyzing the activities that are needed to attain objectives. If your objective is operational cost reductions, the only truly effective way to cut costs is to cut out activities altogether. There is little point in trying to do cheaply what should not be done at all.[2]

Or, if your objective is to grow strategically, consider the advice of strategy guru Michael Porter, who says, "activities are the atoms of strategic advantage."[3]

The quotations from acknowledged thought leaders—Covey, Drucker, and Porter—help explain why ABM is becoming one of the most powerful weapons available in today's management arsenal. The purpose of this book, *Cornerstones of Decision Making: Profiles of Enterprise ABM,* is to help you understand how organizations are now using ABM throughout their operations to dramatically improve their results.

This book goes beyond initial pilots and simple one-time analyses to show you how ABM can be used throughout an enterprise. Case studies from around the globe illustrate a wide variety of uses and implementation techniques. This book also presents the news from the front lines of ABM implementation

1. Steve Player and David Keys, *Activity-Based Management: Arthur Andersen's Lessons from the ABM Battlefield.* Foreword by Stephen R. Covey. New York: MasterMedia Ltd., 1995. Page xi
2. Peter F. Drucker, *The Practice of Management.* New York: Harper Business, 1954.
3. Michael Porter, "Linking Strategy to Activities." Conference speech. Cost Management Conference. October 1997.

teams—their victories and their setbacks. It includes development time lines, difficulties encountered, and lessons learned along the way.

As Covey states, "ABM is not just mere theory. It points with laser clarity to the practical."[4] To that end, this book seeks to provide a firm foundation for you to begin building your own enterprise-wide ABM solutions.

How Companies Use ABM

In preparing this book, we interviewed many companies to serve as case studies. In doing so, we quickly found that organizations implementing enterprise-wide ABM have done so for various business reasons. This confirmed the findings of research performed by the Enterprise-wide ABM Interest Group of the Consortium for Advanced Manufacturing-International (CAM-I). This research group identified over 30 different applications of activity-based information. Those uses, as well as the view of cost they support, are as follows:

Exhibit 1: Uses of Activity-Based Information[5]

Uses of Activity-Based Information	View of Cost
S=Strategic O=Operational F=Financial	
Profitability/Pricing	
Product/service profitability analysis	S
Distribution channel profitability analysis	S
Customer profitability analysis	S
Market segment profitability analysis	S
Product mix rationalization	S
Estimating or bidding on customer work	S
Supporting intercompany chargeouts on shared services	S
Pricing products	S
Process Improvement	
Business process modeling	O
Supporting total quality initiatives	O
Supporting, focusing, or quantifying improvement initiatives	O
Moving or replicating operations	O
Defining accountability or responsibility for activities	O/S
Cost Analysis	
Target costing	S
Operational cost reduction	O

---

4. Player and Keys. *Activity-Based Management: Arthur Andersen's Lessons from the ABM Battlefield.* Page xi.

5. Adapted from John Miller's *Implementing Activity-Based Management in Daily Operations* (New York: John Wiley & Sons, 1996) and expanded by the CAM-I Enterprise-wide ABM Interest Group.

Strategic cost reduction	S
Understanding cost drivers	O
Life cycle costing	S
Evaluating outsourcing	S
Cost driver analysis	O
Inventory valuation	F
Budgeting	
Activity-based budgeting	S
Capital justification	S
Attribute Analysis	
Core, sustaining, and discretionary attributes	O
Four-quadrant analysis (important/urgent/not)	O
Value-added (non-value-added) analysis	O
Cost of quality	O
Time variability analysis (fixed vs. variable, input batch)	O
Primary vs. secondary activity analysis	O
Mission-critical analysis	O
Strategic Decisions	
Strategic planning	S
Strategy deployment	S
Consolidating operations analysis	S
Coordinating new product introductions	S
Acquisition analysis	S
Growing revenues	S
Benchmarking	
Internal benchmarking	S
External benchmarking	S
Process-based costing	S
Activity-based performance measurement	S
Operations Analysis	
What-if analysis	O/S
Project management	O
Capacity management	O/S
Constraint analysis	O

These many applications illustrate the multiple decisions ABM can support. This variety can be achieved because ABM is anchored in a fundamental understanding of the work performed in an enterprise. As the next chapter on the history of ABM points out, Peter Drucker was advocating this approach as early as 1954 in his classic book, *The Practice of Management.*[6]

---

6. Drucker, *The Practice of Management.*

Enabling Technology

The rapid growth of ABM is a result of cost-efficient enabling technology that lets today's manager analyze activities rapidly and repeatedly. As the case studies show, technology has advanced to the point that we can now apply ABM across an entire enterprise and literally around the globe.

Just as ABM can be used for many purposes, various methods and approaches have been developed as companies seek to achieve their objectives. While there are certain core steps to implementing any ABM system, we have found that an organization's approach to implementing ABM often depends on the company's culture, its organizational structure, and sometimes even the perceptions of its employees.

We have termed ABM the "cornerstones of decision making" because ABM provides a fundamental understanding of work and supports a variety of decision making applications. Any cornerstone must provide a solid base on which to build. ABM provides that base through an understanding of activities. Cornerstones set the direction and shape of the structure they anchor. Similarly, the ABM application chosen sets the direction and shape of both the information and analysis needed to support decision making.

As the case studies illustrate, enterprise-wide ABM can be used to achieve dramatic results, such as improving customer profitability, reducing costs, understanding the effects of deregulation, and establishing shared services operations. They also highlight multiple ways to achieve these results. First, however, it is helpful to examine the definition of enterprise-wide ABM and to review some of the background sources for this book.

Enterprise-wide ABM Defined

What does "enterprise-wide ABM" really mean? Enterprise-wide ABM is simply a management information system that uses activity-based information to facilitate decision making across the organization. This simple definition can be better understood by examining its four key elements.

1. *A management information system.* The first element of the definition is ABM as a "management information system." As this implies, ABM is more than a tool: It is part of an ongoing process. Enterprise-wide ABM is used to control and direct operations. It is an active agent used to aid in reaching management's desired outcomes.

2. *Activity-based information.* The second element of the definition is that an ABM system "uses activity-based information." This is a central issue, because activities are the focal point. By examining activities, managers can determine the work that is performed and also the value of that work. While

there are many ways to improve cost information, a focus on activities is the distinguishing factor of an enterprise-wide ABM system.

3. *Facilitating decision making.* Enterprise-wide ABM also "facilitates decision making." This part of the definition emphasizes an orientation toward action. Enterprise-wide ABM is more than a mere recording of activities or presentation of financial results by activity. The focus is constantly on solving key business issues, whether they are strategic or operational in nature. To achieve success, an ABM system must facilitate decision making by the appropriate levels of management.

4. *Across the organization.* ABM works "across the organization." An enterprise-wide ABM system crosses multiple geographic locations, functions within a company, and applications of the information. As a result, the implementation of enterprise-wide ABM typically requires multiple implementations. However, each company's structure comes into play. Depending on the size of the organization and the business reasons behind the analysis, implementation of an ABM system might require a single model covering the entire organization, or it might require more than one hundred models (as in one of our cases).

Providing information across the enterprise is the key source of the power of enterprise-wide ABM systems. ABM can be used to explain cause-and-effect relationships, to benchmark different components of the organization, to analyze the supply chain, to feed performance measurement systems, and to determine overall profitability. These important uses of ABM have prompted many companies to expand their ABM efforts.

Research

Research for this book derives from the following four primary sources:

1. Actual customer enterprise-wide ABM implementations that the authors have assisted.
2. The collaborative efforts and insights from clients and colleagues at Arthur Andersen and Armstrong Laing.
3. ABM best practices studies jointly produced by the American Productivity & Quality Center (APQC), CAM-I and Arthur Andersen.
4. Collaborative research by CAM-I's Enterprise-wide ABM Interest Group, of which the authors are founding members.

Lessons Learned

The key value of this book to you will be the lessons you learn that may help make your enterprise-wide ABM implementation successful. To that end, we have tried to highlight the lessons learned from each case study while also integrating the insights obtained from the ABM Best Practice Studies and the CAM-I Enterprise-wide ABM Interest Group, which are further described below.

Using a series of ABM Best Practices Studies, Arthur Andersen has tracked developments in cost management. The first study began in September 1994 and was sponsored by the APQC and CAM-I. The study team (led by John Miller) identified over 750 ABM implementation sites. The team sent each site a mail survey asking a series of questions designed to identify best practices; 168 responses were received from this mailing. Based on the responses, 40 companies were identified as having some best practices. Site visits were conducted at 15 of these companies to learn more about their practices. In April 1995, the results of this study were published.[7] The Phase 1 Study provides an overall understanding of the status of ABM implementations.

Following the study, Miller worked with his colleagues at Arthur Andersen to identify 52 best practice criteria that provide a comprehensive basis for evaluating ABM efforts. This work has been developed into an "ABM Competency Continuum," which is used as a scorecard to track the progress of an ABM implementation.

In October 1996, the APQC and Arthur Andersen began a second ABM Best Practices Study. While the Phase 1 Study was a broad examination across multiple sites, the Phase 2 Study analyzed the following three issues in depth:

- Transfer of ownership;
- Systems development; and
- Reporting.

The Phase 2 Study also relied on a mail survey covering 400 companies, from which 160 responses were received. The Phase 2 Study was completed in April 1997. A key finding of the Phase 2 Study was the continued expansion of uses for ABM information, as noted in Exhibit 2.

This research is continuing. A Phase 3 Study, which was launched in August 1998, also focuses on a deep analysis of three specific issues. These are as follows:

- Using ABM to grow revenues;
- Activity-based budgeting; and
- Measuring the value and benefit of ABM systems.

In addition to best practices research, CAM-I has been a leading force in ABM

---

7. John A. Miller, ed., *ABM Best Practices Phase 1 Final Report.* Houston, Texas: APQC/CAM-I, 1995.

Exhibit 2: Uses of ABM Information

Application	Not Used	Somewhat	Moderately	Generally	Extensively
Product Costing	24	32	19	38	45
Target Costing	67	30	23	22	13
Make vs. Buy Analysis	52	37	30	28	10
Cost Estimation	23	28	43	35	28
Pricing Models	52	28	27	29	20
Product Profitability Analysis	35	26	23	33	40
Service Profitability Analysis	74	24	16	20	16
Customer Profitability Analysis	65	30	14	20	24
Process Improvement	25	41	35	41	16
Cost Control	18	48	40	32	19
Business Process Reengineering	47	47	31	21	11
Performance Measurement	35	40	32	32	18
Benchmarking	51	47	27	24	7
Budgeting	50	38	18	26	25
Supply Chain Analysis	102	22	15	10	6
Inventory Valuation	92	9	10	13	31

Source: Survey of Best Practices. ABM Phase 2 Final Report. Houston: APQC/Arthur Andersen, January 1998.

research since 1986. The CAM-I Enterprise-wide ABM Interest Group was founded in 1996 as part of CAM-I's Cost Management System program. The ABM Enterprise-wide Interest Group meets quarterly to examine advanced ABM implementations, to review the latest writings on ABM, and to develop leading-edge techniques for implementations.

This book discusses how companies have used ABM to provide an overview of what has been done and how you can use it in your organization. While the paths taken in implementing enterprise-wide ABM may sometimes curve and shift, this is a natural evolution to enterprise-wide ABM. This book will share the learning and education to date of many implementation teams and their management.

In some cases, implementation teams hit dead ends. Yet, rather than quit, these teams changed direction and ultimately succeeded. Their courage reminds us that an occasional stumble or fall can be overcome—if you have the courage to get up, dust yourself off, and continue. Their conviction provides an inspiration for all.

Organization of the Book

The remainder of this introductory section covers two key topics—history and reporting. Chapter 2 provides an overview of the history of ABM as well as the migration from stand-alone pilots to enterprise-wide ABM systems. The history overview should help in understanding the classical thinking that forms the foundation for ABM. It also helps explain why so many great ideas are only now coming into practical application and widespread use.

The discussion of the migration from stand-alone pilots to enterprise-wide illustrates four key trends of this evolution as well as key enablers facilitating these changes. In terms of software, Armstrong Laing is a leader in providing systems enhancements with the enabling functionality and architecture companies need for global, enterprise-wide ABM implementations.

The theme of different uses for ABM is carried forward in Chapter 3, which examines ten techniques for reporting ABM information. Ultimately, the key to any cost system lies in the decisions it facilitates. These reports illustrate the new insights ABM enables and the value it helps managers create.

Section Two provides the real-life stories of 14 enterprise-wide ABM implementations. Each case study begins with company-specific business issues and background information. The case then follows the path taken by the implementers. The fact that these paths often turn out to be winding roads helps to clarify what it takes to be successful with enterprise-wide ABM. The stories describe the setbacks and pitfalls, and more importantly how they were overcome. The cases provide project timelines, project team overviews, results, future plans, and lessons learned. Along the way, exhibits provide examples of the output at each company.

The case studies for this book were selected to provide insight on real-world, enterprise-wide ABM implementations. These cases cover a variety of industries, company sizes, ABM applications, and geographical locations.

The case studies (organized alphabetically) by chapter are as follows:

Chapter	Organization	Industry
4	American Seating	Manufacturing
5	AscoForge Safe	Manufacturing
6	Blue Cross Blue Shield of North Carolina	Insurance
7	Central and South West Corporation	Utilities
8	CinCFleet	Government
9	Dana Commercial Credit Corporation	Leasing
10	DHL	Transportation
11	GTE Supply	Distribution
12	John Deere Health Care, Inc.	Health Care
13	Portugal Telecom	Telecom

These case studies profile companies located in South Africa, the United Kingdom, Portugal, Belgium, France, Canada, and the United States. Many of the companies operate globally. The cases show how successful companies integrate ABM into virtually all decision making.

The final section recaps the emerging trends and key enablers. In addition, it provides linkages between these critical success factors and the case studies profiled earlier in the text.

Finally, the Appendices include several tools for implementation, including a Glossary of Terms, which should help readers understand the principles of ABM. Other tools provided in the appendices include a universal process classification scheme, a sample activity dictionary, a sample activity effort worksheet, and a sample work plan.

2
History of Activity-Based Management and the Evolution Toward Enterprise ABM

Today's trade and professional journals are peppered with stories and case studies about companies that have used activity-based approaches to improve operations, reduce costs, and increase profitability. So much recent publicity probably makes some people view activity-based management (ABM) as just the latest management trend, but its roots run much deeper.

This chapter reviews the history of activity-based costing (ABC) and ABM. It examines the roots of ABM and what has changed to dramatically expand ABM's usage in the 1990s. The chapter also traces the evolution of ABM from stand-alone single models to today's enterprise-wide systems.

How Long Has Activity-Based Costing Existed?

Many people first became aware of ABM in the late 1980s or early 1990s, so they believe ABM is only about ten years old. It is easy to understand their perception—the late 1980s was an anxious time for management accountants.

The landmark book in management accounting in the mid-1980s was *Relevance Lost: The Rise and Fall of Management Accounting,* by H. Thomas Johnson and Robert S. Kaplan.[1] Released in March 1987, *Relevance Lost* clearly articulated the problems with traditional management accounting.

According to Johnson and Kaplan, virtually all management accounting practices in use in the mid-1980s had been developed by around 1925. Even though manufacturing processes had become far more complex and despite the proliferation and diversity of products since the 1920s, management accounting stayed basically the same.

---

1. H. Thomas Johnson and Robert S. Kaplan, *Relevance Lost: The Rise and Fall of Management Accounting* (Boston: Harvard Business School Press, 1987).

Johnson and Kaplan provide an excellent historical perspective on how management accounting had failed to keep pace with business. They advocated that, as management accountants, "we need only understand and adopt the 'cost of transactions' philosophy" that was articulated in the article "The Hidden Factory" by Jeffery G. Miller and Thomas E. Vollmann, which appeared in *Harvard Business Review* (September–October 1985).[2]

But accountants were not the only ones calling for change. Two of the world's leading authorities on productivity—C. Jackson Grayson, Jr. and Carla O'Dell—clearly articulated the problems in their 1988 book *American Business: A Two-Minute Warning:*

> Most financial and cost accounting systems were designed for an earlier era of labor-intensive manufacturing and cannot handle today's decisions regarding capital-intensive flexible manufacturing systems, the greater emphasis on human capital, and the rise of the service sector.

> Trying to make twentieth-century decisions based on eighteenth-century accounting principles is like driving a car with the emergency brake on; you can do it, but there is a lot of smoke and screeching.[3]

While books and articles like these appeared in rapid succession, many significant developments were occurring in the field. The environment for Western (particularly U.S.) business had become highly competitive. Japanese companies, by emphasizing quality and taking a longer-term perspective, were rapidly taking market share. This global threat required strategic investments and a rapid response to changing markets, yet existing accounting systems failed to provide clear pictures of what actions to take.

The broad business community gave widespread recognition of these issues with the publishing of a *Business Week* special issue "The Productivity Paradox" on June 6, 1988. While these and similar articles are often cited as the beginning of ABM, its roots run much deeper.

Early Beginnings

Using numbers to help understand and manage a business has always been the heart of accounting. As Arthur E. Andersen, the founder of the firm that bears his name, said back in 1913:

> Tradition says figures do not lie. Yet, the wrong interpretation of figures may throw the head of the business completely off the track.

---

2. *Ibid,* Chapter 10, page 238.
3. C. Jackson Grayson, Jr., and Carla O'Dell, *American Business: A Two-Minute Warning* (New York: The Free Press, 1988).

Groups of facts must be considered with relation to the right groups of corresponding facts. Both sides of the question must be considered in the tabulated statistics.[4]

Andersen challenged management not only to understand the figures, but also to understand what is *behind the figures.*

While the terminology for ABM developed fairly recently, similar practices have been around for decades. Frederick Taylor recommended breaking down workers' jobs into a set of tasks with standardized times. These tabulated tasks and related times could then be studied to measure costs. By grouping the times needed to perform job tasks and comparing them to the corresponding standards, Taylor found that he could measure and optimize efficiency. In 1903, Taylor presented his conclusions in his famous paper "Shop Management," which marked the beginning of the scientific management movement.[5]

In 1917, H.L. Gantt developed his famous "Gantt Chart," which is a simple graph that measures the activities and tasks that must be performed to achieve a project objective. These charts show expected timelines, projected schedules, and current status. Gantt, who worked directly under Taylor, also devised a task-level wage and bonus system to motivate workers to perform individual activities efficiently.[6]

In the 1920s, Lillian and Frank Gilbreth developed the field of micro-motion study, which divided work into its most fundamental elements. Statistics could then be tabulated for the repetitive steps in a process. These detailed analyses led to simplifying work steps to achieve maximum efficiency while also minimizing the strain on workers.

Adoption of and support for these innovations was mixed. Workers sometimes feared these innovations were merely tools management could use to reduce their wages. Worker organizations lobbied for and helped pass legislation that blocked the use of time studies, though this legislation was later repealed.

During the first 50 years of this century, the global economy changed dramatically—from World War I, the roaring stock market in the 1920s, the crash of 1929 and the Great Depression, and World War II. Modernization brought by World War II was followed by a tremendous post-war expansion. All of these events led up to the writings of perhaps the most influential advocate of activity-based analysis—Peter Drucker.

---

4. Arthur E. Andersen, "Behind the Figures," *System, The Magazine of Business* January 1913. pp. 1–13.
5. Frederick Taylor, *Shop Management* (1903). Out of print.
6. H.L. Gantt, "The Relation Between Production and Costs," Proceeding of the Spring Meeting of the American Society of Mechanical Engineers, June 1915.

In 1954, Peter Drucker wrote his classic book, *The Practice of Management.* In defining the type of structure needed to attain an organization's objectives, Drucker noted the need for activity analysis, decision analysis, and relations analysis:

> To find out what activities are needed to attain the objectives of the business is such an obvious thing to do that it would hardly seem to deserve special mention. But analyzing the activities is as good as unknown to traditional theory. Questions can only be answered by analyzing the activities that are needed to attain objectives.[7]

In more recent years, Drucker continues to advocate an activity-based view of business:

- "Activity-based costing integrates what were once several activities— value analysis, process analysis, quality management and costing;" and
- "If U.S. automakers had used ABC, they would have realized the futility of their competitive blitzes."[8]

The next two decades saw sporadic efforts to use activity-based analysis. The efforts of General Electric in the mid-1960s are reviewed by H. Thomas Johnson in his book *Relevance Regained,* which identifies GE's efforts as the first significant example of the effective use of ABC or ABM in an industrial setting.[9]

Other authors described activity-based approaches in answering questions such as "What do things cost?" Michael Schiff described how to apply activity analysis in the sales and marketing function.[10] In 1971, George Starbus proposed to integrate activity analysis within a transactional accounting model in his book *Activity Analysis and Input-Output Accounting.*[11]

The distribution industry advocated an activity-based approach in 1981 with the publication of *Improving Productivity and Profits in Wholesale Distribution: The Magnifying Glass Technique,* a book written by Arthur Andersen partners Robert J. Grottke and James W. Norris.[12] This book reported the results of a joint research effort by Arthur Andersen and the National Associ-

---

7. Peter Drucker, *The Practice of Management* (New York: Harper & Row Publishers, 1954).

8. Peter Drucker, "The Information Managers Need," Keynote address of the CMC2000 Conference, San Diego, November 1996. (Available through Global Business Research.)

9. H. Thomas Johnson, *Relevance Regained* (New York: The Free Press, 1992). pp. 132–141.

10. For more insight, see *Behavioral Aspects of Accounting* by Michael Schiff, published in 1974.

11. George Starbus, *Activity Analysis and Input-Output Accounting* (New York: Richard D. Irwin, 1971).

12. Robert J. Grottke and James W. Norris, *Improving Productivity and Profits in Wholesale Distribution: The Magnifying Glass Technique* (Washington, DC: National Association of Wholesale Distribution, 1981).

Exhibit 1: Activity Costing Worksheet

NAME: Tim Gallagher
TITLE: Warehouse Supervisor
COMPONENT: Whse #1—Shift 2
TOTAL PEOPLE: 22

ACTIVITY		Component Personnel—% Effort							Component Personnel—$ effort							
NO.	TITLE	Tim Gallagher Supervisor	Georgia Montgomery Assistant	Pickers (12)	Over-the-Counter Pickers (2)	Loaders (3)	Forklift Drivers & Helpers (2)	Clerk	T. Gallagher Supervisor	G. Montgomery Assistant	Pickers (12)	Over-the-Counter Pickers (2)	Loaders (3)	Forklift Drivers & Helpers (2)	Clerk	Total
3.1	SCHDLE. WHSE LABOR FORCE	6	8						2,000	2,400						4,400
3.2	BREAKDOWN & SORT PICKSHEETS			5							15,900					15,900
3.3	ORDER PICKING COORDINATION	26	28	7					8,800	8,400	22,300					39,500
3.4	ORDER PICKING PLUMBING		4	17			16			1,200	54,200			35,300		90,700
3.5	ORDER PICKING ELECT			13			11				41,400			24,200		65,600
3.6	ORDER PICKING H.V.A.C.			3			3				9,400			6,400		15,800
3.7	ORDER PICKING—TRANS. TO ROCKFORD			19			16				60,800			35,300		96,100
	TOTAL EFFORT	100%	100%	100%	100%	100%	100%	100%	34,000	30,000	338,000	54,500	103,500	229,000	16,000	776,300

Source: Improving Productivity and Profits in Wholesale Distribution: The Magnifying Glass Technique, NAW, 1981

ation of Wholesale Distribution aimed at improving profitability and productivity. Exhibit 1 illustrates the activity approach taken to convert functional costs into activity-based costs. The book offered a comprehensive approach with illustrations, examples, and work steps needed for implementations.

While multitudes of these efforts have occurred, none had proved successful for long. This was primarily due to a lack of enabling technology. But by 1985, that was about to change.

Impetus from CAM-I

The spark for rapid and sustainable developments in ABC began in 1985 with a task force assembled by the Consortium for Advanced Manufacturing-International (CAM-I). This international research consortium was founded in 1972 under the name Computer Aided Manufacturing-International; the name was changed in 1992 to more accurately reflect a broadening mission. CAM-I began as a standard-setting body that established protocols to allow machines from different manufacturers to communicate with each other.

In 1985, CAM-I focused on the problems its members were having with traditional standard cost systems. Those systems did a poor job of helping management understand profitability by product and customer, evaluate capital investments, and find ways to better manage rising overhead costs. U.S. manufacturers in the early and mid-1980s faced intense global cost pressure. They were trying to respond rapidly to foreign competitors who had higher quality and shorter cycle times.

A CAM-I Task Force on cost management met several times, ultimately producing a conceptual design for a new cost management system. The Task Force's recommendations were published in 1986 and released to the public in 1988 under the title *Cost Management in Today's Advanced Manufacturing Environment: The CAM-I Conceptual Design.*[13] This book advocated the use of "activity accounting," and the broad-based constituency of CAM-I ensured that activity accounting rapidly obtained wide exposure. This marked the beginning of the modern era of ABC.

In addition to producing the conceptual design document, CAM-I sought to continue the work of the Task Force by launching the Cost Management System (CMS) program in 1986. The CMS program group has continued to meet quarterly to research leading-edge practices in ABC, performance management, target costing, capacity management, and enterprise ABM. It has provided a continuing forum for reforming and improving these techniques. The

---

13. James A. Brimson and Callie Berliner, editors, *Cost Management for Today's Advanced Manufacturing: The CAM-I Conceptual Design* (Boston: Harvard Business School, 1988).

continuity provided by this group has been another key reason that ABM usage has continued to expand.

CAM-I's impact has been widely recognized. In 1992, Peter Drucker noted "CAM-I is just beginning to influence manufacturing practice. But already it has unleashed an intellectual revolution. The most exciting and innovative work in management today is found in accounting theory with new concepts, new approaches, new methodology—even what might be called new economic philosophy—rapidly taking shape."[14]

CAM-I has even had a dramatic effect on the terminology. The term "ABM" came into widespread use following release of version two of the *CAM-I Glossary of Terms*[15] (see the Appendix for the Glossary of Terms). "ABM" connotes a broader use of activity-based data than just understanding what things cost. ABM refers to the use of activity data to manage by and make decisions with.

Many Join In

As the ABM movement began to grow, a need arose for training materials. The American Productivity & Quality Center conducted the first publicly available course in December 1989. It was developed and taught by John Miller. Exhibit 2 presents the course's eight-step process for creating an ABM model.

Exhibit 2: Steps to Create an ABM Model

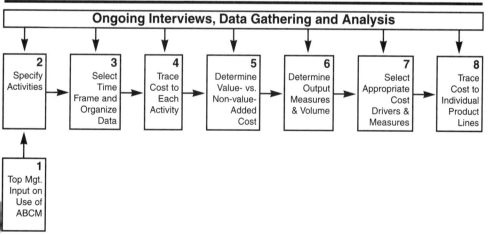

Ongoing Interviews, Data Gathering and Analysis

| **2** Specify Activities | **3** Select Time Frame and Organize Data | **4** Trace Cost to Each Activity | **5** Determine Value- vs. Non-value-Added Cost | **6** Determine Output Measures & Volume | **7** Select Appropriate Cost Drivers & Measures | **8** Trace Cost to Individual Product Lines |

1 Top Mgt. Input on Use of ABCM

Source: John Miller's Original ABC Training Course offered by the APQC, December 1989.

14. Peter F. Drucker, *Managing for the Future* (New York: Truman Talley Books/Dutton, 1992).
15. Norm Raffish and Peter B. B. Turney, editors, *CAM-I Glossary of Terms*. Arlington, TX: CAM-I, 1991. Document: #R-91-CMS-06,v.

Exhibit 3: Activity Analysis Report

Processes & Activities	COST EFFECTIVENESS			EFFICIENCY		
	Value-Added	Non-Value-Added	Cost	OUTPUT		Cost per Unit of Output
				Measure	Volume	
P: Take an order	$45,000	$25,000	$70,000	Completed Orders	25,000	$2.80
P: Bake Cakes						
A: Make Batter	175,000	75,000	250,000	Lbs. Produced	80,000	3.125
A: Bake Layers	110,000	40,000	150,000	Baked Layers	80,000	1.875
A: Frost Cake	75,000	15,000	90,000	Frosted Layers	80,000	1.125
P: Deliver Cakes	70,000	70,000	140,000	Delivered Cakes	60,000	2.33
TOTAL	$475,000	$225,000	$700,000			

Source: John Miller's Original ABC Training Course offered by the APQC, December 1989.

Each of the eight steps is performed to build an ABM model. The training material uses a cake shop as an example. Exhibit 3 illustrates the output of the process through Step 7 "Selection of Cost Drivers and Measures."

By 1992, the number of ABM training courses had skyrocketed, providers included software vendors, consulting firms, professional organizations (such as the Institute of Management Accountants and CAM-I), and many major universities.

As the industry continued to develop, many authors began to write about ABC and ABM. One of the most prolific and insightful of these was Robin Cooper (then of the Harvard Business School, currently at the Peter F.

Drucker Center). A particularly useful series of Cooper's articles appeared in the *Journal of Cost Management* and were subsequently republished in *Emerging Practices in Cost Management.* These include:

- "Does Your Company Need a New Cost System?" Spring 1987;
- "Elements of Activity-Based Costing" (a four-part series) Summer 1988–Spring 1989; and
- "Implementing an Activity-Based Cost System" Spring 1990.

Another key force in developing the ABM industry included publications such as the *Journal of Cost Management, Handbook of Cost Management, Emerging Practices in Cost Management* and *Emerging Practices in ABM.*[16]

Other key authors in this field include Charles T. Horngren, George Foster, John Shank, Vijay Govindarajan, and Bob Howell.

Software

By the early 1990s, there was a rush to develop software to support activity analysis. These efforts propelled the industry in two ways. First, the technology provided by software companies continues to push activity-based solutions to greater usage. Secondly, the marketing by these firms has created a powerful engine that is rapidly educating managers on how these tools can be successfully applied.

By the mid-1990s, various enabling forces had firmly launched the ABM movement. The key enabling forces are:

- Consortium leverage through CAM-I;
- Advocacy by key thought leaders such as Peter Drucker, Jackson Grayson, Carla O'Dell, and Tom Peters;
- Availablility of widespread training opportunities;
- Knowledge-sharing through numerous books and articles;
- Technological developments and marketing efforts by software vendors; and
- Learning through both broad-based and issue-specific best practice studies.

These forces set the stage for the evolution of ABM systems from simple pilot projects into enterprise-wide systems. The next section discusses the key trends of this evolution.

---

16. Barry J. Brinker, editor, *Journal of Cost Management, Handbook of Cost Management*, and *Emerging Practices in Cost Management* (Boston: Warren, Gorham & Lamont, 1990–1997).

Evolution of ABM Systems to Enterprise-wide ABM

Four key trends have converged to make enterprise-wide ABM possible.

- The first key trend is the expansion of simple ABC product costing systems.
- The second trend is the expansion of ABM from strategic to more operational uses.
- The third trend is the expansion to multiple locations which is itself driven by the first two trends.
- The final trend is the expansion of ABM from a finance tool to a management weapon. The combination of these trends—which are discussed in more detail below—can also be seen in the case studies that follow.

Trend One:
Expansion of Simple ABC Product Costing Systems

ABC systems typically began with a simple focus on improving product cost information. Over time, these simple ABC product costing systems expand in scope to include a more complete view of total costs. If ABC could be used for manufacturing overhead, managers reason, why not expand it to also include non-manufacturing costs such as distribution, sales, marketing, and general and administrative areas?

While activity-based systems began migrating to include all functions of the company, they also began to expand in terms of the business uses that activity-based information could address. Primarily through the work of CAM-I, the power and uses of ABC information were explored.

A key landmark in development occurred in 1991 when CAM-I published version two of the *CAM-I Glossary of Terms,* which was edited by Norm Raffish and Peter B.B. Turney. Included in the updated terminology was the "CAM-I Cross," which is shown in Exhibit 4.

This diagram depicts a product costing view on the vertical axis and a process view on the horizontal axis. The process view allows a user to focus on the multiple cost drivers of each activity as well as measurements of activity and process performance. In addition to establishing industry standard terminology, the CAM-I Glossary helps implementers understand how activity analysis can be used to solve operational problems.

Trend Two: Expansion to Operational Uses

Users of ABC quickly began to understand that an operational (as opposed to a strategic) focus on activities could yield dramatic reductions in operating costs. They also understood that each operational and strategic view could be examined independently—product rollups are not needed to focus on opera-

Exhibit 4: CAM-I Cross

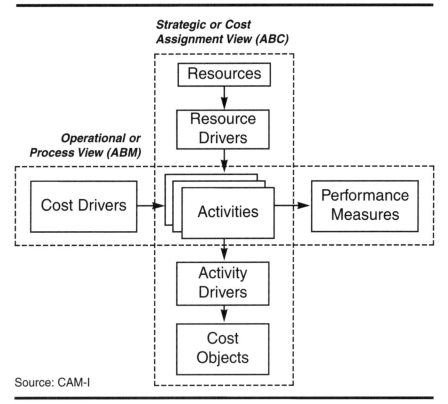

Source: CAM-I

tional cost reductions, and vice versa. This led to an explosion in the operational issues activity-based analysis could be used to help resolve. Seeking a better description of this operational focus, the term *activity-based management* (or ABM) began to be used. A simple definition of ABM was the use of activity-based information to manage.

While the operational use of activity analysis was growing, so was its strategic use for profitability analysis. Inclusion of sales, marketing, and distribution data helped in developing better product costs, but it also shifted the emphasis. Outside of manufacturing, the questions of costing and profitability were expanded to include the cost of serving particular customers, measurement of the value chain, and evaluations of sales-force effectiveness.

Furthermore, even though CAM-I's ABC efforts focused on the manufacturing sector, explosive growth in the usage of ABC was occurring in the service and governmental sectors. Companies in many service industries were demanding better information to address issues such as competition, deregulation, and product and service diversity. Yet these service companies had virtually no product or service cost systems—a lack they shared with non-profit and governmental agencies. Also, growth of ABM implementations in the service, governmental and healthcare sectors has skyrocketed.

Trend Three: Expansion to Multiple Locations

Both of the first two trends—expansion from manufacturing overhead to all overhead areas and moving from a single use in product costing into multiple strategic and operational uses—contribute to the third trend, which is a movement from single location ABM models to multiple location, enterprise-wide ABM systems.

Enterprise-wide ABM systems are (as defined in Chapter 1) management information systems that use activity-based information to facilitate decision-making across the organization. These multi-location enterprise models can take many forms, as the case studies that follow illustrate. These systems can be designed as single models, as with John Deere Health Care and American Seating, which cover the entire organization. Other case studies provide system designs that use multiple models to accommodate separate facilities that may be scattered geographically and do not need to be consolidated for financial reporting purposes. Examples of this approach include Shiloh Industries and Warner-Lambert. Finally, multiple models that are consolidated for enterprise-wide reporting are seen in the Transco and CinCFleet case studies.

Enterprise-wide ABM is not a one-size-fits-all proposition. There are many possible design variations, depending on the organizational structure, culture, and demands placed on the ABM outputs.

Management issues that must be considered when migrating to an enterprise-wide ABM system include local and corporate commitment, consistency of data for reporting, cultural issues, and the level of central control needed.

Trend Four: Expansion from Finance Tool to Management Weapon

The final trend for the evolution to enterprise-wide ABM is the expansion of ABM into a widely used management tool. In many cases, this transition is the most significant factor in determining whether a system is becoming enterprise-wide. The applications used by many best practices companies illustrate this movement to broad use of ABM outside the Finance Department.

At Parker Hannifan, for example, activity analysis is used to evaluate vendors to understand the true, fully-loaded costs of the vendor's products and services. The purchasing managers can analyze and communicate the costs incurred by using vendors that miss delivery dates or whose products have quality problems. Vendors' performance can then be evaluated in light of both activity costs as well as unit purchase costs.

Similarly, the national accounts sales force at TTI, Inc. uses ABC to assist in creating revenue growth. It does so by using ABC to demonstrate the benefits of TTI's automatic replenishment program. Using an ABC template, this national sales team has increased revenues from the automatic replenishment program from $7 million to over $150 million in just three years.

Finally, Johnson & Johnson Medical, Inc. used ABM to measure the impact of its total quality management (TQM) process. ABM became such an important tool that when the Finance Department downsized, key finance staff joined as members of the TQM implementation team.

These brief examples—along with the full text of the case studies that follow—highlight the multitude of companies that have established enterprise-wide ABM systems and how they went about doing it.

3

Decision Making
Using Reporting

One key to decision making is receiving information in a format that highlights the relevant facts. How activity-based management (ABM) data is reported thus becomes a critical consideration, particularly when presenting information to nonfinancial managers.

Reporting Guidelines

Designing an ABM model and collecting the data are major accomplishments in themselves, but reporting the information so that it can be used is critical. If ABM data doesn't meet the needs of the users, all the work is wasted.

Reporting must give users the information they need, when they need it, where they need it, and in both the format and medium they need. The "STAR" acronym below identifies qualities that ABM reports should share:

Support: To facilitate decision making, reporting must support decision makers in taking action. This is achieved by structuring reports in such a way that key facts are highlighted rather than obscured. Well-conceived graphical reports do a far better job than most numeric tables.

Advances in color printing make it possible for reports to use both color and icons (such as directional arrows), which help assimilate and clarify complex data. Because the benefits of any information system derive from the actions it helps users take, these techniques provide a faster way to focus people's attention on the actions needed.

Timely: Unless reports are timely, they lose relevance. To compete in today's global—and increasingly competitive—markets, information must be in "real time." Delays in management information can make the difference between success and failure. Management information must be available when it is needed.

Accurate: Reports must be accurate. The need for timely reports can sometimes pressure the preparers, which increases the risk of inaccurate information. To mitigate the risks, controls are needed to ensure accurate information.

Establishing a formal process for preparing reports allows management to evaluate the degree of accuracy needed and how it will be achieved. Preparation of informative reports should become seamless and automatic. Ad hoc processes increase the potential for error.

Relevant: Unless reports are relevant, they cannot support decision making—notwithstanding their timeliness or accuracy. A decision-maker needs information that, when acted upon, will increase the value of the business. This information should be aligned with the company's goals. Relevance also requires managers to consider the cost and time required to collect and to prepare the information.

Visual Displays of Information

When constructing reports, consider using bar charts, line charts or pie charts. Such visual displays of information can be the most effective manner to communicate results. Each type of chart can be used to help communicate a different message.

For example, a bar chart can be used to compare numerous items. The bars can be presented horizontally or vertically. Bar charts illustrate the relationship between the items.

Line charts work well for displaying actual data relative to targets or for displaying actual information within upper and lower limits. Line charts are also used to display information over time.

Pie charts differ slightly in the message they convey, because they typically represent 100 percent of a particular kind of information. A pie chart is most useful when the user is attempting to understand the relative sizes of related groups of data. Comparative pie charts can also convey relative size by varying the size of the pies (circles).

Users of the information are encouraged to examine different ways of conveying their results. However, try to match the type of graph to the data. Using the wrong type of visual display can result in confusion.

Examples of Reports

To provide examples of how ABM information can be presented, this chapter shows ten reports commonly used to present the output of ABM models. The reports are grouped into the following two categories.

Profitability Reports

- **The "S" curve analysis**: Traditional costs compared with ABC costs.
- **The "Mountain" chart**: Comparison of individual and cumulative profitability.
- **Two-by-two matrix**: Cost per order versus order size.

Cost Analysis Reports

- **Cross-functional activity analysis**: Listing of activity costs by functional area.
- **Pareto analysis**: The top 20 activities in the activity cost matrix.
- **Drill-downs**: Multilevel views of activity cost information.
- **Process map overlays**: Linkage of activity costs to specific elements of the process map.
- **Cost map**: Profiles of cost by process.
- **Cost of quality**: Example of an attribute report.
- **Time-phased view of costs**: Using a cost of quality example.

Each of these reports is discussed in more detail below.

Profitability Reports

The "S" Curve Analysis
(traditional costs compared with ABC costs)

Exhibit 1: The S Curve Analysis

Per Unit Standard Costs Compared to ABC Costs

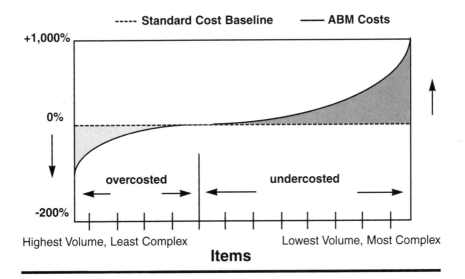

----- Standard Cost Baseline   —— ABM Costs

Highest Volume, Least Complex — overcosted — undercosted — Lowest Volume, Most Complex

Items

The name of this report comes from the shape of the curve that often results, which reminds many users of the letter "S" (see Exhibit 1). The report compares per unit traditional or standard costs to per unit ABC costs. It is prepared by setting the baseline of the graph equal to the existing standard costs. ABC costs are then compared with standard costs on a per unit basis. Items or products are ranked based on the percentage differences from the standard costs. The lowest percentage, which is the greatest negative difference, is posted first. Items are then posted in ascending order, finishing with the items with the greatest positive difference.

All items below the baseline represent products or services that are overcosted by the traditional methods. Typically, these items are produced in high volumes, are low in complexity, or require little technology investment.

All items above the baseline represent products or services that are undercosted by traditional methods. Typically, there are many of these items, and the range of undercosting is usually a much larger percentage, often exceeding 1000 percent. Undercosted products are typically lower in volume, highly complex, or require a large technology investment.

Because an "S" curve analysis maps items on a per unit basis, the area under the curve that is overcosted is typically smaller than the area above the curve, which represents undercosted items. If you were to multiply the items both above and below the curve by the volume of units produced, the resulting areas above and below the baseline would be equal. This is due to the fact that ABC analysis causes neither increases nor decreases in costs: For all items undercosted, like amounts are overcosted.

An "S" curve analysis can be prepared using either total costs or just overhead. Using only overhead leads to far more dramatic differences, because direct materials and direct labor are costed the same way under both traditional and ABM methods—typically by direct tracing. The direct costs are usually as accurate as they are going to be. ABM analysis demonstrates its real strength with overhead, which has typically not been analyzed carefully before, so the differences between the traditional and activity-based costs are often large.

The Mountain Chart
(comparison of individual and cumulative profitability)

As the term "mountain" chart implies, the goal of a business should be to obtain peak profitability. (See Exhibit 2.) Yet companies often pass this peak, because they sell some products or services at a loss. This chart helps to identify how much of this occurs—and where. It sets the stage for individual strategies to improve products or services and to increase the profitability earned from individual customers.

A mountain chart can be used to analyze customer profitability, product profitability, or channel profitability. It first uses a bar chart to rank the profitability of each item beginning with the most profitable and then descending

Exhibit 2: The Mountain Chart

Comparison of Individual and Cumulative Profitability

Cumulative and Individual Customer Profitability

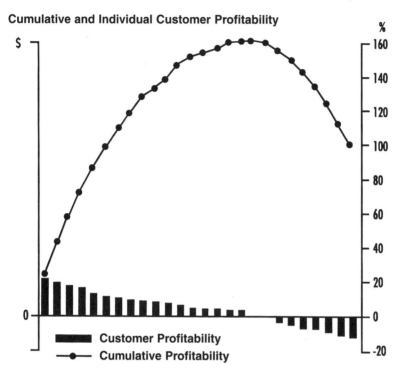

Source: Activity-Based Management: Arthur Andersen's Lessons from the ABM Battlefield (New York: MasterMedia, 1995)

to the least profitable, which is often negative (i.e., it causes a loss). Items such as customers, products, or channels with positive profits are above the zero line, while unprofitable items fall below it. Although this bar chart is useful by itself, it becomes even more relevant when combined with the curve of cumulative profits.

The cumulative profitability curve chart begins at the top of the first bar of the individual chart, which is the most profitable item (assume customers in this example). The next point on the line graph is the sum of the first and second bars, so it represents the cumulative profitability for the first two customers. Similarly, the third point is the sum of the first three bars, and so forth.

The cumulative profit curve will continue to ascend although at a slower rate until it reaches a peak for the last profitable customer. It remains at that peak through all break-even customers, but then it begins to descend at an increasing rate through all unprofitable customers in succession.

The stopping point of the cumulative profitability line equals 100 percent of the company's profits. The percentage of profits from the stopping point back up to the peak represents the profit "leakage" that should be targeted for profit-improvement efforts.

Note, however, that a company may have valid strategic reasons for continuing to carry unprofitable customers, products, or distribution channels. These reasons include:

- Start-up areas are expected to become profitable.
- Loss leaders are used to bring in more business.
- Prestigious accounts add to the firm's credentials.
- Volume spreads the company's fixed costs.
- Competitive actions block gains in market share by others.

Too often, however, companies simply do not know where their losses occur or even why they occur. A mountain chart provides a starting point to answer these questions. It is the first step to developing an improvement plan that focuses on unprofitable customers, products or services, or distribution channels.

Two-by-Two Matrix (*Cost per order versus order size*)

A "two-by-two" matrix is one of the easiest yet most informative ways to communicate information. It can be used to compare virtually any two criteria, one of which is arrayed on the vertical axis, while the other is positioned on the horizontal axis. The information is then positioned into four quadrants.

In the example shown in Exhibit 3, cost per order and order size are the two variables. Thus, the average cost to process each customer's order is displayed in relation to the average size of the order received from that customer. On the vertical axis, the cost per order is plotted, and on the horizontal axis, the size of the order is plotted. The four quadrants identify the desirability of behavior in customers. In this example, the bottom right-hand quadrant is most desirable (low cost per order with high dollars per order). Customer "Z" is clearly the most attractive; assuming that product margins are comparable, the company would profit if it could get more such customers.

Businesses seek to have the greatest throughput at the lowest cost. So it makes sense that companies want to understand the dynamics behind the orders in the bottom right-hand quadrant—big ticket orders that can be processed inexpensively. As the business learns more about the activities that it performs and understands the implications, they gain greater control over the outcomes.

Conversely, the least desirable quadrant is the upper left-hand quadrant

Exhibit 3: Two-by-Two Matrix

Cost per Order versus Order Size

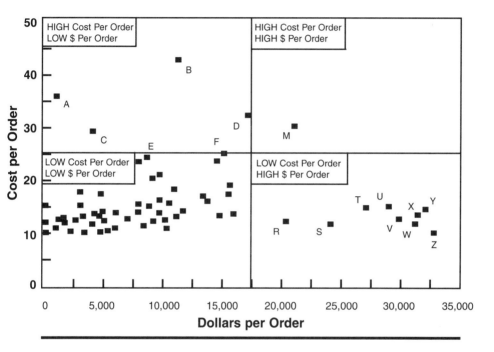

(high cost per order with low dollars per order). Customers like "A" should be examined to see why they are more costly and what might be done to increase their volume.

The behaviors behind the orders in the upper left-hand quadrant are important to understand. The company may decide not to take orders from customers having this profile, or it may implement or modify a minimum-order policy. Other possible actions include changing the process that causes these orders to cost so much. Often customers will not fully understand the effect of their orders on vendors. By identifying undesirable behaviors and working with their customers, many companies find both parties benefit from the new information.

Within the upper right-hand quadrant (high cost per order with high dollars per order) a judgement would have to be made whether the high cost of the order outweighs the high cost incurred to procure it. In evaluating customer "M," questions to be asked would include the following:

- Is this an order or customer that is strategically important to the business, or will it take away capacity that could be devoted to more profitable business?

Exhibit 4: Sample of Cross-Functional Activity Cost Analysis

Act. No.	ACTIVITY	SALES		PURCHASING			MANUFACTURING				WAREHOUSING		DELIVERY		Accounting	EDP
		Industrial Supply and Maint.	Contractors	Plumbing	Electrical	HVAC	Design Engr.	Plant	Mfg. Admin.	Inspt.	Chicago	Rockford	Chicago	Rockford		
1.0	ACQUIRE AND ENTER ORDERS															
1.1	Sales Planning and Forecasting	3	21						3							
1.2	Market Research	4	22													
1.3	Acquire and Develop Accounts	4	96												4	
1.4	Advertising and Sales Promotion		22													
1.5	Sales Call Preparations	4	32													
1.6	Travel Time	9	142													
1.7	Customer Sales Call	5	105													
1.8	Technical Support—Manufacturers	8	33	2	2	1	3			2						
1.9	Technical Support—Customers		118													
1.10	Customer Product Surveys		21					1								
1.11	Taking Telephone Orders	28				6										
1.12	Order Processing	27	10			10										
1.13	Over-the-Counter Orders	5								7						
1.14	Special Orders	18	4													
1.15	Order Expediting	21	44													
1.16	Update Order Book and Check Stock Status	6	54													
1.17	Order Editing		31													
1.18	Customer Inquiries	6	13													
1.19	Customer Complaints	8	52													
1.20	Credit Memos	2	21													
1.21	Received Warehouse Invoice Delivery															
1.22	Handle Salesmen's Inquiries	26														

1.23	Problem Solving	6	100				6
1.24	Special Order Handling		20			3	
1.25	Sales Training	6	55				
1.26	Salesmen's Performance Review	21	21				
1.27	Idle Salesmen Time		34				
1.28	Officers Involvement						
	TOTAL	217	1,071	2	2	20	3
2.0	ACQUIRE AND CONTROL MERCHANDISE						
2.1	Vendor Selection	2	1	2			3
2.2	Product Line Planning		3	3			
2.3	Purchase Order Preparation and Processing						
2.4	Expedite Purchase Orders						
2.5	Schedule Vendor Deliveries						
2.6	Receiving—Physical Handling						
2.7	Receiving—Check-in and Paperwork						
2.8	Straight Stock of Merchandise						
2.9	Breakdown and Repack—Pipe						
2.10	Breakdown and Repack—Fittings						
2.11	Breakdown and Repack—Other						
2.12	Vendor Return						
2.13	Vendor Problems						
2.14							

Source: Arthur Andersen's Cross-Functional Cost Analysis Training

- What is driving up the cost of the order for this customer?
- Can this customer's behavior be improved?

As this example shows, a two-by-two matrix is simple yet very powerful. Two-by-two matrices can also be used for many different kinds of analyses, including:

- Comparison of the number of full-time equivalents performing an activity versus the number of individuals in total performing that activity.
- Comparison of the departmental support activity costs to primary activity costs per product.
- Comparison of each department's mission-critical activities to its non-critical activities to determine the degree of focus.

Cost Analysis Reports

Cross-Functional Activity Analysis
(Listing of activity costs by functional area)
A "cross-functional activity cost analysis" (see Exhibit 4) can be very helpful in understanding the total cost across the company for a particular activity, especially one that is fragmented across many functional responsibilities.

The report lists activities down the vertical axis with the functional responsibilities along the horizontal axis. The functional areas are listed based on the flow of business through the company. This layout should result in a flow of activities from the upper left of the activity analysis to the lower right.

This activity analysis provides a detailed overview of how a company spends its resources. It identifies costs both by functional areas and by activities. This report can be used to show all costs or only payroll related costs. Many companies use this format to analyze activity time, which examines the full-time equivalent effort needed to perform each activity.

A cross-functional activity cost analysis allows a company to identify duplication of efforts, to identify tasks that are no longer necessary, and to understand the flow of work between departments, including the coordination required.

It is also an excellent tool for starting the examination of cause and effect. For instance, in reviewing emergency-maintenance activities, a manager could see if preventative-maintenance activities were also performed previously. Similarly, a manager whose department incurs excess rework activity could check whether employees receive adequate training and supervision. A sales manager could analyze the time sales people spend selling to customers versus the time they spend performing other activities. He might conclude that the number of sales people is adequate, but that they spend too much time on clerical tasks.

By taking a more holistic view, a company can identify ways to combine similar activities. A cross-functional activity cost analysis can raise many important questions, such as:

- Is the activity performed in the correct functional area?
- Are there redundancies?
- Do inefficiencies occur simply because of fragmented processes?
- Are there missing activities that reduce or eliminate the need for other activities?

Without this kind of information, companies have an incomplete picture of what is really going on inside their operations.

Pareto Analysis *(The top 20 activities in the activity cost matrix)*
A "Pareto" analysis focuses managers' attention on activities that are material in size or worth taking action. It can be used at the departmental, process, or enterprise-wide level (see Exhibit 5 for an example of Human Resources Departmental Pareto Analysis).

Pareto analyses simply sort activities from the largest to the smallest cost. Another term sometimes used for a Pareto analysis is "the 80/20 report," which refers to the 80/20 rule (e.g., that 80 percent of total costs are incurred by only 20 percent of the company's activities). Including a running cumulative total on a Pareto analysis report shows whether the 80/20 rule applies in a given case.

To emphasize how useful a Pareto analysis report can be, consider the prerequisites for effective cost control Peter Drucker has enunciated:

> Concentration must center on controlling the costs where they are. It takes approximately as much effort to cut 10 percent off a cost item of $50,000 as it does to cut 10 percent off a cost item of $5 million. Costs too, in other words, are a social phenomenon, with 90 percent or so of the costs incurred by 10 percent or so of the activities.

> The one truly effective way to cut costs is to cut out an activity altogether. To try to cut back costs is rarely effective. There is little point in trying to do cheaply what should not be done at all.[1]

Pareto analysis provides focus to users of the information. In the short-term, a user has a finite amount of time and resources to perform an analysis of what needs to be done and to make decisions. Therefore, users must focus on those activities that might provide the largest returns for their improvement efforts.

---

1. Peter F. Drucker, *Managing for Results* (New York: Harper & Row, 1964)

Exhibit 5: Departmental Pareto Analysis

Rank	Activity Number*	Human Resources Activity Description	$	% of Total	Cumulative %
1	21.06	Explain Personnel Policies	10,693	8.28%	8.28%
2	21.27	Process Cobra	10,506	8.14%	16.42%
3	21.17	Perform Personnel Development Consulting	9,998	7.74%	24.16%
4	19.13	Communicate Benefits Information	9,233	7.15%	31.31%
5	21.16	Update Personnel Records	6,946	5.38%	36.68%
6	14.07	Supervise Staff	6,666	5.16%	41.85%
7	21.26	Process Unemployment Paperwork	6,251	4.84%	46.69%
8	21.15	Review Performance Appraisals	4,999	3.87%	50.56%
9	21.20	Audit Human Resource Files	4,965	3.84%	54.40%
10	19.09	Prepare Welfare/Payment Forms	4,681	3.62%	58.03%
11	19.14	Respond to Other Departments/Locations Requests	4,680	3.62%	61.65%
12	21.12	Conduct Employee Placement	4,167	3.23%	64.88%
13	8.09	Support Alliance Programs	3,667	2.84%	67.72%
14	21.21	Respond to Government Agencies	3,333	2.58%	70.30%
15	21.23	Process Terminations	3,299	2.55%	72.85%
16	6.01	Prepare Written Communications	3,056	2.37%	75.22%
17	6.05	Prepare Summary Reports	3,014	2.33%	77.55%
18	20.12	Answer Payroll-Related Questions	3,014	2.33%	79.89%
19	7.01	File Forms	2,356	1.82%	81.71%
20	21.25	Verify Previous Employment	2,084	1.61%	83.32%
		Top 20 Activity Costs	107,608	83.32%	
		Other Costs (of remaining 28 activities)	21,536	16.68%	
		Total Departmental Costs	129,144	100.00%	100.00%

*Reference number in activity dictionary

All things being equal, if you have ten hours to spend on some activity to reduce its cost by 50 percent, you are better off spending that time on an activity that makes up 25 percent of total costs rather than just 5 percent. Spending time on improving the 25 percent activity would result in an improvement of 12.5 percent overall versus only 2.5 percent for the 5 percent activity.

Pareto analysis also facilitates "drawing the line" to avoid dealing with immaterial activities. A note of caution is in order, however, because smaller activities may turn out to be activities that should receive further investment if the additional investment would add value to the business by causing growth in revenues or by avoiding large costs. The key is to understand how an activity is used and what the activity accomplishes.

Pareto analysis is also helpful when analyzing activities across functional areas. Some activities may appear large when considered only within the context of one department or function. The user should therefore consider the activities performed across the company that, when combined, are still significant for the company as a whole.

Drill-Downs *(Multilevel views of activity cost information)*

A "drill-down" analysis is one of the most common uses of ABM data, because it lets managers quickly review greater detail about the element of cost in a specific cost object. In Exhibit 6, an analyst begins with the first pie chart, which depicts the types of cost incurred in serving Customer "A". This example shows the front-end, back-end, and directly traced costs of a distribution company. The analyst selects the *Front-End Services* category for further analysis.

The second pie chart breaks the Front-End Services slice out to show its components. The analyst reviews these components, then selects *Order Entry* for further review.

In the third pie, the Order Entry slice is dissected into its component activity costs. The largest segment of this pie (58 percent) is the Initial Data Entry activity. *Checking on Order Status* is only 13 percent (or a 4.5-to-1 ratio compared to Order Entry). *Order Quoting* is a relatively low 5 percent. The differences in these relationships between customers begin to provide insight on how their behaviors differ.

The fourth pie illustrates the drill-down of Initial Data Entry into its components, and it shows the cost components of the different elements.

Although these drill-downs show percentages, they also can show dollars, hours, or full-time equivalents. The types of charts used can also vary. At the lowest level, the analyst might choose to compare the cost per fax order to the cost per on-line order using a bar chart. A two-by-two matrix comparing revenue per order with cost per order might also be used.

The key is for users to analyze information in a variety of ways so that they understand what it really means. They can then select reports that properly convey this understanding and cause the appropriate people to take the proper actions.

Many companies have used data similar to that presented in this example. Typically, they seek to determine the lowest-cost method of order entry, then

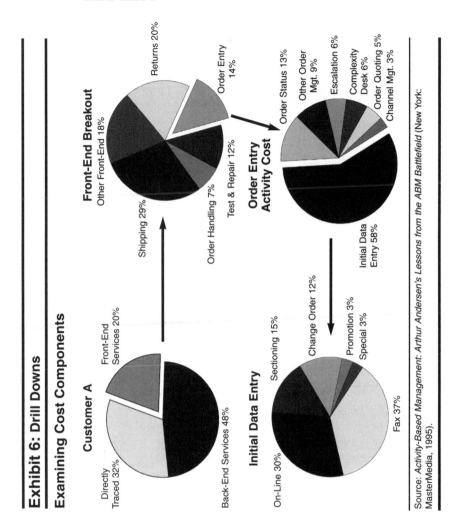

Exhibit 6: Drill Downs

Examining Cost Components

Customer A

Front-End Services 20%

Directly Traced 32%

Back-End Services 48%

Front-End Breakout

Other Front-End 18%

Returns 20%

Order Entry 14%

Test & Repair 12%

Order Handling 7%

Shipping 29%

Order Entry Activity Cost

Order Status 13%

Other Order Mgt. 9%

Escalation 6%

Complexity Desk 6%

Order Quoting 5%

Channel Mgt. 3%

Initial Data Entry 58%

Initial Data Entry

Sectioning 15%

Change Order 12%

Promotion 3%

Special 3%

On-Line 30%

Fax 37%

Source: *Activity-Based Management: Arthur Andersen's Lessons from the ABM Battlefield* (New York: MasterMedia, 1995).

they try to modify the behavior of their customers to take full advantage of the most cost-effective manner for order entry. In many cases, this can lower the costs for both parties.

Drilling down and up helps users rapidly analyze information in many different combinations. This type of analysis is commonly embedded in executive information systems such as Cognos PowerPlay.

Process Map Overlays
(Linkage of activity costs to specific elements of the process map)

A powerful use of ABM information is to overlay it across a process map. This allows an improvement team to understand the magnitude in dollars of the process linkages.

Exhibit 7:
Activity Costs Linked to Process Map

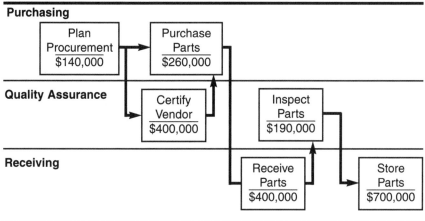

Exhibit 7 shows a simple example by using a basic process map of the procurement process overlaid with the related activity costs in each process step. Using this presentation would tend to focus users on the high-cost activity boxes, such as store parts at $700,000. This type of reporting can also provide

Exhibit 8:
Activity Unit Cost Overlaying Process Map

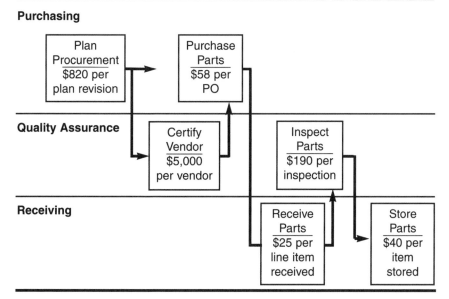

insight on how costs in one area can cause the costs of other areas to increase or decrease.

Exhibit 8 shows a different variation on this approach. This version uses the same process map but overlays "activity unit costs" in each process box. The unit costing provides some view of the volume flowing through the process. This unit data derives from the total activity costs divided by the total of activity driver volumes processed. The underlying data is presented below:

Activity	Total Activity Cost	Activity Driver (output resource)	Output Volume	Unit Activity Cost
Plan Procurement	$140,000	Number of plan revisions	171	$820
Certify Vendor	400,000	Number of vendors certified	80	$5,000
Purchase Parts	260,000	Number of purchase orders issued	4,483	$58
Receive Parts	400,000	Number of line items received	16,000	$25
Inspect Parts	190,000	Number of lots inspected	1,000	$190
Store Parts	700,000	Number of items stored	17,500	$40

When evaluating the unit cost report, a user's attention is drawn to the high-unit-cost activity boxes—certify vendors at $5,000 per vendor, plan procurement at $820 per revision, and inspect parts at $190 per inspection.

Adding color-coded attributes can further improve these graphs. For example, using red boxes to highlight non-value-added activities helps cost reduction teams focus on where major improvements can be made. In these examples, *Inspect Parts* and *Store Parts* would likely be flagged as non-value-added activities. Color-coded attribute boxes help users focus on these non-value-added activities.

Other performance measures can be used in overlays of process maps to present a fuller picture of a process. Exhibit 9 shows the example used in Exhibits 7 and 8 with additional overlays of a cycle-time map and key quality points.

The cycle-time map identifies key delays that dramatically lengthen the overall process. Quality data identifies key process measurement points. Each example seems to focus a user's attention on different areas, as noted in the following chart:

Technique	Key Improvement Areas Noted
Process Map	Inflow and outflow between departments (such as quality assurance)
Total Activity Cost	High total cost activities (store parts)
Unit Activity Cost	High per unit activity costs (certify vendors)
Attribute Flags	Non-value-added activities (e.g., inspect parts, store parts)
Quality Measures	Key measurement points (plan errors, certify receivers, and vendor returns)
Cycle-Time Measures	Points of delay (e.g., between planning and certifying vendors, between inspecting and storing parts)

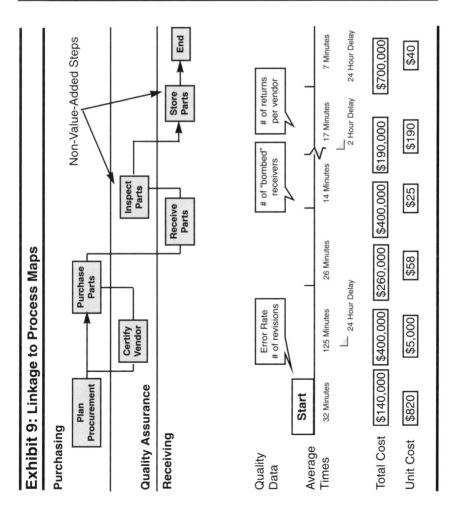

Exhibit 9: Linkage to Process Maps

Exhibit 10: Cost Maps

Cost Map for an International Airline

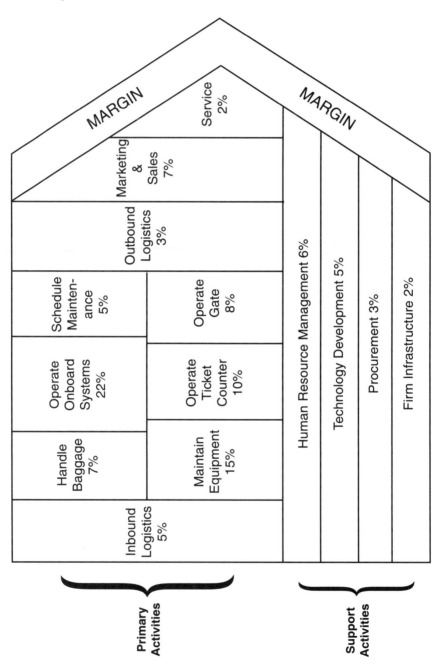

Cost Maps *(Profiles of cost by process)*

Cost maps present another example of overlaying process information with cost data. Exhibit 10 presents a cost map for an international airline that displays the activity costs of each process as a percentage of the entity's total costs. Using percentages makes it possible to compare entities in the same line of business even if size differences exist that might otherwise distort direct comparisons. By making the size of the process boxes relative to their percentages of total costs, this map graphically represents where costs are incurred and to what degree.

Cost maps are often used for value chain analysis. Vertically integrated suppliers have wide cost maps, because they must perform many activities to meet their customers' demands. They can be compared to linked-chained competitors by examining the overall cost maps of their counterparts.

A key point of a cost map is the relationship it depicts to margins. Reductions in costs clearly show greater margins, while expansions reduce it.

Exhibit 11: Cost of Quality Report

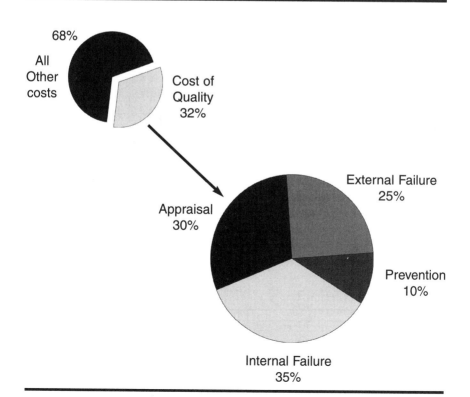

Cost of Quality *(Example of an attribute report)*

A key benefit of ABM is the ability to "attribute" activity-cost detail in a variety of ways. These include:

- Attributes such as "value-added," "non-value-added," and "business-sustaining" costs.
- Characterization of activities as "core," "sustaining," and "discretionary."
- Attributes such as "primary" or "support."
- Characterizations of activities as "mission-critical" or "non-critical."
- Cost of quality attributes.

A "cost of quality" report, such as the one in Exhibit 11, provides a good example of how these attribute reports are used. Activities are reviewed to determine if they are a cost related to quality. If so, they are flagged into one of the four following types of quality costs.

External Failure: Activities that result from quality failures that occur or are identified *after* the customer receives the product or service.

Internal Failure: Activities that result from quality failures within the company before the customer receives the product (or service).

Appraisal: Activities that review for errors.

Prevention: Activities that prevent the occurrence of rework.

Quality costs can be displayed in pie charts that use drill-down features so that users can further analyze costs into their respective elements.

Time-Phased View of Cost *(Using a cost of quality example)*

Another way of depicting cost of quality can be used to illustrate a time-phased view of costs, as shown in the column chart illustrated in Exhibit 12.

This chart provides a total cost of quality as depicted by the size of each column as well as the respective percentage slice of each category. Yearly actual amounts and future goals are also displayed in each column.

This example shows an expected annual decline in the total cost of quality, with reductions coming from reductions in external and internal failures. Both prevention and appraisal activity costs are expected to rise to achieve these overall reductions.

Note how the graph reflects a decline in the cost of appraisal activities in the "Three Year Plan" column, yet appraisal as a percentage of the total continues to climb. This chart provides a good way to understand and illustrate these points.

Exhibit 12: Time Phased View of Cost Using a Cost of Quality Example

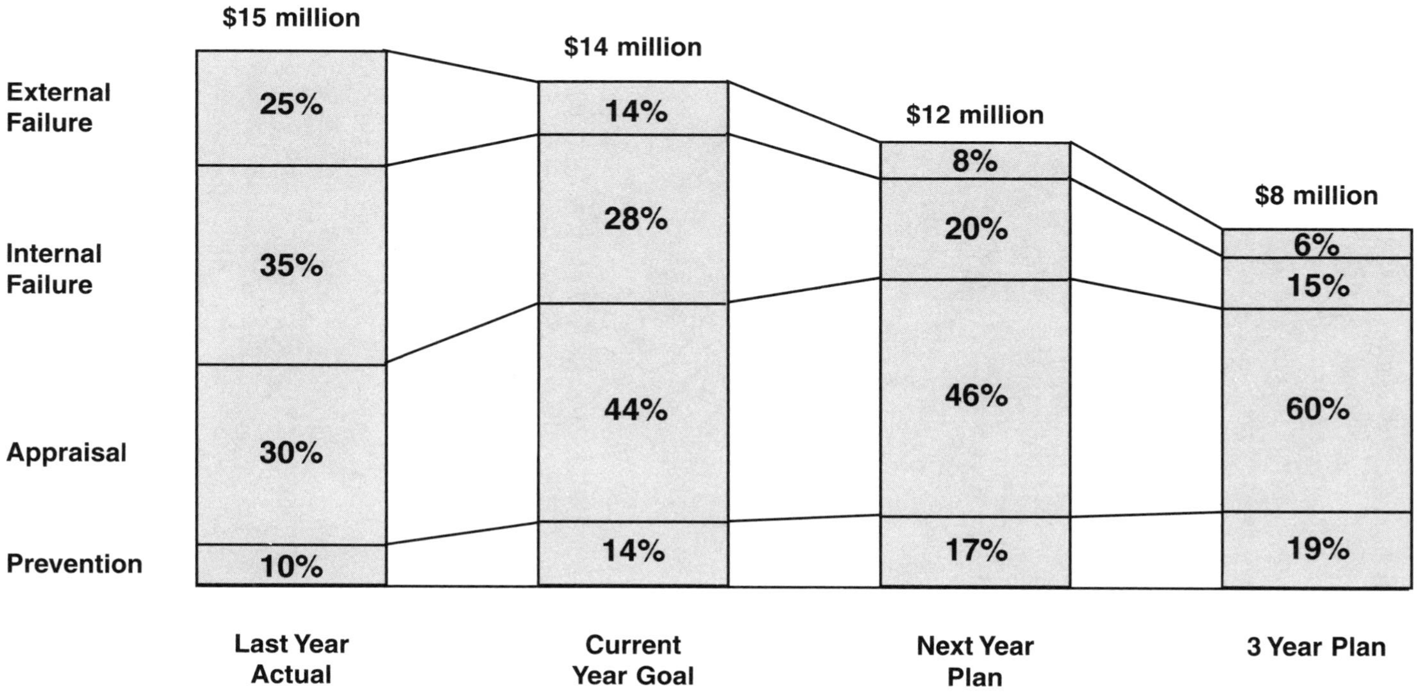

	Last Year Actual	Current Year Goal	Next Year Plan	3 Year Plan
	$15 million	$14 million	$12 million	$8 million
External Failure	25%	14%	8%	6%
Internal Failure	35%	28%	20%	15%
Appraisal	30%	44%	46%	60%
Prevention	10%	14%	17%	19%

Summary

Effective reporting is a *key* to *decision making* for every organization. Don't wait until your ABM models are completed to begin designing reports. As Stephen Covey said, "Begin with the end in mind." This statement rings true with enterprise-wide ABM systems. If you don't began thinking about reporting output early on, you may build ABM models that will not effectively provide required information.

Hopefully, these examples provided will be a basis to start designing your organization's suite of reports. However, remember that each organization is different and will have different reporting needs.

Part II

Case Studies

4

American Seating: Making the Right Decisions with ABM

Written with Michelle Behrenwald, Senior Manager,
Arthur Andersen, Grand Rapids, Michigan

Introduction

As in many industries today, competition is forcing changes in the direction and growth of the seating industry. In transportation seating, for example, companies from Mexico now compete heavily with U.S. companies. And in the stadium-seating arena, an Australian company has made significant inroads into the market share of U.S. companies.

These are just some of the issues facing American Seating, a leading U.S. manufacturer and assembler of seating products, which is headquartered in Grand Rapids, Michigan.

Business Issues

"We were like many leading-edge manufacturers around the world," says Edward Clark, president and CEO of American Seating. "We needed better information to make both strategic and operational business decisions." But when the company turned to existing data, it discovered that—when it came to good cost information—it was data-rich, yet information-poor.

"Our interest in activity-based management (ABM) began during an executive meeting on profitability," says Thomas Bush, CFO of American Seating. "Because our product line is so large, we had concerns with the accuracy of our standard cost system which provided us with our margins. Our executive team needed a better way to identify product profitability information and to strategically pursue certain areas of the business."

Particular product lines and business segments were not achieving their revenue and profit targets due, in part, to changing needs in the marketplace and to the commoditization of certain products. Bush adds, "To be successful, we needed to reduce our non-value-added costs and thereby enhance value-added services to customers. As this became more evident, we began to re-evaluate cost and performance management practices."

Because of the diversity and complexity of its products and product segments, the company needed:

- Economic justification for new product ventures and proposed capital investments;
- Insight into underlying cost structures to support cost estimates and target costing;
- Improved understanding of new product launch costs and the life-cycle impact on profitability;
- Pricing practices separate from standard costs;
- Benchmarking of operations and quantification of continuous improvement; and
- Improved information to help managers make more informed strategic and operational business decisions.

American Seating researched management tools that might provide the information needed. After a site visit to another company that had successfully implemented an integrated cost management system, management decided to launch an activity-based performance management system to provide the answers. Clark explains:

> Performance management offered us a dynamic and flexible process to organize and integrate financial and operational data into meaningful information. It was information we could use to meet our own needs and also the needs of our customers in the marketplace.

ABM Steering Committee

Twelve top executives from various parts of the business formed a steering committee to identify the key issues (see Exhibit 1 for a list of members of the steering committee). They defined a shared vision and developed specific expectations.

According to Bush, American Seating wanted to understand how to maximize profitability and enhance customer satisfaction despite the growth it was experiencing. To do so, the company needed to understand its product cost structure, which was impossible given the company's standard cost system.

The steering committee wanted ABM to answer the following questions:

- Which products, customers, and segments should we target?

- How can American Seating enhance revenue and increase profitability by product and by customer?
- What are our core competencies?
- Are resources being deployed effectively to achieve strategies and improve profits?
- What is the impact of the improvement efforts?

Exhibit 1: American Seating Steering Team Members

President and Chief Executive Officer
Chief Financial Officer
Director of Operations
Director of Marketing
Director of Supplier Development
Vice President of Engineering
Director of Financial Planning
Director of Engineering Services
Manager of Advanced Manufacturing
Director of Pricing/Contracts
Director of Cost
Director of Human Resources

With help from Arthur Andersen, American Seating developed an activity-based performance management solution to more accurately mirror resource consumption by process, product, and customer.

Background

American Seating Company, a midsize manufacturer founded in 1885 in Grand Rapids, Michigan, has a proud heritage based on the simple idea to develop products that provide a comfortable and productive environment at school, at work, and in public facilities. The company which has approximately 900 employees is a leading manufacturer of seating for buses and light-rail systems. It also produces stadium and auditorium seating, office furniture, and ergonomic seating products. These products are produced in four facilities and sold throughout North America. Since American Seating is privately held, revenues are not disclosed.

The company's history includes many firsts:

- Adjustable-height furniture;
- Angle-adjustable desks;

- Desks for both left- and right-handed students;
- Tilt-back and automatic-rising theater seats;
- Self-leveling glides to eliminate table wobble;
- Laminated desktops;
- Body-conforming materials to make seats more comfortable; and
- Cantilevered bus seating.

Each of these innovations has become standard in the seating industry.

American Seating began in schoolrooms and theaters. After World War II, however, the company expanded to meet the growing demand in the transportation market. By the 1960s, the company had also become the leading manufacturer of architectural seating and it later entered the office furniture market, again offering innovations previously unmatched. The company now operates in three primary areas or groups:

- *Interior Systems* (contract seating, tables, and furniture systems).
- *Transportation Products* (bus and light-rail seating).
- *Architectural Products* (auditorium and stadium seating).

ABM Project Rollout

In July 1996, American Seating launched an ABM pilot. The objective was to design a performance management framework that would provide more accurate operational and financial information. Exhibit 2 provides an overview of milestones achieved during the 20-week implementation.

Since completion of the project, the information from the new ABM system has been used for continuous improvement and decision making for issues relating to customer and product profitability. Clark championed the project and Arthur Andersen's Grand Rapids office provided consulting help.

ABM Project Team

The ABM project team included six employees from American Seating and three consultants from Arthur Andersen. The members from American Seating included:

- Director of Cost, who served as the ABM Project Manager;
- Operations Manager;
- Director of Engineering Services;
- Sales and Marketing Education Director; and
- Two Financial and Cost Analysts.

The team worked together over a period of six months to identify leading practices in cost and performance management. They also developed skills

---

Exhibit 2:
American Seating Project Implementation Milestones

- Requirements Assessment (weeks 1–2)
- Team Training (weeks 1–2)
- Interviews & Activity Effort Worksheets (weeks 3–6)
- Process Analysis & Schematics (weeks 7–8)
- Software Selection (weeks 9–10)
- Software Training (weeks 11–12)
- Build Model (weeks 13–15)
- Interpret Results (weeks 14–18)
- Implementation & Integration Planning (week 19)

Total elapsed timeframe - 20 Weeks

---

and tools on process and project management to help implement the pilot project.

The ABM team was dedicated full-time to the successful completion and validation of this project. As Bush says, "We were committed to this project from the CEO down and throughout the organization. We targeted some of our top performers for participation on the ABM team. Although they would be dedicated for about six months, this project was deemed a top priority, and cross-functional leadership and team members were critical to success."

Initial Efforts

Properly training the ABM team was essential. Initial training sessions covered:

- ABM definitions;
- Techniques that would be used;
- How interviews would be conducted; and
- Other project tasks and tools.

The project team then held a series of kickoff meetings which were open to the entire company.

Team members and executives gave presentations to define ABM and explain why ABM was being implemented. Communicating the objectives to the entire organization prevented misconceptions later about the project's structure and goals. The combination of involving employees early and visible support of top management allowed the project team to move swiftly in their implementation.

Next, the cross-functional steering committee conducted a "requirements assessment" to finalize key objectives and questions. The focus included the following:

- Assessing the company's culture;
- Identifying core competencies;
- Matching resources with strategy;
- Targeting key products and services;
- Enhancing profitability and revenues; and
- Measuring the impact of improvement initiatives.

Interviews

Interviews were the next step. The project team began by identifying who would be interviewed and who would conduct which interviews. From the interviews, activity effort worksheets were completed (see Exhibits 3 and 4 for samples of an activity effort worksheet and a completed departmental summary of the forms). The worksheets showed primary activities for each area, time splits for activities, activity drivers, and the resources other than labor that went into the activities.

About 125 people from every work area and various work centers in the manufacturing facilities were interviewed, including managers from functional areas outside of manufacturing. The team used both group and individual interviews, depending on the preference of the manager of each particular area. Before each interview, those who would be interviewed received guidelines such as the number of and significance of activities to be discussed. This framework for the interviewers made it possible to compile the results quickly and consistently.

The project team was divided into three interview teams, each of which had one or two team members from American Seating and one Arthur Andersen consultant. The interviews generally took about 90 minutes to complete, followed by another hour to document and validate the information. It took about four weeks to finish all of the interviews.

Activity Definition

Initially, the people interviewed were allowed to define the activities they wanted in the model, but their inexperience often caused activities to be defined in too much detail. So the process was divided into two stages. The second, or "schematic" phase, rolled activities up to a higher level that would be modeled and maintained. As a result, a total of 228 unique activities were ultimately defined. Activity drivers were then chosen to trace these activities to cost objects.

Software Selection and Model Building

After the schematic phase was complete, the team evaluated the different software products available, weighing the pros and cons of each given American

Exhibit 3: Activity Effort Worksheet

Input	Output	Activity	Activity Description	Driver	Names/Individuals/Groups				
					%Time	%Time	%Time	%Time	%Time
					100%	100%	100%	100%	100%	100%

Non Labor Resources

Exhibit 4: Activity Effort Summary: Sales Department View *

		Total Dept. $	Total Hours	Avg. Hourly Rate
Labor w/ Fringes		$187,002	6,240	$29.97
Non-labor Dollars Allocated		$351,718	6,240	$56.37

Activity	Business Process	Total Hours	Total Labor	Total Non-labor**	Total Dollars	Hours			Driver Volume	Driver Unit $
						Value-Added	Mgt. Required	Non-Value-Added		
Contacting prospects	3a	1,404	$42,075	$52,651	$94,726		1,404		100	$947
Presenting features and benefits of company products and services	6c	1,092	$32,725	$40,951	$73,676		1,092		1,092	$67
Identifying and resolving warranty and non-quality product	13b	858	$25,713	$32,175	$57,888	858			25	$2,316
Developing dealer needs	5a	702	$21,038	$26,325	$47,363		702		5	$9,473
Managing and coordinating area	6c	858	$25,713	$32,175	$57,888		858		9	$6,432
Managing the showroom	6c	0	$0	$117,397	$117,397		0		1	$117,397
Performing administrative responsibilities	10b	1,326	$39,738	$49,726	$89,464		1,326		1,326	$67
Performing independent representative duties	6c	0	$0	$318	$318		0		20	$16
Total		6,240	$187,002	$351,718	$538,720	858	5,382	0		

*Please note the data included in this example is for illustrative purposes only and is not reflective of actual company numbers.
**Breakdown of non-labor includes sales & product literature, showroom, samples, training, and travel & entertainment.

Seating's needs. *Hyper*ABC was selected for its import capabilities, the way it handles multidimensional cost objects, and its reporting flexibility. After the team learned how to use the software, model building began. The selection, training, and model building steps took six weeks to complete.

Validation

Model building was quickly followed by validation of the data. According to Bush, the model was checked to "make sure everything flowed through properly. Then the results could be analyzed." Once costs were traced to the activities, the ABM team returned to the interview groups for final review and approval.

Validation was extremely important to ensure buy-in from the individuals and groups interviewed. The interviewees needed to understand the results as the ABM project progressed. As Bush states, "We wanted everybody to believe the integrity of the numbers when we got to the end." Since the cost objects were identified during the initial executive sessions, they needed only to be finalized during this stage of the project.

Sixty-eight production work cells were costed during the project. These included areas such as the injection molding department, stamping, assembly, and welding (see Exhibit 5 for an example of a work center activity costing report). Costing began at the work-cell level, then rolled up into products, which were summarized into product lines. From there, the product lines were accumulated into customer groups, then from customer groups to business segments.

For the initial pilot project, there were 28 product lines, 16 customer groups, and two fully costed business segments (the third business segment, transportation, was only partially costed). In general all costs were included in the model. The only area not completed in detail was the transportation segment, which will be modeled in the future. Costs for the transportation work cells were aggregated together.

Results and Next Steps

About 14 weeks into the project, the team began to build reports, interpret data, and prepare presentations. The efforts were well rewarded. The following major milestones were accomplished throughout different phases of the pilot:

- Completed an assessment of the company's culture and identified a change management strategy to minimize resistance and ensure lasting change. The assessment was completed on the front end of the project to manage the change process in the pilot.

Exhibit 5: Workcenter Activity Costing Report*
Department ABCD

Activity Costs

Value Class**	Activity	Actual Period Dollars	% of Total Cost	Period Unit Rate	Target Unit Rate	Unit Variance	Cost Driver	Cost Driver Rate	Target Driver Rate	Driver Rate Variance
N	ABCD REWORK	$10,000	1%	$0.02		$0.02	Rework Hrs	$25.00	$25.00	$25.00
N	ABCD DOWNTIME	$40,000	6%	$0.07		$0.07	Downtime Hrs	$400.00		$400.00
V	ABCD RUN PROD	$150,000	21%	$0.26		$0.26	Run Hrs	$60.00		$60.00
N	ABCD SET UP	$180,000	26%	$0.31		$0.31	Set Up Hrs	$60.00		$60.00
N	ABCD MAT HDL	$20,000	3%	$0.03		$0.03	Shop Orders	$3.33		$3.33
N	ABCD HOUSEKEEP	$5,000	1%	$0.01		$0.01	Calc Mach Hrs	$2.50		$2.50
M	ABCD MACH REL COST	$300,000	42%	$0.52		$0.52	Calc Mach Hrs	$150.00	$150.00	$150.00
	Workcenter Total	$705,000	100%	$1.22	$0.00					

Detailed Account Cost Information

	ABCD REWORK	ABCD DOWNTIME	ABCD RUN PROD	ABCD SET UP	ABCD MAT HDL	ABCD HOUSEKEEP	ABCD MACH REL COST	Account Totals
DEPT AB-SHARED MFG SUPPLIES	$0	$0	$10,000	$0	$0	$0	$0	$10,000
ABCD DIRECT LABOR	$10,000	$40,000	$140,000	$180,000	$20,000	$5,000	$0	$395,000
FABCD MACH DEPR	$0	$0	$0	$0	$0	$0	$250,000	$250,000
PERF PREV MAINT	$0	$0	$0	$0	$0	$0	$5,000	$5,000
PERF FWO REQUESTS	$0	$0	$0	$0	$0	$0	$15,000	$15,000
TRBLSHOOT MACH	$0	$0	$0	$0	$0	$0	$30,000	$30,000
Activity Totals	$10,000	$40,000	$150,000	$180,000	$20,000	$5,000	$300,000	$705,000

Workcell Driver Volume Information

	Machine Hrs	Run Hrs	Downtime Hrs	Rework Hrs	Set-up Hrs	Shop Orders
Actuals	2,000	2,500	100	400	3,000	6,000
Planned						
Standard						

Product Mix Information

Product Line Group	Actual Units	Planned Units
Product A	500,000	
Product B	23,100	
Product C	45,000	
Product D	11,000	
	579,100	

*Please note the data included in this example is for illustration purposes only and is not reflective of actual company numbers.

**N = Non-value-added   V = Value-added   M = Management Required

- Developed an activity-based business model with documented model logic. This included a schematic diagram of business processes that identified how resources were consumed. (See Exhibit 6 for the business model.)
- Prepared process-based activity information for each area. This also included an overall management report indicating resource allocation and the relationship of activities to processes.
- Created cost and profitability reports by customer group, product line, and segment.
- Implemented activity-based reporting for each work cell that the shop-floor work teams could use in analyzing and improving their own performance.
- Identified future enhancements, including the desired criteria for performance measurement, such as key customer satisfaction measures, project profitability tracking, alignment of marketing codes and customer groups, and tracking of key cost drivers.
- Identified short- and long-term operational improvements. Those include reduction of non-value-added activities in each area, elimination of ad-hoc reporting, and identification of additional value-added services to help the company exceed customer expectations.

A presentation of the team's findings was made to the cross-functional steering committee. Response to the project was extremely positive. According to Bush, the steering committee was surprised not so much about the profitability of certain product segments as it was about activities. As Bush explains:

> The surprises were in terms of how people were spending their time, how much time we were really spending on planning, and how much time was really dedicated to non-value-added activities.

Value-Added versus Non-Value-Added Analysis

For analysis, activities were classified as either value-added, "management required," or non-value-added activities. A *value-added* activity was defined as adding value from the customer's point of view and represented activities the customer was willing to pay for. A *management required* activity neither added value from the customer's point of view nor was anything the customer was willing to pay for, yet it was nevertheless an activity required to operate the business effectively (e.g., maintaining ISO 9000 certification documents). Finally, a *non-value-added* activity did not add value from the customer's point of view, the customer was not willing to pay for it, and the activity was not even required to operate the business.

According to Bush, "We identified, minimized, and in some cases eliminated non-value-added activities in several areas." The product engineering

Exhibit 6: Business Process Model

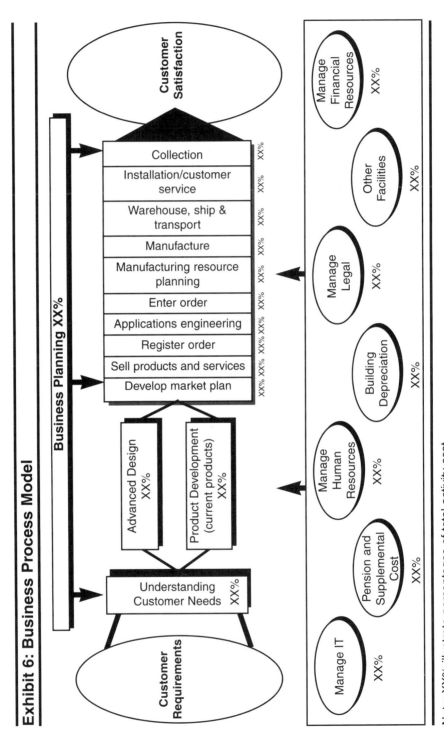

Note: XX% illustrate percentages of total activity cost

area began monitoring some of its key cost drivers, which led to a two-day—or 40 percent—reduction in the special sales order processing cycle. This gave the company a competitive edge in an industry where lead times are compressed and quick response rates are imperative.

Continuous Improvement Efforts

American Seating operates under a "mini-company" concept to focus on continuous improvement. Each team within the concept operates as a mini-company, which means it defines its business plan to support the company's overall strategy. The mini-company also initiates benchmarking and improvement efforts. American Seating evaluates and monitors their mini-companies with respect to quality, safety, morale, and cost. The mini-company concept includes improvements such as reduction of setup time for machines. These improvements bring increased manufacturing flexibility to meet customer requirements and capital-investment justification for new manufacturing technologies.

The information gained by this initiative enabled American Seating to streamline and standardize its product offerings. The company decided to outsource "non-core" manufacturing competencies to increase efficiency and thus provide customers a comparable product at a lower overall cost.

By using the performance management process and its new tools and knowledge, American Seating can now examine specific segments of its product line strategically (auditorium seating for example), to determine if product proliferation has become a problem. The company may then make more accurate decisions about product options customers truly value. This allows the company to match resources with those high value product options. They can also use the performance management process to eliminate non-value-added work and focus efforts on product standardization.

The ABM team began to investigate how many resources were spent on non-value-added functions—and their related cost. They incorporated the information into planning sessions, into the budgeting process, and into their ongoing process improvement efforts.

The process is continuing, as Bush notes:

> Our planning sessions really focus on technology and on how to improve our business processes. Initially, I was worried our people would only think about cost reductions. That is not the case. While the objective is to reduce costs in response to competitive pressures, the business process improvements are also about doing more with the resources available.

Organizational Support and Action

Because of the up-front training and education, reaction to the analysis of non-value-added versus value-added activities was very positive at all levels of the organization. The training emphasized the fact that classifying an activity as non-value-added wasn't a personal assessment. According to Clark:

> The information we gained through the pilot project helped us redeploy resources to better match our strategy and to increase return on investment by focusing limited resources on key business processes.

For example, customer service redeployed resources to focus on the high-value activities through a redesigned process. A specific service administrator is now assigned to each customer order to increase satisfaction and service levels while also reducing inquiry response time. In this way, customer service can concentrate its efforts in areas most important to customers.

Customer-Focused Product Decisions

According to Bush, the entire ABM process helped in making decisions to reduce American Seating's product offerings, which had an impact on both bottom- and top-line results. ABM helped managers identify value-added services and products from the customer's point of view. This knowledge ensured that the company would provide these services and, more importantly, that the value received and the price paid were in line. American Seating ultimately modified its pricing strategies based on what customers consider valuable. As Bush explains:

> A lot of companies look at revenue growth as a way to increase profitability. That wasn't necessarily true for us. We found that we could actually sell less and make more in some instances. So the emphasis is really on how we manage the bottom-line of our company, and how we manage our balance sheet. We don't put the emphasis on the increase in sales as much as we had in the past.

Future Plans

A follow-up executive session focused on how to use the ABM data in the future and what the next steps and priorities should be. Finance was tasked to maintain and improve the ABM database. Finance was also asked to determine how to make ABM an integral part of the company's culture.

ABM information continues to be used for planning purposes, return-on-asset measurements, pricing strategies, and continuous process improvement. According to Bush, the primary focus continues to be on process improvements. "We prioritized the biggest opportunities, and we are working our way down." Future modeling plans call for completing the rollout of ABM throughout the transportation product segment, which is a large growth area for American Seating. Since the company is considering expansion, it is important to complete this analysis soon.

The ABM team as it was originally structured no longer exists because ABM is no longer considered a project. Instead it is now integrated into management decision making. Finance also uses the ABM model to provide data to other functional areas. The information is shared throughout the organization and used by executives in various functions.

"We quickly recognized this new approach was a vast improvement over traditional cost management techniques," says Bush. "We are integrating it with current systems to maximize our capabilities. The information we gain is our basis for business planning, resource redeployment, performance measurement, and increasing stakeholder value."

In the future, American Seating intends to incorporate performance management strategies into its plans for focusing and deploying resources on key customer requirements and specific strategies by segment. As the mini-company concept extends throughout the organization, ABM information will be used to develop strategic plans for each mini-company.

Lessons Learned

- *Executive buy-in is the key to the success of an ABM project.* A senior management group championed by the CEO spearheaded the ABM project at American Seating. Such high-level interest and support ensured a successful project and caused ABM information to be used for daily decision making.
- *Dedicate appropriate resources for the job at hand.* According to Bush, "We wanted a dedicated, full-time team from the beginning and we went after our top people. Even though it took them out of their regular jobs for up to six months, ABM was a priority, and we wanted to do it the right way." If you want to be successful, you must dedicate the appropriate resources. Don't go half way. The team was critical to achieving an enterprise rollout quickly.
- *Select a cross-functional team.* You need cross-functional representation on your ABM team. This will greatly facilitate gaining buy-in from the organization. The functional areas will view it as their project if they have adequate representation. A cross-functional mix will also provide a wealth of knowledge, especially when activities and cost drivers are being defined and validated.

- *Experienced consultants speed the rollout.* Experienced consultants from Arthur Andersen played a critical role in focusing the team. "Having Arthur Andersen involved was a key enabler to our success," notes Bush. "The integration of consultants into the cross-functional team helped us avoid many of the pitfalls we might have otherwise experienced. They kept us on track as we rolled out the project in an extremely short time frame and transferred knowledge to our team members."
- *Don't make ABM a finance project.* From the beginning, the ABM project was championed by the operational side of the business. This emphasis enabled the ABM team to hit the ground running.
- *Perform a requirements assessment at the outset.* You must work with management from across the organization to understand their needs and expectations. For the system to be successful and the information it provides to be actually used, you must solicit management expectations up-front, *not* at the conclusion of the project.
- *Clearly communicate goals, objectives, and strategy to the organization.* Make sure people clearly understand the objectives. Communication helps obtain buy-in from the organization. It also ensures people will not misunderstand the goals you are trying to accomplish. When you use information to eliminate non-value-added activities, employees should understand the purpose is not to eliminate their jobs. Make sure they know you are trying to make them more effective and efficient. Provide examples of how the time saved from the elimination of non-value-added work will be redeployed into value-adding efforts.
- *Focus on integration.* Finding and retaining a dedicated MIS resource for model maintenance and updates can be difficult—and crippling when the proper skill set is lacking.
- *Keep it simple.* Don't build any more complexity into the system than what is needed to accomplish your goals. More doesn't mean better. If Bush had one piece of advice to give on implementing an ABM project, it would be to keep the project as simple as possible: "The information is more valuable if people can understand it and can use it."

5

AscoForge Safe: Improving Profitability with Activity-Based Management

Written with Isabelle Lacombe,
Manager, Arthur Andersen, Paris, France

Introduction

As manufacturing companies around the world have discovered, traditional cost accounting systems do not always provide accurate information about product costs. As companies become more technologically advanced, their overhead increases and their direct labor costs decrease. This change in a company's cost structure can cause overhead to be misallocated if traditional allocation bases (such as a percentage of direct labor or direct labor hours) are used.

Typically, high-volume products are "overcosted" (assigned excess overhead), while low-volume specialty products are "undercosted" (assigned too little overhead). This case study illustrates how costs were misallocated at AscoForge Safe, a French manufacturing company. It shows how management took the steps necessary to cost products correctly by implementing activity-based management (ABM).

Business Issues

Managers at AscoForge Safe found that inaccurate product costs were causing the company to lose potential customers. Sales people did not have the information they needed to prepare accurate price estimates to compete for new customers or to win repeat business from existing customers. Concern intensified as AscoForge Safe realized that only 2 percent of all the estimates the company provided led to orders. The business was barely breaking even, and losses began to loom on the horizon.

Finally, AscoForge Safe appointed a new financial director, who immediately began to assess the situation. Daniel Souloumiac, the new Financial

Director, recalls, "When I arrived, I immediately noticed the lack of cost control and the production of inaccurate product cost information. Indirect costs represented one quarter of the total cost whenever direct costs represented the other three quarters. Indirect costs were being allocated on an equal proportion as well." This practice produced inaccurate product costs, because each product requires a different amount of effort for indirect costs such as design, preparation, production, and quality assurance.

As Souloumiac says, "We didn't have a clear assessment of our margins for our products and customers. Therefore, we urgently needed to take steps to manage costs and institute methods for seeking out opportunities to increase our productivity."

AscoForge Safe's management decided to launch an ABM initiative to address the following business issues:

- Inaccurate product costs;
- A lack of confidence in the company's cost system;
- The need to improve controls over indirect costs;
- The need to increase product and customer profitability; and
- The need for process improvement initiatives.

Background

AscoForge Safe is headquartered in Paris and its 1997 revenues exceeded 600 million francs (US$100 million). The company has 500 employees, including 30 engineers.

As a subsidiary of Usinor, AscoForge Safe manufactures products for the automotive industry, including parts for gearboxes, differentials, axles, and transmissions. Each year, AscoForge Safe produces about 60 million forged steel parts. Most of these parts have a long service life—typically two years of development and a production life that corresponds to the life of the vehicle in which it is placed.

The Old Cost System

AscoForge Safe's previous cost system focused on controlling the direct costs of production. Material costs for each part were calculated based on the steel used, which included adjustments for yield loss. This steel usage was priced out at the purchase cost for steel. Labor costs were tracked based on the time employees spent in the different stages of the production line.

Other direct expenses were also directly linked to products, including electricity costs for the workshop and machine depreciation. As Souloumiac explains, "Manufacturing was the subject of in-depth analysis. We could therefore validate the direct costs linked to the entire manufacturing process."

Indirect costs amounted to 150 million francs (US$25 million), yet the indirect costs had never been analyzed in detail. Indirect costs incurred before and after production roughly equaled to one-third of the company's direct costs. These indirect costs included:

- Research and development costs;
- Engineering costs;
- Quality analysis;
- New product costs;
- Costs of preparing quotations; and
- General and administrative expenses (such as the cost of general management).

Souloumiac notes, "One very simple rule for indirect costs had applied for a long time. To calculate the total cost of the parts, the company had decided to apply indirect costs in proportion to direct costs." While these costs for the entire company represented one-quarter, applying that ratio to individual parts led to distortions in the product costs estimated for each of the products.

Because each product requires a different effort for design, preparation, production, launch, and quality, the actual cost of producing each product varies significantly and is not necessarily proportional to the direct costs incurred. As a result, the company's allocation methods caused high-volume products to be overcosted and low-volume products to be undercosted. (Exhibit 1 illustrates this effect by comparing costs generated by a traditional cost system with costs generated by activity-based costing.)

Because of the inaccurate costs, managers at AscoForge Safe could not rely

Exhibit 1:
Effect of the Direct Cost Method Compared to ABM Costs

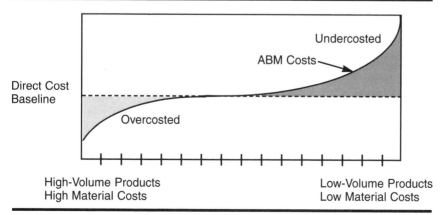

on the costs supplied by the company's management control system. Also, profit margins could not be assessed accurately, which made the bidding and negotiation of contracts even more difficult (and risky).

Initial Efforts

In an effort to address many of AscoForge Safe's business problems, the company's Managing Director launched a management initiative called "Safe 2000," which established various committees to help with the management of the company. (Exhibit 2 shows the organization of the Safe 2000 initiative.) These committees, which ran parallel to the existing management structure, included:

- The Management Committee, which monitored the progress of various other committees;
- Numerous Improvement Committees, which had the following objectives:
  — Design and industrialization;
  — Operational control;
  — Control over the costs of processes and activities; and
  — Optimize human resources.

Exhibit 2: Safe 2000 Organization

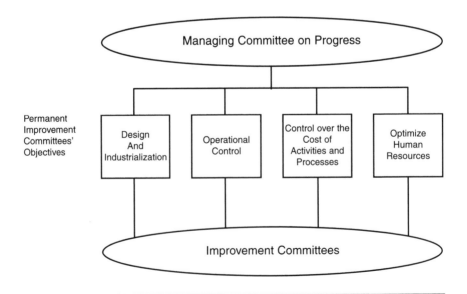

Souloumiac leads the Cost Improvement Committee. Based on his prior experience with ABM at another company, Souloumiac believed that an ABM analysis of indirect costs would quickly provide important information managers needed to address AscoForge Safe's business issues. His goals included establishing a permanent ABM system to address the company's ongoing costing needs. In other words, this was not to be a "one off" project that would disappear after it provided its initial results.

ABM Team

Before kicking off the ABM project, Souloumiac carefully considered who to include on the team. One option was to have a team made up solely of Asco-Forge Safe employees. A second option was to include consultants to speed the process. After carefully weighing the pros and cons, he decided to bring in experienced consultants from Arthur Andersen.

The new ABM team included three members from AscoForge Safe (one full-time member and two part-time members) and two Arthur Andersen consultants. The ABM project was launched in September 1996.

The next step was software selection. After a thorough analysis of software available, the company selected *Hyper*ABC by Armstrong Laing as the software-modeling tool it would use.

Data Collection

The ABM team's first job was to define activities. Since the project's goals were both strategic and operational in nature, the team had to define activities in great detail. Doing so provided detailed cost management information to aid in reengineering. Before ABM was implemented, all cost reduction efforts occurred across the board, with no detailed analysis of where the cuts would do the most good. In evaluating activities such as processing an invoice, training a new employee, or launching a new product, a detailed analysis of activities is far more helpful in detecting potential cost savings.

The project team went through the following project steps to a speedy roll-out of ABM:

- Determine project scope;
- Collect data;
- Build the cost model;
- Evaluate the results; and
- Plan ways to act on the results.

The cost model was designed to provide activity-based analyses of the margins for each customer and each product. The cost information would also be used to provide price quotations and cost estimates.

In building a system to provide cost estimates, indirect expenses were analyzed in detail. The objective was to quickly identify the correlation between specific activities and particular products. This information could then be used to trace indirect costs to specific products, thus providing more accurate product costs.

Two examples of this are transportation/storage costs and capital charges. Cost analyses showed that parts sold to U.S. customers should be assigned a greater share of these costs than parts sold to French customers, because U.S. customers' parts have long storage and transportation delays before they reach the United States. French customers' parts, by contrast, are usually sent to the customer directly from the factory.

The ABM team also analyzed the indirect cost caused by delayed payments, which is now assigned based on particular end customers.

By converting to ABM cost assignments, AscoForge Safe has improved and simplified its cost accounting system. Internal costs that were previously allocated arbitrarily are now analyzed and assigned more accurately. Manager reports now focus on the controllable expenses incurred in each section, which has greatly simplified preparing and monitoring the budget.

Detailed ABM information was also used to launch a reconfiguration of the entire production operation. Activity costs were detailed in the ABM model, which also tracks the tasks included in each activity, then the activities involved in each process. These detailed "maps" were then used to support reengineering.

*Hyper*ABC was used to calculate the results of these sophisticated analyses

Exhibit 3: ABM System Architecture

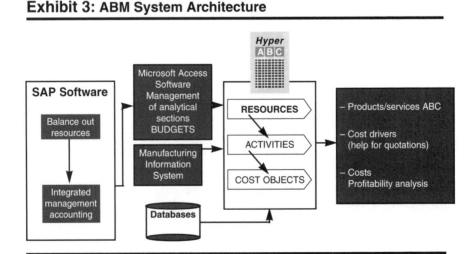

Exhibit 4: ABM Model Volumes

- 165 accounts
- 10 departments
- 67 resource drivers
- 52 activities and 6 processes
- 200 products

(see Exhibit 3 for the ABM system architecture). The ABM system included many types of financial and also operational information. (See Exhibit 4 for ABM model volumes.)

Results and Next Steps

The ABM project has completely changed AscoForge Safe's cost system. Now more than 75 percent of the company's indirect costs can be traced to products. As Souloumiac explains, "It is not possible to trace all indirect costs to products, because the linkage of costs to products is sometimes so indirect that any cost assignment would be arbitrary." Items such as general management costs, certain administrative costs, and certain human resources costs were therefore not traced and were instead allocated. Although all costs are

---

Exhibit 5: Rules of Cost Assignment

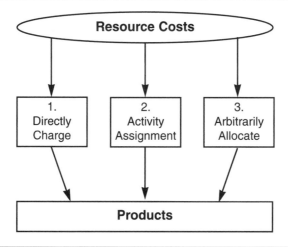

still assigned to products, the costs generated by ABM are far more accurate. (See Exhibit 5 for the rules of cost assignment.)

The ABM team has thoroughly analyzed all activities to find the most coherent way of assigning their related costs. For example, training costs were previously allocated based on a percentage of labor costs and following up on contracts was allocated based on sales revenue by product. After ABM was successfully implemented, AscoForge Safe began using the results to set new product prices.

Other information gained included the discovery that 23 percent of the company's products—all previously considered profitable—were actually unprofitable. (See Exhibit 6 for a comparison of the ABM results with the results generated by the traditional cost system.) For some products, the margin dropped more than 200 percent. Small-volume products that required very high quality and personalized service became many times more costly, while 5 percent of the products previously considered unprofitable actually proved to be profitable. (See Exhibit 7 for differences in margins indicated by the ABM system and the traditional cost system.)

A simple example of why this distortion occurs can be seen by examining the treatment of the cost of quality. The company spends about 9 million

Exhibit 6:
Differences of results on costs calculated with ABM system and with traditional accounting method.

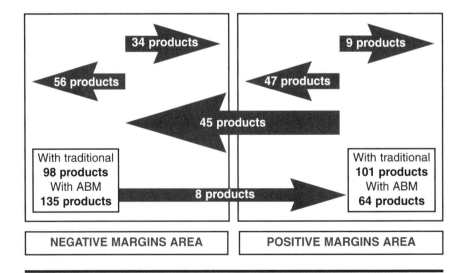

| NEGATIVE MARGINS AREA | POSITIVE MARGINS AREA |

Exhibit 7:
Differences of margins on product costs calculated with ABM and with traditional accounting method

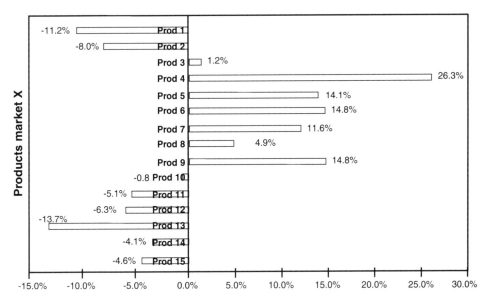

francs (US$1.5 million) to ensure quality. Quality assurance activities include the development of quality standards, implementation of those standards, quality audits, and review of quality controls. These quality costs were previously allocated to each part based on its direct costs. Each part was assigned a quality cost corresponding to 5 percent of its direct costs.

But analyzing the quality activities, the ABM team noted that quality costs vary according to end-customer requirements, not according to the direct cost of each part. This was most noticeable for customers from certain countries that have high quality restrictions. As a result, these parts and customers generated very high quality costs.

The ABM team solved this issue by assigning the cost of quality based on end-customer requirements. They achieved this goal by applying a ratio of quality requirements based on the degree of quality requirements specified by each customer.

The information gained from ABM has also led to numerous policy changes. For example, prices are now set according to the policy adopted for each customer. For example, to motivate certain customers to purchase in large quantities, the company will renegotiate certain sales prices. Management is also considering discontinuing some products.

Future Plans

As Souloumiac notes, "We plan to use ABM information for both internal and external benchmarking. We also plan to use the information to continue our process improvement efforts." AscoForge Safe is also continuing to reduce indirect costs.

Lessons Learned

- *Simplifying basic accounting is a good first step.* AscoForge Safe began by canceling the internal cost allocations it had used. The various business units were made responsible for controlling the expenses of their own units. This simplified budgeting and monitoring costs. It also set the stage for building an understanding of the cause-and-effect relationships of activities.
- *Use experienced consultants.* Implementation usually goes faster by including experienced consultants on the ABM team. They bring vital experience and expertise to complete the skill sets brought by internal members of the project team.
- *Across-the-board cost reductions seldom work.* Attempts to cut costs across-the-board rarely work because some activities are vital. The costs of these activities quickly return in the form of rehired workers, higher outsourcing costs, or higher costs for temporary workers.

  Across-the-board cuts also cause a "hoarding mentality" among managers: Managers tend to hold back (or hoard) excess costs in case another across-the-board cut should occur in the future. This creates a cycle of hoarding that just increases the need for more cost cutting. Detailed activity analysis is needed to identify where costs can be reduced and how to achieve appropriate cost reductions.

6

Blue Cross Blue Shield of North Carolina: Understanding Costs for Improved Pricing Information

Introduction

In the 1990s, health maintenance organizations (HMOs) became increasingly prevalent throughout the United States. The growth in the number and importance of HMOs reflected a major shift in the healthcare industry away from *indemnity* products toward *managed care* products. An indemnity company simply administers and writes insurance policies, whereas HMOs actively manage the healthcare of their members.

This case study explains how Blue Cross Blue Shield of North Carolina (BCBSNC), a healthy not-for-profit organization, used activity-based management (ABM) to strengthen its position in the face of new market dynamics. Although BCBSNC was a leader in its field, it needed better cost information to compete effectively in the rapidly changing healthcare arena. The case shows how BCBSNC turned a failed ABM pilot program into a learning experience, then later implemented a highly successful ABM system throughout the organization.

Business Issues

BCBSNC ranks as one of the stronger Blue Cross and Blue Shield plans in the United States. There were only three HMOs operating in North Carolina in 1993. By 1995, the number of competing HMOs had grown to over 30, which dramatically increased pricing pressures.

BCBSNC's existing cost system primarily provided information for governmental business. However, about 75 percent of BCBSNC's customer base was private (i.e., nongovernmental). As a result, BCBSNC lacked cost information by product and major business segment. To compete effectively, BCBSNC needed cost information to address the following:

- Understand administrative costs by product;
- Manage expenses better;
- Compare its performance with the performance of competitors; and
- Understand the cost structure for competitively pricing products.

To address these issues, BCBSNC decided to use ABM as the means for obtaining the information needed. As BCBSNC's President and CEO Ken Otis states:

> ABM was critical to the organization in helping us gain a better understanding of our costs. It provided us with a foundation for managing expenses better. The cost information about activities provides a benchmark to assess how we are doing against best-in-class and competitors.

Background

BCBSNC was formed through the merger of two competing hospital prepayment plans both founded in the mid-1930s and is now North Carolina's oldest and largest healthcare insurer. Its mission is to be North Carolina's healthcare champion by providing residents of the state affordable, high-quality health insurance, healthcare, and related services.

Organized as a not-for-profit organization, BCBSNC provides coverage to 1.6 million members about 24 percent of North Carolina's insured population. It has about $1.6 billion in revenues and 2,600 employees. BCBSNC's insurance policies are sold through both brokers and a direct sales force. The corporate headquarters are in Durham, though BCBSNC also has offices in Asheville, Greenville, Hickory, Raleigh, Charlotte, Wilmington, and the Triad Area.

In the 1990s the shift throughout the United States toward managed healthcare brought an explosion of competitors. BCBSNC reacted by introducing a series of managed healthcare products, product enhancements, improved marketing methods, and customer-service initiatives. All were designed to give customers health insurance products that suit their needs at competitive prices.

Prior Cost System

Before introducing ABM, BCBSNC's traditional cost system allocated administrative costs to products based on a few key allocation bases ("drivers"), such as the number of members, contracts, and claims. These drivers are appropriate for some operational areas, but they failed to provide an accurate picture of BCBSNC's development and support areas, such as information systems, market development analysis, and healthcare services development.

BCBSNC's management felt the company's old cost system failed to provide the information needed to manage resources or make important business decisions such as product pricing. As Jim Emmons, the Director of Planning and Information, says:

> Activity-based costing is more appropriate for ultimately tracing resource costs to products and services. ABC provides a methodology for tracking administrative costs by product and establishing more appropriate linkages of resources to products through the use of activity analysis.

This need for better information about product costs to support pricing of managed care led BCBSNC to an ABM pilot project.

ABM Project Rollout

BCBSNC's initial pilot began in 1994 with a three-person project team. Although the members of the team all came from the cost accounting department, none of them had experience with ABM. What's more, BCBSNC chose at first to use only internal resources—no consultants were hired. The pilot program focused solely on operations. Its objective was to determine the cost of processing a claim.

The ABM team began by compiling a list activities. Because they had no previously established guidelines on appropriate levels of detail for defining activities, the activity listing quickly grew to over 500 terms, which were defined mainly at the task level. Unfortunately, collecting data at the task level through interviews proved cumbersome—so cumbersome that the difficulty gathering the data caused the project to fail.

But other pitfalls also contributed to the early demise of the initial ABM project. These included:

- Lack of training;
- Lack of project planning;
- Lack of executive buy-in; and
- Lack of clearly defined objectives.

Although ABM was not an instant success at BCBSNC, the company did not abandon the project. Instead, BCBSNC learned from its mistakes and tried again. Its perseverance paid off in the form of valuable information and better management decisions.

Business Issues Still Needed Addressing

Although the first pilot failed, BCBSNC's management still had the strategic goal of transforming BCBSNC from an indemnity company into a managed care company. This created intense pressure to understand administrative costs by product—which, in turn, would lead to better pricing decisions.

According to John Friesen, Vice President of Actuarial and Underwriting at BCBSNC:

> An indemnity company prices products by looking at existing costs and at what the trends have been. The indemnity company then predicts, or forecasts, costs for the next year and uses this information to set the price.

This approach differs dramatically from how competitive HMOs set prices. Friesen explains:

> HMOs set prices differently. HMOs go to the marketplace and ask what is the competitive market rate to sell business. Through market pricing, they determine what the rate has to be and then manage their costs accordingly.

The need for better cost information thus became critical and brought BCBSNC back to implementing ABM.

Second Pilot

About six months after the first pilot failed, two different staff members from BCBSNC's finance and accounting function tried again to launch ABM. A first step was to choose *Hyper*ABC from the Armstrong Laing Group as the ABC software package that would be used for the implementation. A few months later, Armstrong Laing was asked to join the project team and to train managers and employees about ABM. The team had two part-time members from BCBSNC and one part-time member from the Armstrong Laing Group.

The team had learned from the first pilot that planning and buy-in from top management were critical to success. To gain the organizational acceptance and funding required, therefore, the new team focused on "selling" the concept of ABM to BCBSNC's executive staff. Exhibit 1 shows an organizational chart for the executive staff.

To prepare for the meeting with the executive staff, the team researched different approaches to implementing ABM. Key decision points included:

- Project scope (e.g., the entire company, selected divisions, or an incremental rollout);

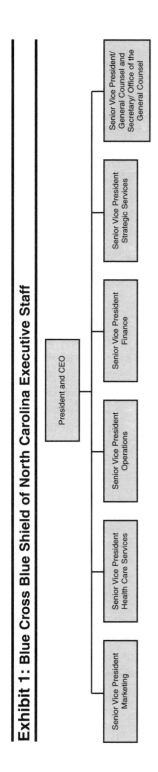

Exhibit 1: Blue Cross Blue Shield of North Carolina Executive Staff

- Number and levels of interviews needed for activity analysis and data collection;
- Resource commitment, including part-time staff, full-time staff, and consultants;
- Start dates and expected delivery dates; and
- Expected outcomes and deliverables.

Exhibit 2 outlines the various approaches the team presented to the executive staff.

The project team faced several challenges in getting the support of the executive staff and the entire organization:

- Overcoming the negative image left by the failure of the original pilot.
- Overcoming the argument that the company already operated effectively—i.e., without yet another large project like ABM. Indeed, BCBSNC was financially healthy despite the increased competition from other HMOs.

As Friesen, the "champion" of the ABM project, says:

> It is easier to change if you are in a crisis mode, because people are looking for solutions; they know they have a problem and have to do something. In this case, BCBSNC was growing and financially healthy, but we needed to do some things differently—like manage expenses differently—because the expenses were affecting the ability to have competitive pricing.

As the "Project Champion," Friesen was the senior leader and supporter throughout the project rollout. He continued to sell and market ABM throughout the organization and he was always available to listen and offer advice as needed. He has continued to play a critical role in the ongoing project success.

Exhibit 2

ABC APPROACHES

Approach	Project Scope	Interview Level	Resource Commitment	ABC Start Date	Outcome	Delivery Date
1	Enterprise-wide	Manager and Analyst	Full Time ITM*	First QTR 96	Activity Analysis / Product Cost	Second QTR 96
2	Enterprise-wide	Manager and Analyst	Part Time ITM*	First QTR 96	Activity Analysis / Product Cost	Third QTR 96
3	Selected Divisions	Director	Part Time ITM*	Second QTR 96	Activity Analysis / Product Cost	Third QTR 96
4	Selected Divisions	Manager and Analyst	Part Time ITM*	First QTR 96	Partial Activity Analysis / Product Cost	Third QTR 96
5	Incremental Approach	Senior Management	Finance Staff	Third QTR 96	Process Analysis	Fourth QTR 96
6	Enterprise-wide	Manager and Analyst	Outside Consulting / No Resources	Fourth QTR 96 / 1997	Activity Analysis / Product Cost Integrate Planning	1997

*Interdivisional Team Member

ABC Approach Implemented

(HYBRID OF ABOVE APPROACHES SELECTED)

Alternative	Project Scope	Interview Level	Resource Commitment	ABC Start Date	Outcome	Delivery Date
	Enterprise-wide	Manager	Finance Staff Outside Consulting	Second QTR 96	Activity Analysis / Product Cost	Third QTR 96

Initial Interviews

The project team used direct contact to sell the ABM project. They interviewed more than 45 people—from the director level to the chief executive officer. The team viewed the people they interviewed as "customers." Their strategy was to explain the specific benefits each area would obtain by having information from the ABM system. Most of the company's managers were sold on the project because of the team's hard work. These interviews and the team's "personal selling" laid important groundwork for change.

The executive staff approved the project, but asked that the ABM project be initiated with as little disruption to normal operations as possible. Therefore, the project team was composed of staff from the finance department and a consultant. Exhibit 3 shows the implementation timeline.

Activity Analysis

The ABM team members made a first cut at the activity dictionary, which they then reviewed with the various directors and vice-presidents. After the team completed this validation process, the dictionary included 67 activities. The validation process included distributing the activity dictionary to key senior

Exhibit 3: Implementation Timeline

	1996 1-Feb	15-Feb	1-Mar	1-May	21-May	1-Jun	22-Jun	1-Jul	20-Aug	1-Sep	30-Nov	31-Dec	1997 1-Jan
Phase 1													
1. Kick Off Meeting	1												
2. Product and Activity Dictionary		2											
3. Driver Methods & Reallocations Defined			3										
4. Relationships Established				4									
5. Inputs into *HyperABC* System					5								
6. Activity Reports Distributed						6							
7. Report Changes Due							7						
8. Product Costing Phase								8					
9. System Changes Completed									9				
10. Phase I Completed										10			
11. Phase II Begins										11			
12. Second Level Activity Process Analysis											12		
13. Second Level Product Costing												13	
14. Integration into Corporate Planning & Budgeting													14

managers for review and acceptance. They also had the opportunity to add additional activities to the dictionary. Before the dictionary was distributed throughout the organization, the team felt it was important to have key individuals approve the dictionary.

Overview binders for the ABM project were compiled for each interviewee. They contained the following:

- An explanation of the project and the requested information;
- An overview of ABM concepts;
- Activity effort forms, instructions, and examples. The forms were used to collect estimates on the activities employees were spending time;
- The activity dictionary;
- A checklist to ensure all requested items were completed and returned;
- Budgeted and actual operating data;
- Full-time equivalent (FTE) counts by cost center; and
- Sample report templates with the types of reports management would receive when ABM results were complete.

Data collection lasted eight weeks and included 350 additional interviews. Most were one-on-one interviews with managers, who ranged from front-line supervisors through the CEO. In addition to gathering activity effort information, the project team used these interviews to explain the benefits of ABM to those they interviewed.

As the activity effort worksheets were received, the team produced reports to show each cost center's activity cost by resource pool. (Exhibit 4 shows an example.) The team also analyzed resources other than labor to determine the most appropriate resource drivers. Validation of the results continued throughout the project to ensure that the managers were buying into the results. This step included returning the results produced to the responsible managers for approval and making corrections when necessary. The team did not want to reach the project's conclusion and have the managers reject the results.

Cost Object and Driver Analysis

With help from BCBSNC's marketing, financial reporting, and actuarial services, the ABM team drafted an initial listing of BCBSNC's products and segments. This list was circulated for validation throughout the organization. The final listing consisted of 11 product combinations and 36 segments as shown in Exhibit 5.

The data collection interviews were also used to discuss which resource drivers and activity drivers should be used. The project team evaluated the suggested drivers to determine the availability and accuracy.

Exhibit 4: Activity Costs by Resource Pool

Cost Center XYZ

Resource Pool	Activities A2.4 Develop Market Positioning	A3.3 Manage Capitalization & Reserves	B1.3 Respond to Customer Inquiries	B2.3 Design Products	B3.3 Prospect Customers	B5.3 Collect Encounters	B7.1 Develop Medical Guidelines	C2.4 Provide Corporate Tax Services	Total
Salaries—Exempt	$18,903	16,402	$4,500	$2,866	$5,012	$1,288	$1,456	$2,733	$53,160
Salaries—Nonexempt	44,500	4,599	2,687		1,234				53,020
Salaries—Part-Time	2,022								2,022
Overtime	1,500								1,500
Consulting				50,000					50,000
Furniture & Equipment	200	200	200	200	200	200	200	200	1,600
Computer Equipment	6,000	3,400	2,000	100			4,400	7,557	23,457
Travel					1,200				1,200
Training			2,000						2,000
Printing	250	5,000	250	250	250	250	250	250	6,750
Office Supplies	50	50	50	50	50	50	50	50	400
Postage	800	550	450			750			2,550
Postage—Express	150				2,580				2,730
Telephone	380	380	380	380	380	380	380	380	3,040
Facility Cost	4,850	1,325	3,300	50	100	100	200	2,500	12,425
Advertising									
Third Party									
Broker Commissions									
Other	50	50	50	50	50	50	50	50	400
Total	$79,655	$31,956	$15,867	$53,946	$11,056	$3,068	$6,986	$13,720	$216,254
Percent of Total	*37%*	*15%*	*8%*	*25%*	*5%*	*1%*	*3%*	*6%*	*100.00%*

Exhibit 5: List of Market Segments and Products

Market Segments	Products
Large Groups (Local)	Comprehensive Major Medical/Traditional
Experience Rated	Preferred Provider Organization (PPO)
Prospectively Rated	Preferred provider Organization (PPO)—Select
Administrative Services Only (ASO)	Preferred Provider Organization (PPO)—Select—Co-Pay
Large Groups (National)	
Experience Rated	MedPoint Point of Service (POS)
Prospectively Rated	Personal Care Plan (PCP)
Administrative Services Only (ASO)	Personal Care Plan (PCP), Inc.
Health Maintenance Organization (HMO)—USA	Dental
	Medical Supplemental
Blue Card Host Plan	Stop Loss
Centralized Processing	Other Products
Inter Plan Data Reporting (Phase Out)	
Government	
Civilian Health and Medical of the Uniformed Forces (CHAMPUS)	
Federal Employee Program (FEP)	
Medicare	
State Administrative Services Only (ASO)	
State Personal Care Plan (PCP)	
Group Insurance Services (GIS), Inc.	
Development	
CORE	
YEAR 2000	
Workers Comprehensive	
Medicare Risk	
Consumer	
Regular	
Conversion	
Blue Assurance	
Grange	
Farm Bureau	
Basicare	
Select	
Select Plus	
Blue Advantage	
Access	
Short Term	
Retired Military	
Medical Supplemental—New	
Medical Supplemental—Old	
Small Groups	
Medium Groups	

When actual data for a recommended driver was unavailable (i.e., number of claims processed by product), alternative or surrogate drivers were evaluated. If cost-effective driver data could not be obtained, the ABM team reverted to percentage estimates. For example, operations managers would provide estimates of the percentage of time spent processing claims by individual products.

In modeling product costs, a full-absorption approach was used. The costs of activities that were not directly assignable or traceable to cost objects (e.g., preparing budgets and providing legal services) were separately identified. This technique provided subtotals to help management understand which costs were controllable and which were not. This allowed management to see the differences in their service and support costs versus their direct costs.

Linking ABM to Other Management Initiatives

In the fall of 1996, a major effort was undertaken to identify and define BCBSNC's most important business processes and to incorporate these into an overall business process model. Emmons was chosen to lead this effort.

In a white paper on BCBSNC's business process model, Emmons pointed out that a process orientation would move BCBSNC from functionally bound "silos" to a process-driven, highly integrated enterprise focused on the customers:

> *Business processes* are the common denominator of the horizontal organization. They allow managers to look across the enterprise to determine the activities that need to be coordinated in order to deliver value to customers.

This project defined a business process as a set of activities that takes inputs, adds value, and produces outputs for internal or external customers. Every process starts with customer requirements and ends with value delivered to the customer. This approach strongly linked ABM with business process modeling.

Exhibit 6 shows a high-level view of BCBSNC's business process model. This model represents the key business processes that BCBSNC performs to deliver value to customers. The "manage the business" process, seven core processes, and the enabling processes, are the components of this high-level model.

As Emmons began business process modeling, he found it critical to align the business process model's activities with the ABM project's activities, so he started to work with the ABM team. As Emmons says:

> We needed to have a consistent view of our processes and activities to identify our cost drivers. We also needed to know what it costs to pro-

duce products within segments. For these reasons, we chose ABM as our strategic and operational weapon.

Emmons and the ABM team worked together closely to standardize activities and processes so that both projects used the same activity definitions. The activity dictionary for the ABM project is more detailed than the business process model, but the activity dictionary maps directly to the business process model.

"The alignment of the business processes with the ABM project ensured our success," said Emmons:

> Without that alignment, it would have been much more difficult to gain the understanding and support from the organization necessary to move these projects forward. The biggest barrier to moving toward a process-based organization is getting people to think horizontally. Most people have risen in the organization and have been successful by performing the tasks, activities, and projects associated with a functional area.

Budgeting Process

ABM is gaining wider usage at BCBSNC as the company's cost management evolves from product costing toward business process modeling. ABM is also expanding in the area of annual budgeting.

Movement toward an activity-based budget began during 1997 as part of the 1998 budgeting cycle. While still functionally organized, BCBSNC now produces a 12-month line-item budget. When each cost center produces a line-item budget, it also predicts how the budgeted resources will be traced to activities for the coming year. This process ensures that the resource-level budgets line up with the expected activities, and—in turn—allows BCBSNC to set benchmarks for projected activity costs, which can be monitored throughout the year.

Management hopes its budgeting process will evolve into one that is completely activity-based. The budgeting process would then start by determining expected customer outputs (i.e., number of products). Next, activity-based relationships would be used to calculate the number of activities required to produce those outputs, then activities needed would determine the resource levels required.

Results and Next Steps

BCBSNC constructed a strategic ABM model using an aggressive timeline. ABM is now being used at BCBSNC to support the business process model and to push the planning process down to budgeted activity costs.

Exhibit 6: BCBSNC Business Process Model

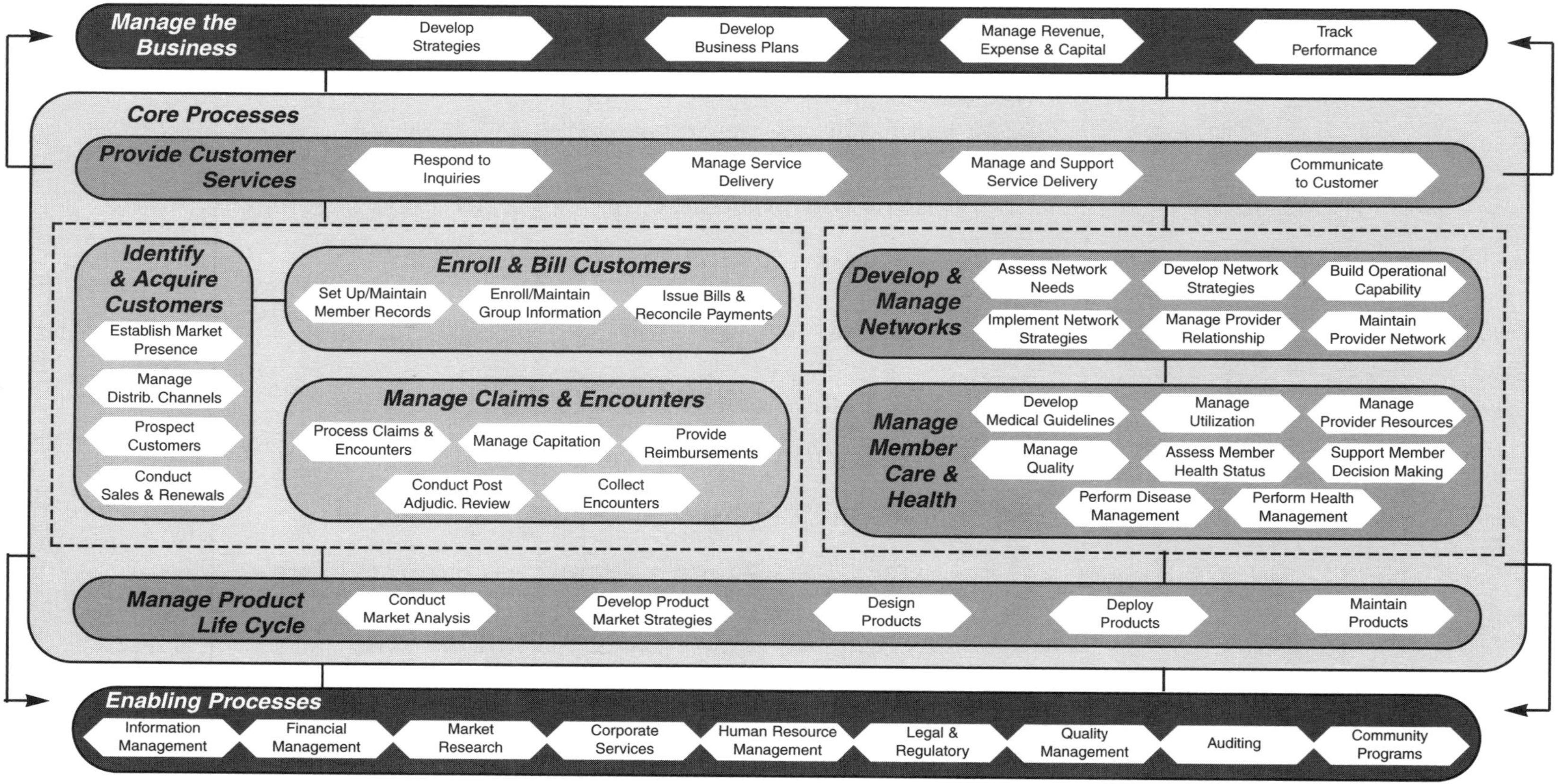

Manage the Business

- Develop Strategies
- Develop Business Plans
- Manage Revenue, Expense & Capital
- Track Performance

Core Processes

Provide Customer Services

- Respond to Inquiries
- Manage Service Delivery
- Manage and Support Service Delivery
- Communicate to Customer

Identify & Acquire Customers

- Establish Market Presence
- Manage Distrib. Channels
- Prospect Customers
- Conduct Sales & Renewals

Enroll & Bill Customers

- Set Up/Maintain Member Records
- Enroll/Maintain Group Information
- Issue Bills & Reconcile Payments

Manage Claims & Encounters

- Process Claims & Encounters
- Conduct Post Adjudic. Review
- Manage Capitation
- Collect Encounters
- Provide Reimbursements

Develop & Manage Networks

- Assess Network Needs
- Implement Network Strategies
- Develop Network Strategies
- Manage Provider Relationship
- Build Operational Capability
- Maintain Provider Network

Manage Member Care & Health

- Develop Medical Guidelines
- Manage Quality
- Perform Disease Management
- Manage Utilization
- Assess Member Health Status
- Perform Health Management
- Manage Provider Resources
- Support Member Decision Making

Manage Product Life Cycle

- Conduct Market Analysis
- Develop Product Market Strategies
- Design Products
- Deploy Products
- Maintain Products

Enabling Processes

- Information Management
- Financial Management
- Market Research
- Corporate Services
- Human Resource Management
- Legal & Regulatory
- Quality Management
- Auditing
- Community Programs

Activity-based information has significantly increased management's awareness of how costs flow to products at BCBSNC. The dynamic model has made ongoing contributions in the following key areas:

- New business: Cost information helps the company bid on and acquire new contracts.
- Operations: Financial information helps senior managers to operate the business.

Future Plans for the ABM Model

BCBSNC plans to update its ABM model monthly and to expand the products and segments tracked. Top management also plans to expand the dimensions viewed by bringing in analyses of regions and groups. The reports developed from the ABM model should ultimately become part of the monthly financial reports for management. BCBSNC also plans to integrate ABM by implementing full activity-based budgeting.

Otis noted, "We have been effectively using ABM for identifying costs associated with products and setting the right prices. We now plan to extend ABM's application into areas beyond product pricing."

Lessons Learned

- *Establish guidelines to limit the level of detail in both the activity dictionary and the list of cost objects.* More detail can be added after the initial implementation. It is better to discover the major cost sources and seek more detailed information later, than to become mired in the minutiae of an overly detailed ABM model.
- *Implementation teams need ABM expertise.* If you lack the expertise, hire it or engage experienced consultants to guide and train the team. Otherwise the project may quickly fail, which will make it harder to gain support for ABM later.
- *The commitment of top management is critical to the success of the project.* Having the support of top management makes it easier to deal with the inevitable obstacles to any ABM project.
- *Proper planning and realistic goals are essential.* Set appropriate milestones throughout the project. Communicate these goals to the organization, and publicize your success when goals are reached.
- *Coordinate ABM with other major projects to gain additional visibility and credibility.* Linkage to other important projects can give each project greater power. Enabling other initiatives is a great way to win support for an ABM project.

- *Clearly defined objectives are critical.* Make sure that ABM objectives are clearly aligned with key business issues and objectives.
- *Training is essential, though often overlooked.* All members of the ABM team should be trained in ABM concepts, implementation practices, use of the ABM software, and project management. Valuable resources are wasted if team members lack proper training. Those who receive activity-based information should also be trained so that they know how to interpret the information and how to use it appropriately.

7

Central and South West Corporation: Heating Up the Electric Utility Industry with Activity-Based Management

Introduction

Until recently, investors considered utilities safe, stable investments that could be depended on for steady rates of return. Utilities such as Central and South West Corporation (CSW), an international electric holding company headquartered in Dallas, Texas, operated as monopolies. Their prices were based on assets and recovery of annual costs. While the company's returns may not have been spectacular, they were consistent.

But things are changing rapidly for utilities. Deregulation, which is sweeping across the United States and other countries as well, is forcing dramatic shifts in pricing—and in the information needs of managers. Now utility executives need to know not only the profiles of their customer segments, but also the underlying profits and costs that those segments generate.

In a deregulated world, competitors are coming in to take those highly profitable accounts, potentially leaving the utility with a collection of less profitable customers. In today's world, understanding costs and which customers drive them is not only enlightening, but it is essential to keeping a utility company ahead of the competition. The experience of CSW discussed in this case study demonstrates how utilities can use activity-based management (ABM) to better understand profitability in a deregulated environment.

Business Issues

Utilities have traditionally been characterized by regulation at every level—federal, state, regional, and local. Deregulation in the electric industry, however, is ever increasing. And, while electric utilities have always needed to manage costs, deregulation makes this information even more vital due to competition in the marketplace of the future.

Many utilities have not fully understood the total cost of providing products to customer groups according to Bryan Kaiser, Senior Coordinating Consultant at CSW:

> As an industry, we have managed in terms of direct cost. Overhead items did not enter the picture. But it is imperative for all of us to recognize the full cost of doing business—and to attempt to make the information available in usable form.

Most electric utilities are vertically integrated which means that they are involved in all aspects of providing the product. They generate electricity, transmit it across a power grid, distribute it to individual homes and businesses, and also offer retail services.

But in recent years, companies have begun to move towards "unbundling" of their vertically integrated structure. Unbundling has caused electric utilities to review their strategies and goals in order to remain profitable. Companies such as CSW continue to modify their business environment by making adjustments both geographically and in areas of business served. Accurate cost information is a key to knowing where to add and where to cut.

Background

CSW, which owns and operates four electric utilities in the United States, serves 1.7 million people located in an area covering more than 150,000 square miles. In addition to its domestic electric operating companies, CSW's business structure includes:

- A regional electric company in the United Kingdom (SEEBOARD);
- Domestic and foreign independent generation facilities;
- Foreign electric delivery systems;
- A domestic communications company;
- Three energy-related service companies; and
- Financial subsidiaries.

Therefore, CSW owns, operates, and manages generation facilities, transmission and distribution electric delivery systems, communication delivery systems, customer-relations call centers, and area offices.

The company's domestic electric business provides electric service to residential, commercial, industrial, and wholesale customers in four states. CSW's U.S. electric business is supported by approximately 7,000 employees and had revenues in 1997 of some $3.3 billion.

Early in 1995, CSW's management recognized that the corporation needed "something more" from its management accounting. According to Kaiser, "Managers were not getting the cost information they needed to manage their businesses." While a wealth of good financial accounting information was available, the information was not useful from a process or operational perspective.

Initial Pilot and Project Rollout

Management's need for better cost information led to CSW's original ABM project, which began with a feasibility study facilitated by Arthur Andersen. The study began with no preconceived ideas as to which methodology would be selected, only the goal to determine what tools would most efficiently and effectively meet CSW's cost management needs.

As part of this three-month project, CSW members conducted interviews with about 50 CSW vice-presidents, executives, and managers from throughout the organization.

The results of the study confirmed a need to provide improved costing information. After results of the interviews were compiled, the project team chose ABM as the best tool to help them reach the company's goals. The team believed that by analyzing activities with ABM, they could identify the underlying drivers of costs.

The Pilot Project

Based on earlier recommendations a pilot project was begun in June 1995 to determine if ABM would provide the information CSW needed and wanted. The Controller of CSW sponsored this pilot project and asked Arthur Andersen to help once again.

Fifteen team members selected from all areas of the company were trained about ABM concepts, then sent back to their business units to define the major activities. This effort led to a list of activities. The initial focus was on CSW's domestic electric business, which represented about 95 percent of the company's total business at that time.

The initial implementation was linked to a market segmentation study by CSW's market research group. This market segmentation study sought to learn more about different characteristics of CSW's various customers. The market research group had expressed interest in understanding each segment's costs and related profits. The goal of the ABM team was to understand the cost structure and profitability of different segments or markets, including residential, commercial, and industrial customers.

A Strategic ABM Model

Once the decision was made to link ABM to the market segmentation study, the project team designed a strategic ABM model that would calculate relative profits generated by each segment.

But when this model was designed, the ABM team discovered that the model had to include the entire corporation, because shared-services organizations existed throughout the company. CSW's shared services organizations support the generation, delivery, and after-sales support of electricity as well as its unregulated businesses. Therefore, the costs of shared services had to be assigned to all internal consumers of each service; otherwise the cost assignments would be invalid.

Employees from each of the business units having to do with domestic electric activities conducted interviews in their major departments. Interviewers used a standard data collection form (see Exhibit 1). On this form, the interviewers recorded the activities performed by each department and also the percentage of time devoted to each activity.

Exhibit 1: Data Collection Form

Department Name	Activity Name	Resource Driver	Resource Driver Volume/Percentage

Activity Definitions

Much of the initial information was extremely detailed—even activities like opening mail and preparing time sheets were defined. As a result, some 1,000 task-level activities were later "rolled up" into a broader set of activities that allowed the team to focus on profitability by market segment.

Because of the strategic purpose of the model, it was unnecessary to use hundreds of activities to determine profitability by customer segment (see Exhibit 2). Instead, criteria were established using a baseline materiality level of $2 million dollars (0.1% of CSW's $2.4 billion cost structure). Activities that did not have at least $2 million dollars assigned to them were rolled up into other activities.

Exhibit 2: ABM Success Plan

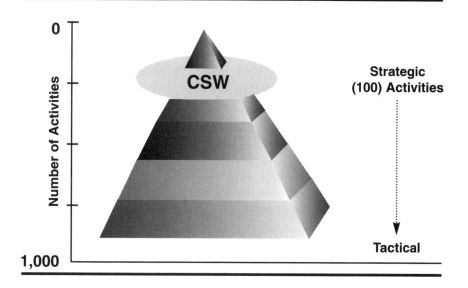

Kaiser explains the logic for defining activities for the pilot, as follows:

> Focusing on how any given activity affected customer profitability was imperative. There were a number of tasks we couldn't relate to cost objects. Things like copy work and so forth were rolled up. We had to reduce the number of activities, because we had nearly 1,000 at first, which would have made data collection extremely difficult.

The 1,000 activities originally identified were therefore consolidated into about 100 strategic activities. For example, the ABM team discovered that as it focused on customer profitability, 30 activities for the transmission area provided too much detail. Most of the activities provided no insight into the profitability of customer segments; having only one or two activities was sufficient. The 30 activities were thus consolidated into only two—one for lines and one for substations. Similarly, about 30 activities originally defined in distribution were deemed unnecessary and therefore were consolidated.

Kaiser explains the team's process for defining the activities associated with power generation as follows:

> Instead of breaking generation down into detailed work activities, we broke it down into generating plants. Each generating plant was an activity in our model, which meant that the team could determine product costs for each generating station. The generation business unit was

already preparing income statements for each generation station. We wanted to give them information that supplemented what was already being done.

The Strategic ABM Model

CSW's strategic ABM model, which used *Hyper*ABC software from Armstrong Laing, was completed in June 1996. The model (see Exhibit 3) included the following:

- 15 ABM cost pools (which were consolidated from over 3,000 general ledger accounts);
- 2,100 departmental cost centers (the costs came from the general ledger);
- 100 strategic activities;
- 2 products (capacity and kilowatt hours);
- 2 delivery channels (transmission and distribution); and
- 22 customer market segments.

Exhibit 3: Data Gathering and Modeling

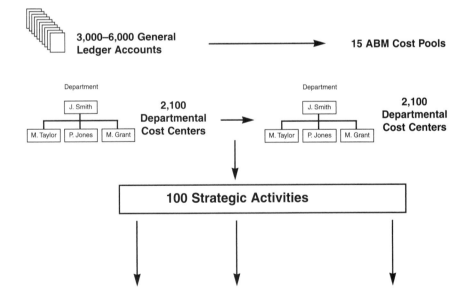

The ABM model calculated the profitability of these domestic segments as-signing $2.4 billion of costs to activities and then assigning those activities to cost objects. These costs represented 90–95 percent of CSW's domestic costs. The ABM model included fuel and purchased power cost, operating and maintenance cost, depreciation and amortization, debt and preferred equity capital cost, and other miscellaneous cost. These costs were reconciled to the general ledger to validate the data. The validation step ensured that the proper data was downloaded from the general ledger into the ABM system.

The initial strategic ABM project took 12 months to complete. The length of the project took its toll on the ABM team, which shrank from 15 part-time members at the beginning to only two full-time members at completion. In retrospect, Kaiser recommends that an enterprise-wide pilot be broken down into shorter, more manageable pieces.

Ongoing ABM Initiative

During the pilot, it became apparent that cost information was not the only ben-efit of ABM. Management needed additional performance measurement infor-mation to make better decisions. To address this need, an ongoing "activity-based costing and performance measurement" (ABC&PM) team was formed. This team included seven full-time members who are responsible for preparing performance scorecards, including unit cost measures. The team also provides cost and profitability analyses for products, channels and customers.

The ABC&PM function reports to CSW's Controller through the "Plan-ning and Analysis" department. Team members were selected from different areas of the company, including:

- Generation engineering;
- Transmission and distribution engineering;
- Customer service;
- Human resources;
- Information technology;
- Financial systems and controls; and
- Financial planning and accounting.

The ABM model at CSW is now updated semi-annually. (Exhibit 4 shows a project timeline.) Resource driver information is updated using both data collection forms and face-to-face interviews. Usually, existing information is presented, then the ABC&PM team determines if the information remains valid or needs updating.

CSW continues to use *Hyper*ABC for modeling. Kaiser says that the soft-ware offers great flexibility for the cost and profitability analyses users need.

CSW also plans to develop a more tactical (or operational) version of the ABM model, which will use an expanded set of activities.

Exhibit 4: Central and South West Project Timeline

Project Milestone	1995 Mar	Jun	Sep	Dec	1996 Mar	Jun	Sep	Dec	1997 Mar	Jun	Sep	Dec	1998 Mar	Jun	Sep	Dec
1. Arthur Anderson Feasibility Study	1															
2. Original Cross-Functional Team Formed		2														
3. *HyperABC* Software Selected			3													
4. Activities Defined and Validated			4													
5. Initial Activity Costing Completed				5												
6. Calculated Complete Model						6										
7. Segment Profitability Reporting						7										
8. Full time ABM Team Selected								8								
9. Performance Scorecard Initiated									9							
10. Business Unit Profitability									10							
11. Update Model with '97 Volumes and Cost										11						
12. Formalized Electronic Reporting														12		
13. Benchmarking Studies to be Initiated																13

Automating Data Collection

The ABC&PM team has automated the activity output data collection to the greatest extent possible by using commercially available software products and other data extraction tools. Data comes from many major systems including the following:

- The general ledger;
- The property system (CSW's version of a fixed asset system);
- The human resources system;
- The materials management system;
- The customer information system; and
- The accounts payable system.

As Kaiser explains:

> We have done a proof-of-concept pilot using Oracle database tools, and we plan on using them more in the future to store extracted data. The ABC&PM team has also created formatted templates for clients who need to provide us with data that does not reside in mainframe or other major systems.

Since this is the first time that some of the data has been needed (or needed at this level of detail), the ABC&PM team has occasionally needed to work with client groups to "scrub" or fix the data. Although the results generated by the ABM model may not match the financial results generated by the traditional financial system (because of different cost-flow assumptions), the team always reconciles to the original cost data (including trial balances, income statements, and balance sheets). This ensures the validity of the ABM output and helps explain the results to managers who have only seen financial data.

Reporting is a very simple process. Dynamic software links provided by *Hyper*ABC are used to view and report the results in Microsoft Access. This lets users of Microsoft Access perform their own queries and customize their own reports.

The ABC&PM team is now trying to place cost information on CSW's intranet. Their goal is to use all available technology to put information into managers' hands. The data can be shared by attaching files to e-mail, using an internal on-line publication tool, reporting the data through CSW's website, and by providing the Microsoft Access tables. The one thing the team does not do is mail paper reports. As Kaiser says, "We do not have the staff to produce and mail a stack of reports just in case a manager wants to look at them."

Integration with Other Initiatives

By integrating activity costing with performance scorecards, a natural link was created between ABM and process decision analysis. CSW has marketed this approach to leaders of its strategic business units.

Cost Efficiency

The ABC&PM team works extensively with groups that have a strategic focus on cost efficiency. These business units (which include power generation, energy delivery, customer relations, the supply chain, information technology, and telecommunications) have begun to use cost and performance information for internal benchmarking. As a result, they can develop standardization and process improvement activities.

To link ABM efforts to corporate and business unit strategies, business plans are used to develop performance scorecards for internal clients. These *balanced scorecards* cover the following four areas:

- Financial and economic factors;
- Products, markets, and customers;
- Product or service delivery processes; and,
- Culture, innovation, and technology.

As scorecards are being developed, strategies are classified into one of these categories, then the appropriate business measurement is chosen to help achieve the strategy. (Exhibit 5 shows the underlying measures used at the corporate level.) Each business unit develops a set of measures that link up to the corporate measures.

Results and Next Steps

One of the most important contributions of the ABM model has been in shared service cost transfers. CSW spends much time assigning shared service costs based on the volume of consumption of a particular service. The best output volume for a particular service is determined, then information is gathered to determine how much of the output each department consumes. Costs are assigned to internal consumers based on the cost per unit consumed multiplied by the units consumed. These cost assignments are based on information provided by the ABM model. The information is of great interest to clients that use internal shared services.

Shared service providers have begun using the information to manage their unit costs, because the process provides a full picture of activity costs. Before ABM was implemented, costs remained within the functional area that provided the service, so the true profitability of products and segments was unknown.

Exhibit 5: Corporate Balanced Scorecard

Culture/Innovation/Technology	Financial/Economic
• Domestic Utilities Residential Consumer Satisfaction Indices • International Utilities Customer Satisfaction • Research and Development Expenditures (Tentative)	• Economic Value • Free Cash Flow • Operating Cash Flow • Earnings Per Share • Return on Equity

Product/Service Delivery Process	Products/Markets/Customers
• Domestic Utilities Reliability Indices • Domestic Utilities Performing Commitments • Consolidated Net Operating Profit After Tax • Consolidated Operating Margin • Consolidated Return on Net Investment	• Domestic Energy Kilowatt Hour Growth • Domestic Energy Capital Growth • International Energy/Utilities Revenue Growth • International Energy/Utilities Capital Growth • Related Retail Services Revenue Growth

---

Important benefits also came from the integration of activity costing with the balanced scorecard performance reporting. This information will be used to help CSW's managers see how individual activities affect economic value—and the relationship this has to performance improvement.

A third area where ABM has produced important results is profitability analysis which was developed in the pilot for different market segments. This is a critical area for utility companies like CSW that face the increased competition brought by deregulation. CSW's strategic ABM models provide insight into where the company can gain profitable revenues from other competitors as well as which markets CSW should defend.

Using ABM to Manage

CSW's vision of the future includes expanding the use of ABM as a management tool rather than simply a method for gathering costs. The objective is to enable managers to make operating decisions that maximize long-term economic value. Plans call for integration of ABM into every aspect of its management, beginning with the planning and budgeting process and ending with performance appraisals and incentive programs. According to ABM team members, "If we are going to manage by activities, it must be all-encompassing or it won't work."

This vision is not universally accepted yet at CSW. Those who do not understand the possible benefits may consider ABM a replacement or alternative for other necessary efforts, such as financial reporting or the need to plan, budget, and allocate resources. In fact, ABM builds upon and enhances other financial tools rather than replacing them.

It takes time for everyone in a large organization to accept that the costs of activities can be used to strategically understand customer profitability. Constant education and communication are required. According to Kaiser, "Getting ABM integrated into the daily thinking and decision making of a large corporation is a very slow process. Be patient and never give up."

Lessons Learned

- *Manage expectations.* Kaiser notes that the most important task for an ABM team is "to manage expectations for the organization. You need to clearly communicate what type of information is to come out of the project, what the information will be used for, and what it will not be used for."
- *Use cross-functional teams.* Campaign diligently for cross-functional representation on the ABM team. Having a broad-based team will facilitate communication and buy-in from the entire organization. Also, diversity on the team broadens its knowledge base.
- *Teach managers how to use ABM information.* Market ABM information constantly as a way to make better management decisions. Again, ongoing marketing and communications efforts are critical to keep the project team on track. These efforts must emphasize the benefits of ABM information so that ABM is integrated into daily thinking and decision making.
- *Plan the project.* Determine the project's objectives at the outset. Meet with internal customers to learn their expectations. As the author Stephen R. Covey says, "You must begin with the end in mind."
- *Train the team and users on ABM concepts.* Make sure that the team is properly trained about ABM concepts and implementation techniques. Similarly, those who will use the information have to be trained to understand the reports generated, which will present costs in an unfamiliar format.
- *Select a motivated, high-energy ABM team.* Obstacles are inevitable with any significant change in management processes. The team should have tremendous energy and perseverance to overcome these obstacles.
- *Continuous selling is critical.* Even when an ABM project has the support of top management, people cannot be forced to use the information. Leaders must be convinced that ABM will help them attain their business goals. Explain the benefits of ABM and how it provides information they need to manage their businesses better. Persistence counts.

8

CinCFleet: Military Might with Activity-Based Management

Introduction

Focusing successful organizations on cost management can be difficult, especially when that organization's mission is military readiness. Because of budget cutbacks, military leaders throughout the world have had to face the important question of how cost management can help military commanders meet their goals—defending their countries in a time of lessened tension—while also keeping military men and women ready for war.

This case study shows how the British Navy's Commander in Chief Fleet (CinCFleet) recently implemented activity-based management (ABM) to help its leaders understand the full costs of naval operations.

Business Issues

Ministries of the British Government prepare many financial reports these days that were never required several years ago. British Ministries are moving away from cash accounting toward accrual accounting. They are now required to produce a complete set of financial statements, including full cost accounting reports, cash flow statements, and balance sheets.

What's more, CinCFleet recently introduced ABM throughout the department. As the ABM Project Manager* of CinCFleet states:

> We in the Ministry of Defence—and CinCFleet in particular—are working on a key initiative that is part of the accrual accounting directive called *output costing*. We needed to identify our cost objects in a reasonable way so we could facilitate what we call "cost communication" between budgetary areas. Historically, we have been requesting X million

---

*By policy of the Ministry of Defence, names of CinCFleet personnel cannot be given here.

pounds for manpower and X million pounds for fuel, but not explaining *why* we needed the funding. We knew the inputs, but not where the money went. Now we want to see the outputs or services produced by CinCFleet.

CinCFleet also wanted to understand the shared costs among departments or areas.

Effective costing procedures make it much simpler for CinCFleet to identify internal charges and to understand the full cost of a product or service—even if the activity in question does not incur an actual or "hard" charge in the budget.

In the past, CinCFleet could not identify the complete costs of its outputs. Under the new cost system, however, CinCFleet will receive "memo billings" from other Ministry of Defence (MoD) departments, but no hard charge or transfer of cost to the general ledger.

When a ship goes from sea into a base, for example, it must be pulled by a tugboat. The tugboat used may fall under the auspices of another unit of the Royal Navy. In the past, CinCFleet's system could not capture the full cost of getting the ship into base; an *activity cost* like pulling the ship by tugboat could not be transferred or memo billed. Yet activity costs such as the cost of tugboats were exactly what CinCFleet desperately wanted to understand.

To gain a better understanding of full costs, CinCFleet decided to develop a system that reflected those costs, and ABM was chosen as the tool to provide that information.

Background

CinCFleet is one of the 13 units of the MoD sometimes called *top-level budgets,* or TLBs (see Exhibit 1 for the budgetary structure of the MoD). But CinCFleet is not only a management area of the MoD; the term also refers to the person who is Commander in Chief (CinC) of the Royal Navy. CinCFleet is responsible for the operational capability of the Royal Navy, including all ships and submarines. All naval operations under the direction of CinCFleet are directed from Northwood, a military installation just outside of London.

CinCFleet itself has the following six budget areas (called *higher-level budgets,* or HLBs):

- Submarines.
- Surface Flotilla.
- Naval Aviators.
- Royal Marines.
- Royal Fleet Auxiliary.

- Fleet Headquarters (which provides command and control for all the other areas).

Exhibit 1: British Ministry of Defence Budgetary Structure

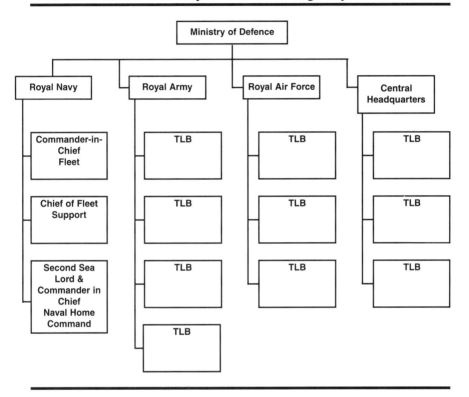

These HLBs refer to distinct areas of operation within CinCFleet (see Exhibit 2 for CinCFleet's organizational chart).

The total annual operating budget for CinCFleet is £1.1 billion—roughly U.S.$1.8 billion. ABM is now used solely for cash costs. Although noncash charges such as depreciation are not yet included in CinCFleet's ABM models, CinCFleet is moving toward full costing.

Several of the HLBs are further broken down into basic-level budgets (BLBs), which depend on the structure of the particular organization. For example, the Royal Marines has several BLBs based on various geographical areas. Regardless of their location, BLBs report to their HLB, which reports in turn to CinCFleet.

Exhibit 2: Organization Chart of the Commander in Chief Fleet

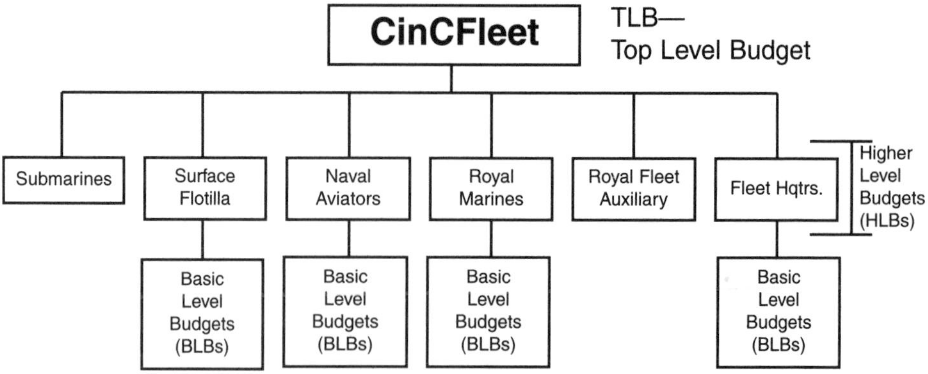

Note: The number of BLBs may vary depending on the structure of the HLB. Submarines and the Royal Fleet Auxiliary do not have any BLBs.

Project Rollout

After CinCFleet received the general directive in the mid-1990s to implement accrual accounting, research began at the Northwood facility to determine a methodology to help CinCFleet implement full output costing. The naval command had to determine which tool could be used to calculate the full cost of all services. Ultimately, ABM was the methodology selected.

ABM Team

The ABM project began in late 1994 with a team composed of three management accountants. The rollout to the HLBs began in early 1995. The ABM team provided support and assistance to the various HLBs, each of which was held responsible for building its own models. This requirement was based on the conviction that each HLB would know infinitely more about its own activities than anyone else. About 50 people in the field were involved in building ABM models.

The ABM team was responsible for collecting all of the models from the HLBs, consolidating the information, and producing the necessary reports, which were distributed to the appropriate users of the information.

Initial Efforts

In early stages of the ABM project, the goal was to support an annual costing process known as *long-term costing,* an annual projection of operating and cash requirements ten years into the future. The ABM Project Manager described long-term costing as follows:

Because of the nature of our business, a ship wears out and we have to project that far ahead. This way, we ensure that when a ship is being decommissioned, there is another ship coming along to replace it. The ABM system was put into place initially to provide long-term cost figures in *output* terms—rather than in purely input terms or resource costs. Its purpose was to justify funding requests made to the British Parliament. However, the goal was to take the input terms and relate them directly to specific activities. What we wanted to determine was a better definition of the outputs. If we spend a certain amount of money, what exactly is accomplished for that amount of money? Where does it go? And what is the exact benefit derived?

The ABM Project Manager, who arrived at CinCFleet in 1995, joined the three management accountants on the ABM team. He was responsible for determining the direct outputs of the costs being consumed.

The first year, according to the Project Manager, was a "dummy exercise" (see the Enterprise Rollout Timeline in Exhibit 3). The team made several broad assumptions and produced what they called "shadow" *output costing*. Input and output terms were not calculated: The goal was simply to prove that ABM worked and to win support for using ABM. Based on the successful achievement of these objectives, the ABM project moved to the next stage.

Fiscal Year

CinCFleet operates on a fiscal year that begins in April and ends in March. After the successful shadow costing exercise, the group began its development of HLB models using 1996–97 planning figures and nine additional forecasted years. After the fiscal year ended, the ABM figures were produced and made available in time for a meeting held in September 1996. During that time, discussions occurred about the structure of the models. In particular, attempts were made to achieve a common structure for activities. As the ABM Project Manager said, "We had long discussions about the activities, and ultimately we achieved the uniformity desired. We wanted to be able to look at cost measures across CinCFleet."

Long-term costing in 1997 focused on outputs for the first time and was completed in September 1996. The full long-term costing included output terms at the TLB, HLB, and BLB levels. The BLBs "rolled up" into an HLB, and the HLBs rolled up into a TLB. (See Exhibit 2 for CinCFleet's internal structure.) CinCFleet's senior management was very pleased to receive this information. ABM provided information they needed to complete the long-term forecasting required.

Exhibit 3: CINCFLEET Enterprise Rollout Timeline

Project Milestone	1994				1995				1996				1997				1998			
	Mar	Jun	Sep	Dec	Mar	Jun	Sep	Dec	Mar	Jun	Sep	Dec	Mar	Jun	Sep	Dec	Mar	Jun	Sep	Dec
1. Initiated Project				1																
2. *HyperABC* Software Selected					2															
3. Present ABM Project Manager joined project						3														
4. Rollout to HLBs						4														
5. Shadow output costing						5														
6. Preparation for LTC '97									6											
7. Customized training developed and provided									7											
8. Completed LTC '97											8									
9. Preparation for LTC '98													9							
10. Completed LTC '98															10					
11. Reevaluation of model detail																	11			
12. Evaluation of use for performance measurement																		12		
13. Preparation for LTC '99																		13		
14. Evaluation for monthly forecasting in output terms																			14	

HLB—Higher Level Budget
LTC—Long-Term Costing

Internal Reorganization

In late 1996, certain weaknesses were identified in the ABM rollout. Simultaneously, an internal reorganization occurred. In June 1996, the three management accountants were reassigned to other responsibilities, which left only the ABM Project Manager: "When it fell to me, I knew there were some issues within the HLB areas that had to be dealt with. There was a lot of mistrust and a lot of disillusionment with the ABM system." The ABM Project Manager conducted full-scale troubleshooting in each area to determine the problems not only with the system, but also with the ABM methodology that had been followed.

What he discovered were major misunderstandings of the system and of the methodology. No one could really get his or her arms around it. Because of these misunderstandings, support for the project was waning. Fortunately, the CinC—the senior executive in the organization—was very committed to the ABM project, so the Project Manager set out to make immediate changes.

Change can be difficult in any organization, and CinCFleet had definite change management issues. As the ABM Project Manager puts it, "The attitude of many people here is 'How will full-cost information help me engage in military activities?' We had to deal with these cultural issues and attitudes. Change management has been the biggest challenge, even with the CinC's active interest."

ABM Training

The ABM Project Manager first took time to evaluate the implementation, then he introduced various training and support activities to encourage a better understanding of both the system and the methodology. The ABM Project Manager traveled throughout the country to all areas involved in the rollout, where he provided extensive support. He taught the local units how to work with the ABM model, how to report the information, and what it could do for them: "If you are going to introduce something from the top, there are always personnel at outstations far removed from the headquarters. They receive this new system from above and, without training, can find it difficult to use."

The ABM Project Manager's goal was to provide all the hands-on support needed. Working with a training instructor from the Armstrong Laing Group (ALG), he developed and wrote a course designed especially for CinCFleet with modeling terminology specific to the organization. For example, CinCFleet does not use the term "departments." Instead "Unit Identity Numbers" are used. The course incorporated these changes to facilitate acceptance of the system within CinCFleet. ALG also tailored the *Hyper*ABC software for CinCFleet by incorporating terminology specific to CinCFleet.

The system is not complicated, but the original terminology differed significantly from CinCFleet's terminology. Everyone believed the intended users of the system would be more receptive to information that used terminology they were familiar with—and, thus, they would be more likely to use it. Changing the terminology to reflect CinCFleet activities helped bridge the gap and move towards accomplishing that goal.

Although the extensive training and support provided was time consuming, the response was positive. The participants in the training understood the system and began to see the benefits of ABM. According to the ABM Project Manager, the training and support made a huge difference to the successful outcome of the project.

ABM Models

About 60 people in the field work with the system. They use one or more of nearly 20 models. Models from the HLBs are sent to the ABM Project Manager. Depending on the area, the HLB may have five or six BLBs. The Project Manager may get an amalgamation of those lower-level models or he may receive individual models for each. The Project Manager notes:

> I would like to know more about the underlying elements in many of the activities. It would help me to fully understand what goes on within each HLB and its specific problems. I argue that if you can show full costs, you will have a position of strength, because you will be able to tell exactly what your costs are and why. They will be fully justified in a reasonable manner. But it is a change of culture and that always takes time.

A typical HLB operates with approximately six high-level activities that deal specifically with the activities of support areas. These "drill down" to about 100 lower-level activities. Some of these activities are similar across all the HLBs, while others differ according to the area (e.g., aircrafts versus ships).

Future Plans

The CinC is very interested in determining the full cost of "task ready days," which is the full daily cost of a ship at sea. There are also different levels or "readiness states." If a ship is fully trained, fully manned, and fully armed, it is at a different state than another ship not quite up to that standard. Knowledge about the cost differences between readiness states will help the Commander make decisions about how many ships are kept at what readiness states.

According to the ABM Project Manager, the information available from full costing would allow CinCFleet to better understand its resources:

> I believe that, if we don't have an understanding of full costs, how can we understand the product itself? How do we recognize the military task or know if a ship is actually as effective as it could be? These days, when government is looking for efficiencies, we must be able to justify ourselves and our actions, and to a greater extent.

The ABM Project Manager compares CinCFleet's need to better understand its costs to a chef trying to prepare a dish using an incomplete recipe:

> Perhaps you have the recipe, and the ingredients, but you don't know the quantities or how to mix them together. Or you don't know how long to cook it. The finished product may be raw or it may be burned. Like the chef in the story, we have to know how best to utilize the resources available to us.

Users of ABM Information

The primary users of ABM information have been CinCFleet's central staff. Because the ABM information is geared toward annual budgeting and costing reports, the basic-level operational managers have not fully used ABM information, though this is a goal for the future. CinCFleet plans to move beyond providing only strategic information. The plan is to implement ABM soon at the operational level so that it provides better management information. Ships engaged in training exercises, for example, incur radically different costs than ships that visit foreign ports for diplomatic reasons. An ABM system can measure and project those costs.

Recent changes in CinCFleet have reduced the length of the long-term costing process from ten years to four. CinCFleet also has until the end of the decade to move from its present accounting system toward accrual accounting. (The same directive applies to all government ministries.) When full accrual accounting begins in 2001, CinCFleet's reports will have to be published and audited by the United Kingdom's National Audit Office in NATO.

Results and Next Steps

ABM provides CinCFleet's senior management output costing information that helps with the annual budgetary process. This has been seen as an improvement by senior management, but there is still a long way to go.

As with all new systems, there have been some nonbelievers. But there is a growing recognition that CinCFleet needs a fuller understanding of its costs. Sometimes it is difficult for people to measure the benefits of ABM. It is a valid question, moreover, to ask whether knowing and understanding costs will help run a war or drive a ship: A war is not run on costs. Yet, as more and more budget cutbacks appear on the horizon, the better CinCFleet understands and controls its costs, the better its chances of successfully defending the budget requests it makes. To achieve optimum readiness, CinCFleet must know the actual cost of a ship, whether the ship is put to sea or docked at the base.

CinCFleet will be taking a close look at its ABM systems in the near future to reevaluate the detail captured for annual budgeting. Those knowledgeable about ABM have concluded that they have gone into too much detail for this annual process. However, they are looking into the need for providing key operational information more frequently for management purposes and for monthly forecasting. Additional plans now call for using ABM information to facilitate performance management.

Finally, CinCFleet must meet MoD's requirements concerning accrual accounting: CinCFleet has led the way within the MoD in preparing for the mandates for the year 2001. The ABM implementation has thus proved successful, and CinCFleet looks forward to continuing its ABM journey.

Lessons Learned

- *Complete a proper business analysis.* It is important to thoroughly analyze the business issues you want to resolve, and to do so at the very start of the project. CinCFleet's experience testifies to the fact that it is much simpler to get where you are going if you have a map to guide the way—in this case, a well-defined ABM map with well-defined parameters. Much like driving a ship safely into harbor.
- *Executive buy-in is essential.* The key to this project's success was the involvement of the CinC and his Management Board. The CinC continued to champion the ABM effort because of his belief in both the cause and the results produced. Having a top-level champion helps tremendously in smoothing the waves when you run into turbulent waters along the way to an effective implementation of ABM.
- *Consistency is key for enterprise-wide analysis.* It is important to achieve some sort of commonality between areas. If you have different functions in different areas, you need an activity map to provide some consistency across each of the areas. There must also be a valid measure of what is happening within the organization.
- *Keep your models as simple as possible.* Determine through your early analysis what type of information you are going to provide from your models. If the models are strategic in nature, keep detail to a minimum. Don't go into any more detail than what is needed for the analysis. Too much de-

tail slows the process down and confuses users. Focus on controllable costs, because that is where management can make the most immediate change.

- *Properly train participants at all levels.* Training is extremely important when you implement an ABM system. Don't expect people to understand the methodology, software, or process if they haven't been thoroughly trained. ABM is totally new, so everyone involved in model building, data collection, and reporting has to be trained so that they can use the system effectively and analyze the reports received. Also customize your training by using terminology people understand, which will help them learn the material faster.
- *Provide ongoing support.* In addition to formal training, provide ongoing support for those in the field who build models. When a project is directed from the top, those who are out doing the legwork must have the resources they need—and when they are needed. Without this support the participants will become frustrated and disillusioned.

9

Dana Commercial Credit Corporation: The Road to ABM Excellence

Introduction

What does a great company do to get better? Implement activity-based management (ABM). In 1996, Dana Commercial Credit Corporation (DCC) was at the pinnacle of success. DCC had just won the prestigious Malcolm Baldrige National Quality Award in the seldom-awarded service company category. Benchmarking results showed that DCC won dramatically in virtually every category, from return on equity to customer satisfaction. This case study discusses why DCC chose to implement ABM and how ABM is being used to better satisfy DCC's customers.

Background

DCC began operations in 1980 with a $2.5 million investment from its ultimate corporate parent, Dana Corporation (Dana). With annual revenues exceeding $250 million and about $2 billion in assets, DCC has grown to be one of the largest leasing and financing companies in North America.

DCC has expanded internationally; it now has offices throughout the United States, Canada, the United Kingdom, and continental Europe. DCC has various subsidiaries, divisions, and operating groups. Each operates independently, though they share certain management, administration, and marketing functions.

DCC, which has over 750 employees, has the following six product groups:

- Diversified Capital;
- Capital Markets;
- Dealer Products;
- Technology Management;
- Asset Management Services; and
- Shannon Properties.

Because of DCC's decentralized approach, about 75 percent of its employees in the product groups have direct contact with customers. What's more, each product group is empowered to manage its own customer relationships and to devote the resources needed to meet and exceed customers' expectations.

As Jim Beckham, DCC's Director of Quality, explains:

> If you asked to see our strategic plan I couldn't show it to you. I could show you six strategic plans. Each product group is a self-contained business unit. We want to give employees a sense of responsibility that they will be around tomorrow because of the actions they take today.

This philosophy is ingrained into decision making at DCC. Senior management does not mandate projects such as ABM. Instead, when a business issue arises within a product group, the product group itself determines what approach will be taken to address the issue.

Business Issues

Winning the 1996 Baldrige Award merely provided validation of the fact that DCC was an extremely well-managed company. Yet, as a service company in an unregulated industry, DCC had no existing cost system other than its general ledger. Consequently, although the company was experiencing tremendous growth and record profits, it had no firm grasp on the costs of its products and services.

Some may find it difficult to understand how an extremely profitable, well-managed company can be so successful without a cost system. The answer lies in the company's focus on quality, which leads directly to low cost and operational excellence.

As Beckham notes:

> When you look at the Baldrige criteria, effectiveness and efficiency stand out. In other words, if you focus on the effectiveness of a process, you are focusing on the customer, and then ultimately efficiency will be achieved.

Baldrige Criteria

DCC increased its focus on quality in 1993, when its parent Dana implemented its own quality award based on the following seven Baldrige criteria (Malcolm Baldrige National Quality Award - 1996 Award Criteria):

1. Leadership: Examines senior executives' personal leadership and involvement in creating and sustaining a customer focus, clear values and expectations, and a leadership system that promotes performance excellence.

2. Information and analysis: Examines the management and effectiveness of the use of data and information to support customer-driven performance excellence and marketplace success.
3. Strategic planning: Examines how the company sets strategic directions, and how it determines key plan requirements.
4. Human resource development and management: Examines how the work force is enabled to develop and utilize its full potential, aligned with the company's performance objectives.
5. Process management: Examines the key aspects of process management, including customer-focused design, product and service delivery processes, support services, and supply management involving all work units, including research and development.
6. Business results: Examines the company's performance and improvement in key business areas—product and service quality, productivity and operational effectiveness, supply quality, and financial performance indicators linked to these areas.
7. Customer focus and satisfaction: Examines the company's systems for customer learning and for building and maintaining customer relationships.

(See Exhibit 1—Baldrige Award Criteria Framework)

Interestingly, the trigger to implement ABM came at DCC from a customer satisfaction requirement.

Need for a Cost System

During a strategic planning session with the Diversified Capital Group, the issue of cost of servicing DCC's largest customer was at the top of the agenda. According to Gerry Fuller, DCC's controller:

> We were negotiating fees, and the customer was under the impression that they were paying more than they should. We believed they weren't paying enough. We knew that we must focus on our customer's needs. To make this customer comfortable with the pricing, we needed a cost system.

Ed Shultz, the CEO of DCC, had previously voiced the belief that DCC might benefit from ABM. As Fuller notes, "We did our research on ABM and decided to embark upon a pilot to respond to this customer need and to better understand the cost structure." The pilot focused on the Diversified Capital Group, which is a midsize leasing group that specializes in leases that range in value from $50,000 to $2 million. The main cost objects were the programs, customers, and channels of the Group.

Exhibit 1: Baldrige Award Criteria Framework

Dynamic Relationships

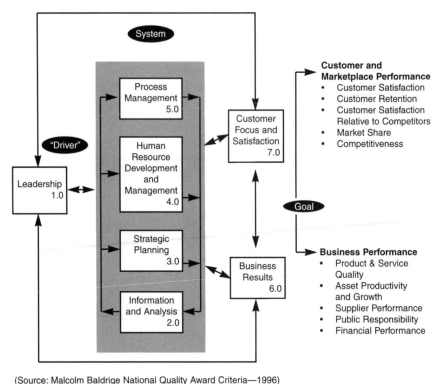

(Source: Malcolm Baldrige National Quality Award Criteria—1996)

Project Rollout

The ABM pilot was launched in April 1997, and followed a four-phase implementation (see Exhibit 2—ABM Implementation Steps). While a steering committee was not used, the ABM team appointed did have the full backing of senior management, including Shultz, the CEO, and Rod Filcek, the CFO.

DCC's ten-member, cross-functional, ABM team included the following:

- The ABM manager;
- The controller;
- The accounting manager;
- An accounting analyst;
- The supervisor of business systems and processes;
- The supervisor of portfolio administration;

- A portfolio administrator;
- Two investment analysts; and
- A lease administrator.

Each of the team members participated in the interviews and the model building.

Exhibit 2: ABM Implementation Steps

Phase I	Phase II	Phase III	Phase IV
• Define business needs/ project scope • Form cross-functional team • Educate participants • Select software	• Define business processes • Define activities • Define tasks	• Conduct interviews • Assign time • Define activity drivers	• Calculate model • Perform "Sanity Tests" • Research open issues • Report to management

Training and Communication

As Brad Gillespie, DCC's ABM manager, notes:

> One key to success has been the provision of adequate training and education for project participants. This included the team as well as each employee of the Diversified Capital Group. Following on the concept that DCC believes people are our most important asset, we believe that we need to continually educate our employees and keep them informed and not surprised.

Two training sessions were held before the interviews began. The first focused on ABM concepts, methodologies, terminology, and the reasons behind the ABM implementation. The second training session covered the terms *value-added* versus *non-value-added*.

As Gillespie notes:

> We planned to perform non-value-added activity analysis, and we wanted to avoid misconceptions. During the training, we did not want people to take offense to the term non-value-added. We emphasized that the focus was on the activity and not the person.

The training proved to be beneficial. In the interviews, employees were very forthcoming in providing information about their participation in non-value-added activities.

Employees themselves categorized an activity as either value-added or non-value-added. Because training and education had removed their fear of identifying non-value-added activities they had to perform, they freely provided this information. Value-added activities were defined as those activities that a customer is willing to pay for or that the government requires. All other activities are considered non-value-added.

In addition to providing training, the ABM team also began an aggressive communication plan to keep employees posted about ABM developments. The team even published a monthly newsletter—the *ABM Examiner*—with articles about ABM and progress reports about the results.

The training and newsletter articles were put on DCC's Intranet website, thus making them continuously available to all employees (see Exhibit 3 for overview of the ABC website).

Software Selection

DCC reviewed ten ABM software packages, then narrowed the search to two finalists. One key criterion was to find a program that worked well with what the company already had in place. Another was to feel comfortable with the people who would provide technical support.

The four-person selection committee unanimously chose *Hyper*ABC by Armstrong Laing because of its use of multidimensional cost objects, support for users, and ease of use. But, the overriding factor was the comfort level members of the ABM team had with Armstrong Laing.

Data Collection

To define activities, the team conducted about 50 interviews, with at least two team members at each interview. The interviews were quite extensive, each lasting two to three hours. When the team assembled the information they had collected, they found 162 activities that they had identified (though many of these were actually tasks rather than activities).

In the first round of interviews, the people interviewed categorized the activities that they performed as either value-added or non-value-added. As Gillespie notes:

> We also allowed interviewees to designate an activity as only partially non-value-added. For example, if they felt that an activity was 75 percent value-added and only 25 percent non-value-added, they could note that on their survey, which facilitated the process.

After compiling the results of the interviews, the ABM team concluded that, by identifying 162 activities, they had gone into too much detail. They worked to

---

Exhibit 3: ABC Web Site

▼ Home
▼ Search
▼ Feedback

ACTIVITY-BASED COSTING

Diversified Capital Group

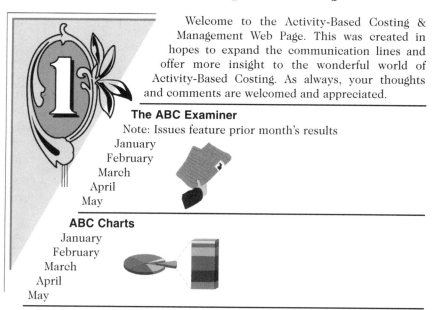

Welcome to the Activity-Based Costing & Management Web Page. This was created in hopes to expand the communication lines and offer more insight to the wonderful world of Activity-Based Costing. As always, your thoughts and comments are welcomed and appreciated.

The ABC Examiner
Note: Issues feature prior month's results
January
February
March
April
May

ABC Charts
January
February
March
April
May

ABC Guide:
ABC team members, glossary, methodologies, DCG's implementation story.

Article "World Class Practices: Activity-Based Costing":
Synopsis of what ABC is and how it works.

Activity Dictionary:
List of activities, characteristics (primary/secondary, value-added/non-value-added)

Monthly Measurables:
Easy access to the measurables presentations.

Other Web Pages:
  • Dana Commercial Credit Web Page
  • Dana Corporation Web Page

consolidate some of the activities, after which the number of activities was reduced to 75. An activity dictionary was used to capture base, or starting data for each activity. (See Exhibit 4 for a sample page from the activity dictionary.)

The team conducted a second round of interviews with the same people. The purpose of the second interview was to explain the consolidation process. Gillespie says, "We didn't want anyone to feel that we had just discarded all the information they previously provided." The second interviews lasted less than an hour and reconfirmed that the team still had support from the people they had interviewed.

The first activity costs were produced three months into the project, then cost objects were calculated about six months into the project. The cost objects were Diversified Capital Group's seven programs. Customers were also included in this first model.

The model included all operational expenses except for taxes, interest, and depreciation of the operating-lease portfolio. This resulted in the model including about 70 percent of all costs.

The model began producing results in July 1997. As Gillespie says, "Things just started to fall into place as people started becoming more familiar with everything. It just seems like we have been continually improving." In the third quarter, the team began breaking costs down by program, and by the fourth quarter, Gillespie really started feeling confident with the numbers.

Exhibit 4: Activity Dictionary Sample

Activity Process	Procure Lease Equipment Documentation & Booking
Activity Definition	The process of purchasing equipment for lease purposes. This includes all accounts payable functions, issuing purchase orders, speaking with vendor contacts, etc.
Inputs	Purchase order/voucher
Outputs	Payable check for lease equipment
Activity Driver	Number of equipment purchases
Activity Characteristics	Primary, value-added

Continuous Improvement

The ABM team increased its validation effort, which Gillespie describes as follows:

> We would perform sanity tests on the results just to make sure they made sense. For instance, to evaluate the "book a contract" activity, we would extract the total time the model reflected that it took to perform the activity (labor costs divided by activity driver volume to determine labor cost per activity which was then restated in terms of minutes per activity). We'd then go back to the lease administrator and ask—how long does it really take you to book a contract? Results would be compared to see how closely they matched the previous calculations.

In this way, the team could validate the results from the model and make everyone comfortable that the numbers were reasonable.

Estimates

Fuller expressed the team's concern that the model relied significantly on estimates of time spent on various activities. In November 1997, the team formally addressed this concern by putting together a time-tracking system. This effort gained impetus after the annual controllers' conference when people asked if the ABM results were mainly estimates or guesswork. Although the team believed the results were only 50 percent accurate due to the estimates involved, they had no way of knowing for sure. The problem was compounded by the fact that the model was updated only quarterly, and it took six weeks to assemble the data each time.

To eliminate people's concern about estimates, the ABM team implemented a time-tracking system to obtain time information daily and to improve the model's accuracy. Using a Microsoft Excel spreadsheet, team members developed a point-and-click system that improved accuracy to 80–90 percent because people were now recording their time daily.

Using pull-down menus, employees can now record time information in just five minutes per day (see Exhibit 5 for a sample time tracking screen). Icons on the screen are used to send data through the network to the ABM Manager, where it is automatically consolidated into a file that is downloaded into *Hyper*ABC. It used to take six weeks each quarter to accumulate data. Now it takes only two days each month—and with much higher reliability.

To make the system more user-friendly, the team added simple pop-up reminder buttons. These reminders appear whenever Excel is opened, when a user's computer is opened in the morning, and also when the user shuts the system down.

Exhibit 5: Sample Time Tracking Screen

DCC

Diversified Capital Group
Activity-Based Costing
Time Tracking Program
Version 3.0

Reset | Save | Chart | Submit | About | Hot List

Employee: Gillespie, Brad
Month: July
Hours Entered: 169.00 of 169.00
Last Update: 7/31/98 4:08 PM

	Activity:	Program:	Customer:	Qty:	Hours:	Minutes (Hours in Month):
1	Provide Administrative Support	ALL		0	35	15
2	Perform Strategic Planning	Program 2		1	7	0
3	Perform Residual Analysis	Program 3		2	8	15
4	Generate Proposals (Q)	Program 5		1	6	30
5	Price Contract (Q)	Program 4		3	24	30
6	Process Cash	Program 1		540	40	15
7	Clear Suspense Account	Program 1		58	17	45
8	Setup/Book Contract	Program 6		16	7	30
9	Perform Credit Evaluation (Q)	Program 7		15	6	0
10	Perform Month End Close	ALL		0	16	0
11				0	0	0
12				0	0	0

The team introduced the new time-tracking system in another educational session. They explained the need for higher accuracy and the benefits of spending a maximum of five minutes a day versus trying to recall how your time was spent three weeks ago. These educational efforts and the user-friendly system for tracking time have converted most staff.

The tracking system also allows DCC to track lost productivity caused by system downtime. It allows the cost to be broken down further, which makes it possible to trace costs to the proper program. For example, data processing charges previously charged out based on headcount can be broken down into specific journals by person so that each employee's costs can be charged to the appropriate program.

As Fuller notes, "The time keeping system has also increased buy-in from management. Now that we have taken a lot of the guesswork out, they are more comfortable with the results."

Results and Next Steps

When the ABM results had been produced and validated, they confirmed what many had suspected all along: They had been underpricing their services. DCC provided its major customer with the results. As Gillespie notes:

> We met with the customer and walked them through the ABM methodology and the ABM model. We showed them the breakdown by process and activity, and also how we performed the cost assignments. They would have liked to have seen the costs lower, but they accepted the methodology.

DCC is using the ABM results as a pricing tool. Before ABM information was available, a straight percentage was used to assign indirect costs to leasing prices—even though each program consumes indirect costs differently. Using ABM to assign indirect costs means that the prices generated better reflect the true economics. As Gillespie says, "We have gone from being in a reactive mode to being in a proactive mode when pricing leases."

ABM information at DCC is now used for process improvement. As Gillespie notes:

> We also decided to outsource our Uniform Commercial Code (UCC) filings. Every time we purchase contracts or initiate leasing agreements, we have to file them with the UCC. We had quite a backload of the UCCs that we were having trouble finding the time to complete. We outsourced this activity, which saved us approximately 50 percent of the costs of keeping the activity in-house.

There has been an added benefit. Before ABM costing information was available, there was some concern about the number of meetings being held. After DCC quantified how much those meetings were costing, many of those meetings were eliminated.

Future Plans

In 1998, ABM moved into a maintenance mode for the Diversified Capital Group. Updates are performed monthly and reports distributed. Gillespie continues to work full-time on ABM. Although the ABM team is still together, the members now spend limited time on ABM initiatives.

ABM implementation in the Asset Management Services Group began in mid-1998. As Gillespie says:

> I'm hoping with the second implementation it will give us even more publicity. It will help that they can utilize the lessons we learned from the first rollout, so it should be an even smoother process.

A successful implementation in the Asset Management Services Group should pave the way for implementation in DCC's other product groups. Implementing customer profitability analysis is next on the agenda.

ABM in Shared Services

The tremendous success of the pilot project at DCC has caused management to consider implementing ABM in shared services. Each product group is now charged a monthly allocated cost for shared services. Because the allocations are perceived as somewhat arbitrary, the product groups have asked for clear, understandable cost assignments based on actual consumption of the shared services.

Other plans at DCC include using a *balanced scorecard* of performance measurements. Through annual employee surveys, DCC received feedback that its current performance measurement systems could be improved. DCC wants to increase the value of performance measurement by using a balanced scorecard and marrying it to ABM. There are plans to make performance measurements available through the Intranet so that the visibility of the measures is increased and feedback is immediate.

Continuous improvement is part of the Dana style. The ABM results led to a "hit list" of process improvements that were ranked according to their priority. The ABM Manager will continue to work closely with the business systems analysts to implement these initiatives.

Lessons Learned

- *Educate your audience.* You must educate both managers and employees about ABM, including how the new system will be used. No one should ever be surprised. Throughout the project, all ABM team meetings should be open. Anyone who wants to attend should be welcome to do so.
- *Make your model manageable.* Don't put unnecessary detail in your model. In particular, do not include *tasks* when defining activities. The ABM team at DCC originally defined activities in too much detail. Remember for strategic analysis, activities can usually be aggregated to make the detail more manageable.
- *Buy-in from top management speeds rollout.* Even though DCC has a decentralized structure and top senior management does not impose projects on the business units, it still provides a comfort level when you have the CEO and CFO supporting your project, as was the case at DCC.
- *A cross-functional team is essential.* To perform any type of activity or process analysis properly, an ABM team needs members from different areas of the business. Cross-functional representation also helps in obtaining buy-in, analyzing activities, and collecting data.
- *Experienced consultants can be invaluable.* DCC used minimal consulting for its ABM project, but the knowledge gained from the consultants was invaluable. Having an experienced person available to answer questions helps keep ABM on the right path. This assistance smoothed out a lot of bumps in the road.
- *Get employees involved in the ABM rollout.* Solicit comments and feedback from as many people as possible. Note, however, that if you ask for feedback, you must carefully listen to the people who provide it. Dana is dedicated to the belief that people are its most important asset. This is true in everything the company does, including the ABM project.
- *Communicate and share results.* Communication is the only way to avoid misconceptions. After you educate people about ABM and why you are implementing it, keep people informed about what is happening with the project. To help with communication, the ABM team had an open door policy. All employees were invited to the meetings to listen and share ideas. Employees at DCC proved to be more than willing to come and talk to the ABM team because they knew that the team would seriously consider their ideas. Other communication tools used included an ABM web page, newsletters, and widely distributed ABM reports.

10
DHL: Taking Activity-Based Management Around the Globe

Introduction

While many companies talk of going global, few match the geographic coverage of the air express transport company DHL. Operating on such a large and geographically wide scale creates many unique management challenges. In particular, DHL has faced fierce competition and shrinking margins. This case discusses how DHL (which operates 2,321 delivery stations serving 225 countries) uses activity-based management (ABM) to help meet those challenges.

Business Issues

DHL's initial ABM implementation efforts were driven by a need to understand customer profitability. ABM was used to assist in setting prices for individual customers. Even today, customer profitability analysis and margin management are key uses of DHL's ABM system.

But as these strategic needs have been addressed, the ABM team at DHL has seen greater demand for information to help managers better understand and manage costs. As Costing Manager, Martin Holton, says, "Uses of the information for cost management represent a growing need as we seek to better utilize the infrastructure we have put in place."

Background

With a current revenue growth rate of 15 percent per year, DHL is estimated to hold a 38 percent share of the global air express market. Since its founding in 1969, DHL has remained committed to providing the fastest, most reliable, and most flexible door-to-door express delivery service that customers can buy.

The company offers the following four major product types:

* Document express service;
* Parcel express service (for items that must be declared through customs);

- European Community express (for packages moving within the European Community); and
- Logistics (total logistics solutions and express logistics services).

To provide these services DHL uses 14,635 ground vehicles and 217 aircraft, all of which are operated by DHL's 59,000 employees. The typical flow of express packages begins as an outbound shipment from a pickup vehicle or station, which flows into one of 34 hubs. Parcels are then sorted and transferred between hubs, and then sent out to a delivery station. From there, the package is delivered to the receiving customer.

The growth of this industry has spawned a multitude of fierce competitors at every level—local, regional, national, and global—which has resulted in a highly competitive, tight-margin business. The need to invest in a complete global infrastructure, coupled with constant market pressure on prices, has focused DHL's management team on the need for improved margin-management tools, which in turn require detailed knowledge of a complex cost base.

Initial Costing Efforts

Initial efforts to improve costing at DHL began in 1987. Driven by a need for pricing support, the company built a spreadsheet allocation model. This simple costing tool used 30 cost pools that were assigned to customers based on five key drivers (see Exhibit 1). The output of this tool was used in two ways:

- It fed a simple customer profitability system; and
- It fed a mainframe profitability system connected to the monthly billing system.

Exhibit 1: Initial Costing Tool

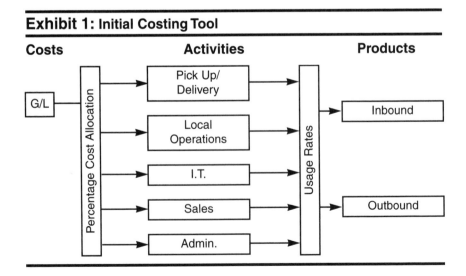

ABM Rollout

After using the system for some time, DHL began to have doubts about the validity of the results. Finally by 1992, DHL realized that the spreadsheet did not provide the information managers needed, so an ABM project was initiated. (See Exhibit 2 for a Global Rollout Timeline for ABM). After examining the cost data, managers and analysts noted some abnormalities in the spreadsheet cost flow. As Holton says:

> Banks appeared to be very unprofitable customers, whereas heavy manufacturers appeared to be very profitable. This was bad news because we had a lot more banking customers than heavy manufacturing customers.

A detailed review of the costs showed that the drivers being used (such as the number of shipments) were distorting the true cost picture. These drivers failed to adequately reflect key causal factors such as the impact of package weights and the treatment of overhead costs, so misleading results were produced. Because of these findings, DHL management decided to implement a more robust ABM system.

Pilot in the Netherlands

DHL launched a "second generation" ABM project in January 1993. The implementation team in the Europe Africa region began with a pilot project in the Netherlands. To ensure widespread support, the company used a cross-functional steering committee of 20 people. The ABM project team was small: a part-time leader, an ABM specialist, and two consultants.

The ABM team spent four months analyzing cost behavior at the local level. By May 1993, the paper-based cost analysis phase was completed. The steering team approved the conceptual cost flows. In July, the team selected *Hyper*ABC as its software and built the cost modeling system. The results were presented to top management, who were quite pleased with the study and made the decision to continue the rollout.

Pilot in the United Kingdom

In November 1993, a new pilot in the United Kingdom extended the ABM effort at DHL. This second pilot, which was completed in four months, allowed the project team to compare activities between the operations in both the United Kingdom and the Netherlands. While the operations were very similar in their practices, each operation had some significant differences that needed to be captured. The project team added a few additional activities to accommodate this difference.

Exhibit 2: DHL ABM Global Rollout Timeline

Project Milestone	1992	1993	1994	1995	1996	1997	1998
1. Initial simplified costing efforts (1987)							
2. Need for new system recognized	2						
3. Pilot in the Netherlands		3					
4. Software implementation		4					
5. Pilot in U.K.		5					
6. Pilot in Ireland			6				
7. Global rollout planning			7				
8. Global rollout training			8			→	
9. Version 2 of ABM manual released				9			
10. Global rollout continues				10			→
11. Software customization complete						11	
12. Ongoing reporting and maintenance		12					→

The U.K. pilot led to significant changes. As Holton notes, "The U.K. pilot was successful in getting useful results. It helped people really understand what drivers should be measured and managed in order to control costs." For example, a review of the trucking fleet's activities in the United Kingdom showed that the weight transported was a main driver of cost, yet this factor was not routinely tracked or examined. As a result, tracking of weight soon began.

Pilot in Ireland

After completing these two pilots, DHL was almost ready for rollout. First, however, a third and final pilot was conducted in Ireland. In early March 1994, a three-person team went to Ireland to work with local management. The objective, Holton notes, was to see how fast ABM could be implemented:

> It was like a dress rehearsal for a full rollout. We went in with a list of activities already defined. We had the methodology fully documented, and we wanted to see how quickly we could build a model and rollout the process.

The Irish pilot project was successful: The team completed the work in five weeks. The team made several slight changes to the chart of activities, which afterwards contained 85 activities. Forty-seven potential drivers were identified (although some of the drivers were mutually exclusive). This pilot helped DHL understand what the rollout would require in terms of training, methodology, manuals, and software support. Exhibit 3 shows the ABM System Flow Diagram.

Rollout Planning

In May 1994, the project team began developing these materials in preparation for the global rollout. Over the next four months the team completed documentation of the ABM methodology manual (see Exhibit 4 for an overview of the ABM manual). The ABM manual includes extensive training and educational materials, along with a chart of activities and a list of activity drivers. The team believed that consistency was a key to obtaining meaningful results from the ABM process, which was one of the reasons for creating a standard chart of activities and the list of activity drivers. (See Exhibit 5 for a sample page from the chart of activities and Exhibit 6 for a sample page from the list of activity drivers.)

For ease of use, the team organized the chart of activities into 15 categories (see Exhibit 7 for a list of the categories). They also developed a five-day training course that covered the concepts of ABM, preparation of a project

Exhibit 3: The ABM System Flow Diagram

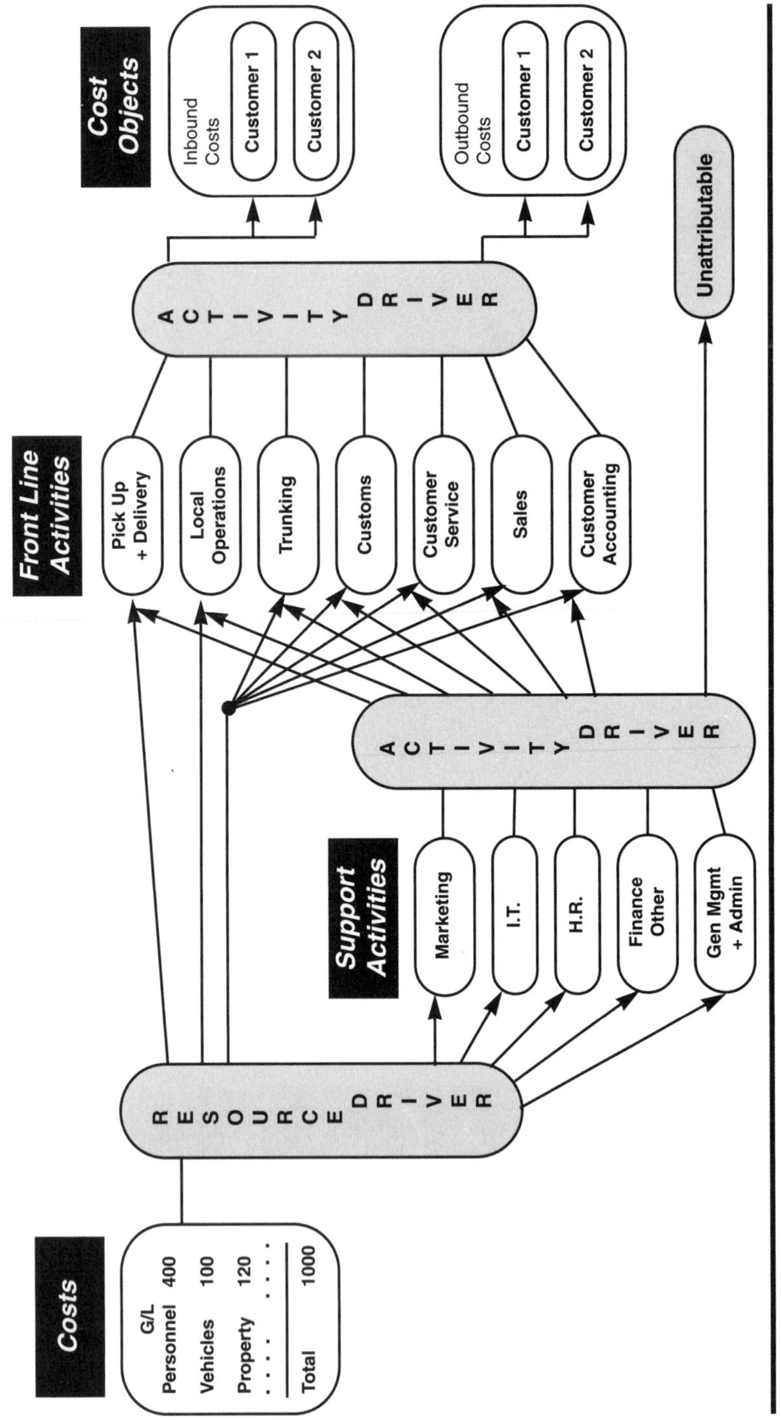

Exhibit 4: Overview of ABM Manual

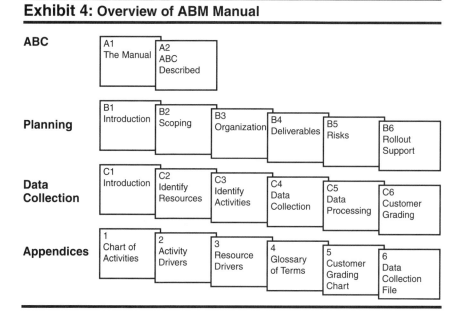

ABC
- A1 The Manual
- A2 ABC Described

Planning
- B1 Introduction
- B2 Scoping
- B3 Organization
- B4 Deliverables
- B5 Risks
- B6 Rollout Support

Data Collection
- C1 Introduction
- C2 Identify Resources
- C3 Identify Activities
- C4 Data Collection
- C5 Data Processing
- C6 Customer Grading

Appendices
- 1 Chart of Activities
- 2 Activity Drivers
- 3 Resource Drivers
- 4 Glossary of Terms
- 5 Customer Grading Chart
- 6 Data Collection File

plan, pointers on "selling" ABM to management, interviewing techniques, and assumptions for data collection.

The global rollout emphasized the ongoing ABM work to be performed by local employees of the individual countries with DHL operations. Therefore, the training and support material had to make them self-sufficient.

In addition to training, the ABM team made a final software selection for use in the global rollout. The team sought a stand-alone, commercial off-the-shelf ABC software. DHL selected *Hyper*ABC (which had also been used in the pilots) because of its ease of use and the way it handled complex reassignments of costs. With the signing of a global software license agreement, all the elements for rollout were in place.

Rollout Support

Beginning in September 1994, the first rollout training was held. A typical five-day training class included eight to twelve people from about six different countries. Upon completion of the training, the people in the class would return to their home countries, develop project plans, and begin collecting data.

After collecting most of their data, the trainees would return for two more days of training—this time on software modeling. The software training was separated from the training about data collection to simplify and modularize the implementation.

Exhibit 5: Sample Page from the Chart of Activities

Category A: Pick-up and Delivery
Unit of Measurement: Stops made by DHL couriers

Activity code: A00199STN0
Activity description: Picking up and completing shipments
Activity type: Front-Line OUTBOUND
Level: Station specific
Driven by: Customers demand of couriers' time on pick-ups
Driver measured by: Courier minutes outbound
Driver code: DRV0299STNO

Activity Definition:
Collection of shipments by a courier at the customer's premises. This involves an act of transferring possession. Activities related to missed pick-ups should also be considered here.

It also includes pick-up of shipments at drop boxes, but not activities related to shipments left by the customer at DHL locations (see activity A00399CTYO). It includes pre-scheduled, occasional and cash pick-ups.

This primary activity would typically include:

- Obtain details of all shipment(s) to be picked up;
- Plan and assess route workload (individual courier);
- Go to location;
- Find location and make contact (leave DHL calling card if unsuccessful attempt);
- Validate acceptance of picked up shipment (no prohibited items, full and accurate description);
- Ensure conformity with customs requirements and availability of supporting documentation;
- Check packaging;
- Provide predicted transit time information to customer; and
- Provide insurance.

After the software modeling training, the trainees would return home and begin model creation at their own entities. The regional offices would provide additional help in modeling.

Over the course of a year, the ABM team trained implementers from over 40 countries. The company also launched user group meetings.

In September 1995, the ABM team released version 2 of the ABM manual. Version 2 increased the number of activities from 85 to 106. This greater detail facilitated identifying the costs of special projects. The revisions also increased the use of weight as a cost driver.

Exhibit 6: Sample Page from the Activity Driver List

Activity Driver Description
Pick-up and Delivery

Driver code:	DRV0199CTYO
Driver description:	Shipments received at the front counter
Activity code:	A00399CTYO
Activity description:	Receiving shipments at the front counter
Activity driver definition:	Total number of outbound shipments that are dropped off at a DHL premises by a customer

---

Current Status

DHL has continued to roll out ABM worldwide. Holton believes that the company has reached maturity in its rollout. Currently, 80 percent of all costs are modeled using ABM.

Twenty-five countries regularly report full ABM costing information (using the 106 activities). The greatest concentration of these countries is in the Europe Africa region, which generates a very large proportion of DHL's

---

Exhibit 7: Chart of Activities Categories

Category A	Pick-up and Delivery Activities
Category B	Local Operations Activities
Category C	Trunking Activities
Category D	Customs Activities
Category E	International Sorting Activities
Category F	International Transportation Activities
Category G	Customer Services Activities
Category H	Sales Activities
Category I	Marketing Activities
Category J	Information Technology Activities
Category K	Human Resources Activities
Category L	Customer Accounting Activities
Category M	Finance Activities
Category N	General Management and Administration Activities
Category O	Other Activities

revenues. The full ABM system focuses on customer costing. About another 50 countries use a simplified version of ABM (which uses 50 activities). This simpler ABM system focuses on product costing, which can also be used to estimate customer costs.

The remaining countries have smaller operations that make preparing ABM information unwarranted. Instead, these operations use a quick calculation of costs on spreadsheets. This makes the point that the complexity of a company's costs determines the sophistication of the cost system it needs. Implementation teams must make sure that the value of the information to be gained from a new system exceeds the cost of providing it. As Holton notes:

> We use the quick spreadsheet calculation in countries where a simple cost of delivery is all that is needed. In those countries, the cost of sending someone over to calculate the numbers would exceed any benefits from the greater precision ABM would provide.

Modeling and Data Collection

Pulling data from legacy systems proved to be quite a challenge for DHL, primarily because of the diversity of DHL's operations. Each country is allowed to keep its own general ledger. Consequently, there is a wide variety in the level of detail maintained. The number of cost centers also widely varies. Statutory, financial and managerial accounts are maintained. The books may be designed to comply either with generally accepted accounting principles (GAAP) of the host country or of the United States. In addition to accounting rules, the ABM system needed multi-currency capabilities. The implementation team's instructions had to accommodate these many variables.

The ABM team responded to these challenges by creating standardized approaches, including the chart of activities and the chart of drivers. The ABM team requested that information efforts begin with the management accounts, which had to be stated in U.S. dollars and in accordance with U.S. GAAP.

After the initial model is constructed, data from the general ledger is set to upload routinely into the ABM system. Drivers are also pulled from four or five operational systems. While system-generated data was preferred, the cost models also utilized data from interviews and, in some cases, from detailed time records (see Exhibit 8 for a DHL Systems Map).

To further speed processing, DHL worked with Armstrong Laing to develop new features for *Hyper*ABC's Application Programming Interface (API), which linked a Microsoft Access database directly to the *Hyper*ABC engine. This enhancement allows local managers to input costs, driver volumes, and allocation values directly through "DHL forms" that use familiar terminology and systems.

Exhibit 8: DHL Systems Map

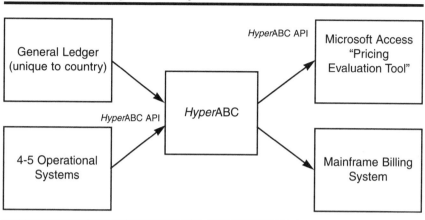

On demand, the automated links transfer the cost and driver volume detail directly into *Hyper*ABC where the model is automatically calculated. The results are fed back through the same automated links into the results tables, again using Microsoft Access and DHL forms. These reports can then be uploaded and used in other systems.

Local managers now have access to detailed ABM cost information without having to learn how to build or interpret a complex ABM model. Managers can upload this data to feed other tools (such as margin-management applications). They can also export the data to another database. The data can also be transmitted to regional and worldwide headquarters for analysis as part of the corporate data warehouse. This system was completed and rolled out by the end of 1997.

Two main applications use this information. The first is the "Pricing Evaluation Tool" (or PET), which is in Microsoft Access. This application uses ABM data to estimate appropriate pricing levels. The other application is a mainframe system that calculates the profitability of customers based on monthly billings.

ABM data is updated twice a year. In either December or January, the ABM systems are run using the following year's budgeted numbers. In February or March, the system is run again using the prior year's actual data. These actuals are compared against budgeted amounts as a reasonableness check. Factors that have caused significant variations include:

- Dramatic changes in exchange rates;
- Wars and civil unrest; and
- Sudden changes in the economic environment.

ABM Team

Holton led the initial ABM pilot in the Netherlands while serving as part of the finance staff for the Europe Africa Region. As the ABM effort grew to a global scale, Holton moved into a global support role.

The initial ABM team was organized by the region and used a small team. It pulled regional finance people into a regional cost team that also included two consultants. As the project progressed, this team expanded to eight people located in a central office in Brussels. In addition to the ABM team, the implementations require two or three people in each larger country and one in the smaller countries.

Training, software, and other support tools make it possible to cut implementation times from the initial four-month efforts down to three to four weeks. Smaller countries take only one to two weeks. Because the costing needs are not continuous, most ABM Managers in the field also perform a variety of other finance responsibilities.

The ABM team has used a mixture of permanent members and temporary members who rotate through on an assignment away from their home country. These rotations provide excellent training for the temporary member who returns to serve as the ABM Manager for his local office. These assignments which last from three to twelve months are expensive because of the added travel and living expenses, but they greatly enhance DHL's abilities. According to Holton, "These assignments have assisted in enabling DHL's success. They provide detailed, hands-on training as well as a way to build team cohesion and deepen relationships with team members around the globe."

The key responsibilities of the team include maintaining the ABM system, supporting the process improvement efforts, and providing information to improve the marketing strategy. The team primarily comes from within DHL, although few have a finance background. As Holton emphasizes, "an accounting background may be a deterrent." The basic requirement is someone who has strong analytical skills and is good with numbers. The hiring has tended to focus on MBAs.

In addition to the training courses and modeling support, the ABM team also maintains a cost library, attends (and makes presentations at) public seminars and supports cost management courses at European business schools.

Results and Next Steps

ABM information has become the primary source for customer profitability information at DHL, which has invested about U.S. $6 to $7 million creating this system. This estimate includes the costs of all internal resources as well as out-of-pocket costs. It is difficult to quantify the benefits received from supporting process improvement initiatives. However, the "Pricing Evaluation Tool" is used to evaluate over $500 million of revenues per year. Each 1 percent margin improvement driven by greater understanding of customer profitability generates $5 million in greater profits, and the Pricing Evaluation Tool clearly drives specific customer strategies.

According to Holton:

> The thing we consider critical is the grading of our major customers according to how much of our time they consume. Using the ABM information, we have gone to our customers to discuss how we can better work together. This helps us as well as the customers. When we work more closely together we save the customer time and money too.

ABM has been used to negotiate price increases, but rarely have any major customers been completely dropped. According to Holton, "This is due to a concern that an investment has been made in acquiring a customer relationship, so dropping that customer would waste that investment. It is preferable to look at opportunities for cost reductions or renegotiations of discounts." There is also concern that a reduction in revenues may not result in an ability to reduce costs. Lastly, DHL doesn't want to have to encounter the motivational impact of any headcount-related cost reductions caused by eliminating a customer when this can be avoided.

Future Plans

Since virtually all the ABM models necessary are now in place, DHL has an excellent understanding of its customer costs and how to best manage margins. In the future, DHL faces the challenges of spreading the use of these tools for cost management and process improvements. As Holton notes:

> We are investigating ways to use the ABM information for performance measurement and process improvement. Although the ABM information is supposed to be used to serve multiple purposes, it is presently skewed towards margin management. We are looking at ways of skewing it back to a more cost management point of view.

The process improvement group has done considerable work. They have performed business modeling and have linked this modeling to ABM activities. They are mapping out processes with a view of improving them. Holton notes, "We are looking at ways we can extract more action points from the data. We want to present management with clear recommendations for business decisions that will enable improvements in the business."

Lessons Learned

- *Get buy-in from the managers that count.* When starting a project of this magnitude, it is critical to get buy-in from key managers, though this may not always require starting at the top. At DHL, ABM was "sold" first to the directors and financial controllers. The work that goes into selling this type of effort is both formal such as presentations and meetings and informal such as hanging around the coffee machine to lobby key decision makers. Much of the real change in companies starts in the middle of an organization and works its way out.

- *Gain momentum from initial successes.* The successful pilot in the Netherlands allowed the ABM team to take on a larger pilot in the United Kingdom, which led to the pilot in Ireland, and finally made a global rollout possible. Plan your steps so that success builds. Start in locations that ask for ABM to help make them successful. Those who volunteer are more likely to use the results of ABM efforts.

- *Global coordination requires well-documented support.* To be successful on a global scale, the DHL implementation team had to develop a well-documented and well-explained process. This step was achieved through an in-depth ABM manual, an extensive training course, and a standardized software tool that others could build on. These tools were critical to creating self-sufficient ABM champions in each key country.

- *Training should be focused and delivered when needed.* Training begins at DHL with a five-day introductory course that covers not only ABM concepts, but also key implementation skills such as interviewing, how to sell the project, and how to develop the project plan. Later, a two-day software modeling school is delivered in a just-in-time fashion. The ABM team has also added a training course titled, "Now that I have an ABM model, what do I do with it?" This course focuses managers on getting more out of their existing ABM system. Topics covered include process improvement, benchmarking, and activity-based budgeting.

- *Global reach means you must work through others.* Widely dispersed operations require you to work through others to achieve your objectives. With ABM, this first means making sure that people at the local operation fully own their own modeling efforts. This requires them to buy-in to the value of the information that an ABM system produces. Secondly, the local employees must be adequately trained in what they are being asked to do. This includes providing manuals and ongoing support services. Thirdly, make sure that the quality of the data used is as good as it should be by building validation checks into the process.

11

GTE Supply: Improving Billing Systems with Menu-Based Pricing

Introduction

GTE Supply is an international distributor of telecommunications equipment and network-support products. This case study about GTE Supply's activity-based management (ABM) project shows how cost systems evolve over time—and also the importance of persistence. As the case illustrates, the many twists in the road toward an ABM system may render challenges, but they can also lead to a deeper understanding and greater success.

As in many organizations, ABM is only one of several improvement initiatives at GTE Supply, each of which competes for resources. When the company-wide demand-based planning initiative appeared to have a higher priority, the company's ABM team offered to redirect its efforts. But GTE Supply's management insisted that they needed the ABM information to feed the supply-chain initiative and make menu-based pricing possible. Menu-based pricing is the unbundling of product and service costs to give customers an option of choosing from a "menu" only those activities they desire to purchase. Fortunately, management understood that accurate cost information was critical to effective strategic and operational decision making.

Business Issues

GTE Supply supports the telecommunications industry, which faces tremendous competitive pressures and a dramatically expanding demand for services. Because of alternative technologies that are becoming available, communication companies can choose many different ways to compete. These trends, coupled with the deregulation of the industry, combine to make a highly competitive industry with relentlessly downward pricing pressures.

The expanding economy, broader uses of technology, and greater worker mobility all serve to increase the demand for communications services. Also, the expanding use of home computers and the growth in Internet traffic has led to many diverse uses of technology.

Because of these changes, the average number of telephone lines per customer has increased dramatically, and networks must operate at faster speeds and higher capacities. Another result of these developments has been greater worker mobility, because many people now find it possible to be telecommuters by working at home.

To meet the increased demand, the communications industry has accelerated the commercialization of alternative technologies. Fiber-optics technologies have dramatically increased call-volume capacity over that available from traditional copper wires. New switches, faster software, and more reliable electronic hardware have also expanded the options available. For example, technology has now made it possible for new competitors to provide services such as calls over the Internet, which can go through cable systems or via the wiring provided by utility companies.

Competitive Pressure

Competitive pressure brought by the deregulation of the communications industry in recent years has dramatically reduced the barriers to entry, which has also played an important role in the many changes in the industry. As a result, new companies have sprung up to "cherrypick" the most profitable niches of the traditional phone companies—that is, they skim off the profitable business and leave the less profitable business to the old-line companies.

The industry giants have also begun to invade each other's traditional territories, each seeking to maintain its historical growth and profitability. The mindset of the entire industry is shifting. The old "cost plus a regulated return" way of doing business is being replaced by the sharply downward pressure on prices, which means a corresponding need to cut costs. Because of the high network infrastructure costs in the industry, there are tremendous incentives for companies to build volume as quickly as possible.

At GTE Supply, these industry dynamics all pointed to the following two imperatives:

- To reduce costs continuously by eliminating waste; and
- To understand the cost and profitability of each customer.

To achieve these objectives, GTE Supply needed cost information—information that was difficult to find or not available in its existing information systems. As a result, the company is using ABM to assist with its understanding of cost and profitability.

Background

GTE Supply provides procurement, materials management, distribution, electronic repair, and logistics services. As a subsidiary of GTE Corporation, it supports its sister companies ("affiliates"), though it also sells to other telecommunications and high tech companies ("nonaffiliates").

With thousands of employees operating in regions, GTE Supply supports its affiliate business through regional logistics centers, electronic repair facilities, and customer care centers. Nonaffiliate customers are served through three *national logistics centers* (NLCs), which are in California, Indiana, and Georgia. Affiliates can also draw from the NLCs.

Initial Efforts

In 1993, GTE Supply began to utilize ABM with a pilot project in the purchasing department. Exhibit 1 shows the Project Timeline for the pilot.

In reviewing the motivation for ABM, Don Miller, manager of Business Planning, notes:

> The project was initiated and championed by the Director of Finance, who recognized activity-based management as a tool that GTE Supply could use to benefit the company by providing better management information.

The company's purchasing group includes more than 150 people. The pilot effort, a detailed study that lasted about eight months, focused on understanding the activity costs of purchasing. These activity costs were used for analysis in billing, which gave managers a far better understanding of the cost differences between customers.

The pilot produced an activity dictionary that included 50 activities for the Purchasing department alone. While the information generated was interesting, the department's managers did not understand how to use the data for improvement. Miller explains the situation as follows:

> I remember our champion trying to engage the purchasing managers, and it was a real challenge. Because ABM was a new concept at the time, they had a hard time understanding what he was trying to accomplish.

Building on the Pilot

In late 1994, Warren Rappleye, GTE Supply's ABM Manager, transferred from inventory accounting to this new job, where he built on the success of the ABM pilot. Rappleye tried to get the purchasing managers to make better use of the ABM information, but the emphasis of the ABM efforts shifted in-

Exhibit 1: GTE Supply Project Timeline

1993	1994	10/94	3/95	10/95	1996	7/96	8/96	11/96	1997	7/97	3/98
1st ABC Pilot Conducted in Purchasing		2nd Pilot Conducted Covering Purchasing. 3rd Pilot Expanding to ERS	Enterprise-wide Activity Effort Survey Completed			Focused on Using ABM Data for Billing		Converted to New Logistics System; Updated All Driver Links		Updated Activity Data Using Manager Surveys	Prepare to Support Menu Based Pricing
	New ABM Team Formed		Decision Made for Enterprise-wide ABM Effort		ABM Team Reviews Non-Value-Added Activities		Switched to HyperABC		Began Using ABM for External Benchmarking		

creasingly toward *process improvement.* In particular, the focus became gaining an understanding of value-added versus non-value-added activities, which would make it possible to understand—and eliminate—waste.

In addition to projects in materials management and procurement activities, the company's ABM team decided to extend ABM to Electronic Repair Services (ERS). This extension of ABM provided a broader view of costs in the materials area.

Two Quick Pilots

Rappleye's ABM team completed the revised studies of procurement and ERS in two months. The team also reduced much of the detail of the prior models by redefining activities at a broader level. Specifically, activities were restricted to work that consume at least 5 percent of someone's time.

The initial ABM pilot was made more difficult by all the detail considered. The mountains of data caused users to feel overwhelmed and, thus, less likely to use the information. The revised approach reduced the activities included in the activity dictionary from about 50 activities for the Purchasing department alone to about 20 activities for both Purchasing and ERS. This higher-level approach to defining activities proved very successful.

Rollout Throughout the Enterprise

Based on this success, the ABM team was asked to complete an ABM review throughout the company by the end of 1995. In March 1995, a cross-functional ABM team was assembled to start interviews. The team included two full-time team members from finance and ten part-time members from various functions in the company. (Exhibit 2 shows the composition of the ABM Team.) The part-time members spent 10–15 percent of their time helping with ABM efforts in their respective functional areas.

The ABM team conducted hundreds of interviews. In large departments, only managers were interviewed. In some areas, including finance, virtually everyone was interviewed. The team then compared notes on the activities performed to eliminate redundant activities. The resulting activity dictionary listed some 300 activities for the entire company.

The main focus, according to Rappleye, was to identify the costs of *processes:* "We grouped activities into core processes identified by the directors." As such, GTE Supply identified six core processes. (See Exhibit 3 for GTE's core business processes.)

After the ABM team completed interviewing, defining activities, and collecting data, it compiled activity cost reports. As Rappleye notes, "We were able to create reports reflecting different slices of the data. This provided

---

Exhibit 2: GTE Supply ABM Team Composition

Human Resources (1)

Logistics (2)

General Accounting (1)

Contract Management (1)

Systems (2)

Finance (2)

Electronic Repair Service (1)

Commercial Markets (2)

---

process costs and activity costs, and it also helped us to understand where our costs were located."

Focus on Non-Value-Added Activities

The ABM team also focused on the activity attributes "value-added" versus "non-value-added." In defining non-value-added activities, management sought to identify those activities that provided no benefit to customers. The goal was to stop performing those activities.

Examples of non-value-added activities include the following:

- Investigating shipping errors;
- Resolving receiving errors; and
- Reconciling matching errors in procurement.

Ultimately, the ABM team determined that about 20 percent of the company's activity costs could be categorized as non-value-added.

GTE Supply's management was impressed with the data and reports, but they asked the ABM team to analyze the data and suggest ways the company could improve. Although the ABM team made significant progress toward this goal, it also encountered conflict. In particular, ABM teams face problems when they ask employees to supply information that may later be used to improve efficiencies by reducing costs in the employees' departments.

Rappleye explains this stage of the project and the composition of the ABM team project as follows:

> In retrospect, using a cross-functional team to identify the improvements would have been easier if we had included as members of the team those who do the work rather than just people from finance. As a finance group we didn't know the processes as well as the people who perform

Exhibit 3: GTE Core Business Processes

Order Management	Material Acquisition	Bid Management	Supply Chain Finance and Planning	Supply Chain Related MIS Costs	Electronic Repair Services

Support

the processes and neither did we have the authority to make any changes.

Despite these challenges, Miller notes:

> The ABM team identified several good opportunities for improvement and also achieved some solid results. Putting a spotlight on non-value-added activities such as matching errors in procurement provided the focus for ultimately implementing process improvements.

Improvements to Billing

After finishing the process improvement project, the ABM team launched an effort to improve billing through the use of menu-based pricing. For this project, the team needed to eliminate some of the detail previously used. For strategic issues such as billing and pricing, they simply didn't need all the detail required for their previous project, which was more operational in nature.

An improved billing system is of interest to both the sales department and to GTE Supply's customers. Miller explained, "We provide a service. We charge for that service and our customers are interested in keeping their costs down." Rappleye agreed. Both internal and external parties, he says, "would become interested in the ABM project if they were being billed" on an ABM basis.

In July 1996, the ABM team began once again to broaden the definitions of activities included in the activity dictionary. The 300 activities for the company as a whole were consolidated into only 48. These activities were then grouped into high-level processes in much the same way that activities had been combined into processes previously. These activities were linked to activity drivers that were generated from the legacy systems. Defining these activity drivers and writing programs to extract them from the legacy systems was a large job. Although much of the information needed already existed, the ABM team had to identify ways to capture and use it.

This step was complicated by the fact the company was moving away from its old data processing systems. Like many large companies, GTE Supply has multiple legacy systems that operate in various locations. While useful source data usually exists in these older systems, capturing it in the proper format for use in ABM systems can be time consuming.

When legacy systems are converted, the work of writing programs to extract the activity drivers must often be repeated. Therefore, maintenance costs are a major concern for operating ongoing systems throughout a company. GTE Supply's upgrading of its systems merely complicated the work.

Positive Customer Feedback

As work progressed, the ABM team began to see encouraging signs from users. As Rappleye says:

> Our customers were excited. They could see a real need for menu-based pricing. They were providing ideas along the way about what kind of menu prices to include. This dialogue helped us determine what information we needed to capture.

Customers were highly interested in receiving billings that more closely related to their actual usage of services. The old billing process was based on a load rate, which spread GTE Supply's overhead based over the dollar value of purchases. Higher-cost purchases therefore were burdened with more overhead than lower-cost purchases, regardless of the underlying activity costs incurred to provide the items purchased.

Incorporating External Benchmarking

During the process of converting the activity dictionary from 300 to 48 activities, the ABM team collected external benchmarking data. In converting the existing dictionary of 300 activities into a shorter, more strategic list of activities, the team reviewed the external benchmark data for comparisons. Rappleye notes "benchmarking gave us more validity on the activity side." This also enhanced the output of the ABM team, because the team could provide both internal and external benchmark comparisons.

After completing the new and shorter list of activities, the ABM team resurveyed managers since the ABM dictionary had been radically revised. The revised activity analysis used the 48 activities and fed the data collected regarding time spent on activities into a Microsoft Access database for consolidation. The ABM team provided each manager both prior detailed activities and the revised format for input. This additional information helped managers map their time into the higher-level activities. As Rappleye explains, "The activity rollup was much easier for the managers to complete, because not only were there fewer activities, but also because the format was intuitive to them."

In August 1996, the ABM team also switched ABC software in conjunction with this more strategic approach. A more sophisticated system was needed to avoid the burden of having to input data manually. The ABM team selected *Hyper*ABC from Armstrong Laing to automate the input of data. The activity driver volumes and financial data were mapped into the system.

After loading the data into *Hyper*ABC, the ABM team generated new menu-based prices. These prices generated new customer billings, which were compared to GTE Supply's existing billing amounts. The proposed menu prices consisted of 60 different customers (50 of which are affiliated), 40 different order types, and 8 different product groups.

Validation of the Model

During the validation process, the ABM team had to make changes to the model. These changes were to ensure that overhead costs directly associated with the support of certain customers or customer groups were included in their activity costs (menu-based prices). This step was taken for benchmarking purposes and included only the menu-based prices for those customers.

The ABM team discovered that they could use features in *Hyper*ABC to separate direct costs by customer and product when tracing costs from activities to cost objects. After this revision in the model, the results more closely matched the results generated by the old cost system. There were still some differences, but this is only to be expected because of the new costing methodology. Nonetheless, the new costs were much more in line with what people had expected. As Rappleye notes:

> Menu-based pricing led to profitability analysis, which included the development of customer segmentation to identify profitability by group. This information was so well received by marketing, they are now requesting the information by individual customer. We are currently in the process of expanding the system to provide that information.

According to Jenny Xu, another member of the ABM team, "the new menu-based pricing system gives GTE Supply the flexibility to customize reports and better meet our customers' needs for cost information."

Activity Collection Examples

GTE Supply has collected activity data in several ways. This effort has typically begun with interviews by the ABM team. These interviews provide the information needed to compile an activity dictionary, which includes a listing and description of all activities.

The company's most comprehensive collection of activity information occurred in October 1995, when all employees in the workforce were surveyed. The ABM team used a machine-readable survey form to automate data entry and minimize keypunch errors. These forms were downloaded into a Microsoft Excel spreadsheet, which was linked to files in the Human Resources department to produce activity information by job title. Activity costs were calculated based on job code.

Results and Next Steps

As the ABM migration has evolved over the years at GTE Supply, it has produced various types of cost information giving new insights as to what it costs to do business. The ABM team has supported process improvement initiatives, value analysis, both internal and external benchmarking, and, finally, they have created menu-based pricing using ABM information.

The present model provides approximately 20,000 menu prices, which will be a significant improvement to the existing billing system.

Future Plans

In 1998, the ABM team is working to refine the inputs and outputs of the model providing more menu-based pricing detail for customers. This effort is expected to lead to full menu pricing by early 1999. Achieving this goal is expected to require additional discussions with top management and internal customers to achieve full buy-in.

Transaction level profitability analysis is also a key goal of the ABM team. This data will provide new insights as to what, how and whom the product should be sold.

The ABM team is also seeking to incorporate activity-based results into the annual budgeting and planning process giving management the ability to better plan and react to changes in the marketplace.

Lessons Learned

- *Maintain a clear vision of your objectives.* This case study illustrates many uses of ABM data. In retrospect, however, one important lesson learned was to keep a clear vision of what you are trying to achieve and which business issues you are trying to address. Doing so will keep the activity detail (and thus data collection efforts) at a manageable level. Also, it is critical to manage the expectations of top management. Nonetheless, as your company's needs change, you should be willing to change the direction of your ABM project giving management the ability to focus on what is important.
- *Use a full-time cross-functional team.* The ABM team believes that its efforts could have been completed faster if fully dedicated help had been available. The full-time members of the team should come from operating and marketing areas, not just finance. Key roles on an ABM team include the overall project manager, an ABC modeler, technologists to help with data collection, and both operational and functional experts to help capture how the business works. These experts are especially important for training and "embedding"ABM into different areas of the company.
- *Persistence is required.* The ABM team lived through various times when the ABM effort at GTE Supply might have been abandoned, yet they persisted in their efforts. Their experience illustrates the role that commitment plays in the success of an ABM project.
- *Learn from each step.* The ABM team has been successful because of their ability to adapt and learn. If an approach failed, the team learned from the effort and changed the approach used.
- *Train managers on how to use ABM information.* ABM information is powerful, but few managers know how to use it. ABM teams need to train managers on both the operational and strategic uses of ABM. They should also be specific about how managers can use the information in their own work.
- *Focus the level of detail for activities.* GTE Supply has used various levels of detail in defining activities. If activities are defined too minutely, the sheer detail makes the analysis difficult to use. If the detail ever becomes cumbersome, consider consolidating activities to simplify the model.

12

John Deere Health Care, Inc.: Partnering Operations with Finance for ABM Excellence

Introduction

In the healthcare industry, medical costs have risen continuously, but so have administrative costs as well. Many service companies have lacked the tools required to accurately track and identify administrative costs by product or by line of business. This case explains the issues surrounding rising administrative costs at John Deere Health Care, Inc. (JDHC) and how the company went about resolving those issues.

Business Issues

Keith Wilson, JDHC's Director, Financial Planning explains how the company turned to activity-based management (ABM):

> Several issues led to the implementation of activity-based management, but the most significant challenge we faced was brought on by the explosive growth in our business, which reached an annual growth rate of 20 percent. Staffing levels increased, driving up administrative costs at an even faster rate than our business growth.

Chuck Parsons, Vice President of Operations at JDHC, became the driving force behind the ABM initiative. As Parsons notes:

> Operations have a keen interest in cost management. To truly manage costs, you must look at the processes involved. When you focus on processes, you ultimately focus on the customer, and that's where you want to be.

Other business needs driving the ABM implementation included the following:

- A need to support continuous improvement initiatives;
- A need for a better way to assign costs to the various lines of business and operational sites;
- A need to provide process costs to the process teams for analysis;

- A need for a robust platform to provide a basis for launching more detailed cost studies in the future; and
- A need for a tool to facilitate internal and external benchmarking.

Background

John Deere Health Care, Inc. was created from a simple concept: If you want something done right, you often have to do it yourself. By 1971, healthcare costs at Deere & Company (Deere) had skyrocketed. Healthcare costs were becoming the expense with the highest growth rate. Management determined that something needed to be done.

When Deere's management investigated, they found that very little was being done to manage healthcare costs, so Deere shifted to a self-insurance plan, thus bringing the processing of healthcare claims in-house. Then, in 1978, Deere formed a dedicated department to manage healthcare costs.

In the early 1980s, Deere led an effort with other companies to establish HMOs. In 1985, this resulted in the formation of JDHC, a wholly owned subsidiary of Deere & Company. Through one HMO, Deere extended healthcare management to other Deere locations and also to other companies.

With membership on the rise, JDHC has expanded to three HMOs that cover more than 400,000 members. The membership comes from more than 1,700 employer's groups and has access to more than 6,000 network physicians. JDHC has about 825 employees and annual revenues of more than $400 million.

Early ABM Efforts

In 1995, JDHC chartered a team to initiate activity-based costing (ABC). But, because the team had minimal cross-functional involvement, it was viewed primarily as an accounting project. Wilson notes that this initial effort failed because it lacked the buy-in of both operations and top management.

But Wilson and his supervisor were determined to keep "that little spark" burning. Concerned about the rise of administrative costs, management created requirements for a new set of operational and financial reports. These *financial management reports* analyze profitability by line of business and are compiled for each of JDHC's 20 operational units. Operations wanted these reports produced quickly; the accuracy of the administrative expense allocations could be worried about later.

When the new reports were released in late 1995, considerable discussion followed. The operations people were pleased with the results, however, they questioned how the administrative costs had been assigned to the lines of business. As Wilson notes, "They wanted the information to be more refined and, basically, asked us if we could do a better job." This request by operations led to a better method for cost assignment; it paved the way for ABM.

A Better Way to Assign Costs

When Wilson met with representatives from operations, he assured them that finance would be able to assign administrative costs to the lines of business more accurately in the future (see Exhibit 1 for a listing of the lines of business). Wilson notes:

> We told them we could provide all operational managers with reporting that allows them to see how their resources are being consumed by activities—and how activities are being consumed by the lines of business.

Exhibit 1: John Deere Health Care—Lines of Business

---

1. Heritage Standard HMO
2. Heritage Preferred HMO
3. Heritage PCC
4. Medicare Risk
5. Heritage Medicaid
6. Other Self Insured
7. Administrative Services Only (ASO)
8. Deere Self Insured

Operational managers were eager for this information. Wilson's team embarked on this project with a clear understanding of their needs and a clear requirement for operational support, which operations—led by Chuck Parsons—fully supported.

At JDHC, all projects seeking funding must develop a charter that must be approved by the Planning Council, which is composed of the president, senior vice presidents, and vice presidents. To provide a closer link to the continuous process improvement efforts, management chose to call its ABM initiative *process-based costing* (PBC).

Process Management

Process teams had been established at JDHC in 1992, to facilitate continuous process improvement. These teams had identified six core processes and also an administrative support process (see Exhibit 2 for a listing of core processes and subprocesses). Individual teams are assigned to particular processes to work on improving and simplifying the processes. JDHC's management

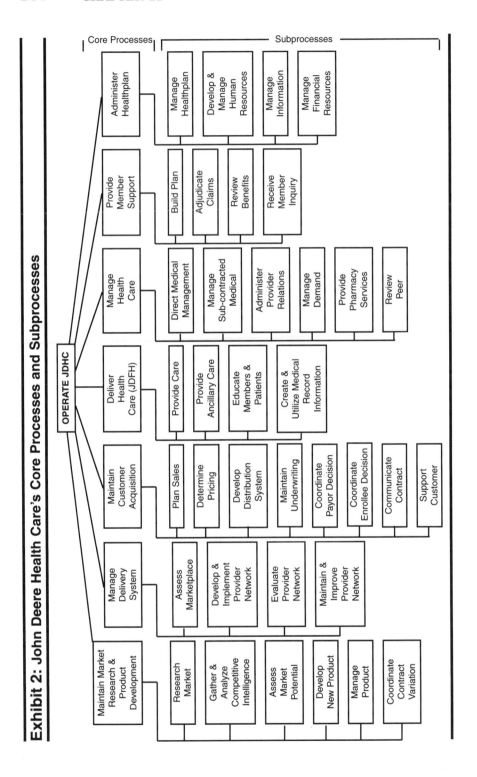

Exhibit 2: John Deere Health Care's Core Processes and Subprocesses

planned to link the PBC initiative to these existing process teams.

JDHC has continually reviewed the company in terms of its core processes. Yet, as Parsons notes, "When you are organized vertically by department (as most companies are), it is difficult to think horizontally—across processes." While JDHC used cross-functional teams to focus horizontally on core processes, difficulties still existed because there were no process and activity costs available for analysis. Processes were an aggregation of related activities that made up the process.

As Parsons says:

> Each year, we fell back on the annual functional budgeting process. Process-based costing provided our first opportunity to convert the functional budget into process costing. It allowed us to look at what *drives* the cost of the individual processes.

The project charter for PBC was first presented to the CFO and the individual operations managers, which generated grass-roots support. When the idea was later formally presented to the Planning Council, Parsons convinced the Council that operations needed this critical information. With this joint approach by finance and operations, the project was approved.

Initial Efforts

The implementation at JDHC started with software selection. This task was performed by the finance department's staff after a clear understanding of the mandate was received from operations (see Exhibit 3 for a project timeline).

After software selection, a PBC team was formed to develop activity definitions, validate those definitions, and collect activity effort information regarding how much time employees spent on activities. The new team was linked to JDHC's process teams to provide process costs. Finally, the team had to select appropriate activity drivers. Overall, the PBC effort took 15 months.

Software Selection

The finance department selected software after the PBC project received approval but before the PBC team was formed. As Wilson notes:

> We didn't want the team to get bogged down in the software selection process, so we handled it first. We reviewed five different softwares and selected *Hyper*ABC based on the product's flexibility. We have a very complex operational structure and *Hyper*ABC could handle this better than the other packages.

The members of the finance department who were slated to be on the PBC team made the selection. Operations had made it clear beforehand exactly

Exhibit 3: John Deere Health Care Project Timeline

Project Milestone	1994 Mar	Jun	Sep	Dec	1995 Mar	Jun	Sep	Dec	1996 Mar	Jun	Sep	Dec	1997 Mar	Jun	Sep	Dec	1998 Mar	Jun	Sep	Dec
1. First ABC Pilot				1																
2. Financial Mgt. Reports Designed						2														
3. Initial Financial Mgt. Reports distributed								3												
4. PBC Pilot Approved									4											
5. HyperABC Software Selected										5										
6. PBC Team Selected										6										
7. PBC Project Launched											7									
8. Preliminary PBC Dictionary Compiled											8									
9. Validated PBC Dictionary												9								
10. Collected Activity Effort Information													10							
11. Preliminary Activity Costs													11							
12. Activity Driver Collection														12						
13. Model Completed/Cost Object Results															13					
14. Model Refinement															14 →					
15. Fully Incorporated into Financial Management Reports																	15			
16. Cost Reduction Initiatives															16 →					
17. Target Costing Rollout																		17 →		

what the operational personnel needed from the new PBC system. This hard-earned knowledge had been gained previously when the finance management reports were being developed and also through discussions with operations.

The Process-Based Costing Team

The PBC team was a key enabler of success. Wilson sought out a cross-functional team with top people from throughout the organization. The 12 members of the team were carefully selected to represent the different areas of the company. (See Exhibit 4 for a complete listing of Project Team Members.)

Exhibit 4: John Deere Health Care—Project Team Members

Vice President, Operations—Champion
Director, Financial Planning—Team Leader
Operations Manager
Actuary
Systems Analyst
Operations Development Coordinator
Accounting Intern
Manager, Quality Deployment
Finance Manager
Managed Care Representative
Accounting Supervisor
Budget Accountant

Subcommittees of the PBC team were used to conquer specific tasks throughout the implementation, including communications and education, resource assignment, activity driver determination, and various other implementation tasks. As Craig Srajer, JDHC's Manager of Medicare and Cost Reporting, notes:

> Subcommittees were helpful in accomplishing specific tasks in an expedient manner. We took advantage of the team members' skills and abilities when assigning them to the subcommittees. By doing so, we used the skills of our team members to their fullest.

Activity Definition

After the PBC team received training on ABM concepts and methodology, its members began defining activities by linking the process teams to the PBC effort. (See Exhibit 5 for a breakdown of a core process into subprocesses and then into activities.) As Srajer notes:

> Leveraging off the existing process teams was a key to the project's success. They assisted with development of the activity dictionary.

Neither the PBC team nor accounting owned the activity dictionary: Rather, the process teams owned it.

After a preliminary activity dictionary was compiled, the team began validating it. As Ross Lund, cost accountant, says:

> We wanted the front-line managers involved, so we took the original activity dictionary to them to validate. This step was key to getting an accurate activity dictionary and also essential to gaining additional buy-in for the project.

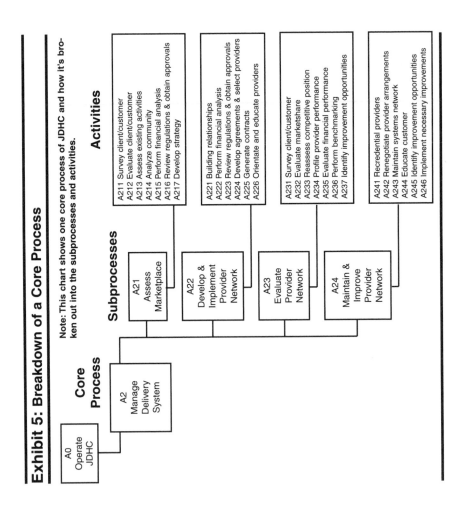

Exhibit 5: Breakdown of a Core Process

Note: This chart shows one core process of JDHC and how it's broken out into the subprocesses and activities.

Core Process

A0 Operate JDHC

A2 Manage Delivery System

Subprocesses

A21 Assess Marketplace

A22 Develop & Implement Provider Network

A23 Evaluate Provider Network

A24 Maintain & Improve Provider Network

Activities

A211 Survey client/customer
A212 Evaluate client/customer
A213 Assess existing activities
A214 Analyze community
A215 Perform financial analysis
A216 Review regulations & obtain approvals
A217 Develop strategy

A221 Building relationships
A222 Perform financial analysis
A223 Review regulations & obtain approvals
A224 Develop agreements & select providers
A225 Generate contracts
A226 Orientate and educate providers

A231 Survey client/customer
A232 Evaluate marketshare
A233 Reassess competitive position
A234 Profile provider performance
A235 Evaluate financial performance
A236 Perform benchmarking
A237 Identify improvement opportunities

A241 Recredential providers
A242 Renegotiate provider arrangements
A243 Maintain systems network
A244 Educate customer
A245 Identify improvement opportunities
A246 Implement necessary improvements

The PBC team contacted the 60 managers who had budget responsibility, then held meetings with six to eight managers at a time. During these meetings, the team educated the managers about PBC and its benefits. The team also asked the managers to define the activities performed in their departments.

After the managers had defined their activities, the project team asked them to map the activities to the preliminary activity dictionary previously proposed by the process teams. As Lund notes, "We took their feedback and distilled it into the dictionary."

A tremendous amount of work went into validation of the activities, but doing so was extremely important. Because the PBC team worked closely with the managers, the managers felt included in the PBC project rather than being forced to cooperate by corporate or finance. As Lund says:

> We also created a process map that illustrated the different roles of the process teams, the PBC team, and the departmental managers. This map was extremely helpful in explaining how the different roles interacted.

Exhibit 6 shows a flowchart of the various participants' roles.

Data Collection

In total, the work of defining and validating activities took four months. After the activity dictionary was validated, the PBC team began collecting activity effort information. They validated the dictionary by distributing it throughout the organization for review and acceptance. The resource assignment subcommittee designed an electronic form for collecting activity effort surveys. The form, which was distributed by e-mail, required front-line managers to estimate the time spent by each member of their department on various activities for a given time period. In the first phase, data was collected for all of 1996.

The project team distributed the forms throughout the organization. After data had been collected and input, the full team had much less to do. Most of the work fell to the members of the team from accounting. Time estimates for each person were weighted based on the person's salary, then consolidated into the overall percentage for the department. This approach allowed the team to reflect differing compensation levels while still keeping the salaries of individual employees private.

Collecting and analyzing all this data—including activity data for more than 800 employees—took between three and four months. Unfortunately, the team had allowed only three weeks on the work plan for this work—which points out the need for conservatism in estimating the time needed for data collection.

Preliminary activity costs were produced based on the activity effort surveys and the departmental salary costs collected. These activity costs were detailed by department to let managers analyze the work done. The PBC team

---

Exhibit 6: Flowchart of Participants' Roles

Process-Based Costing Team Plan

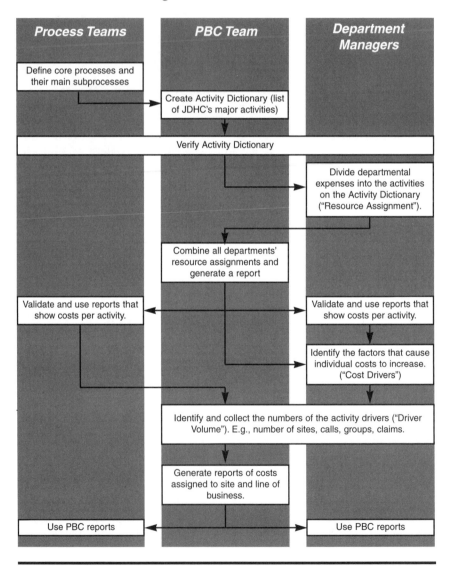

then had to determine the volume and cost of output produced. This was done by completing an analysis of activity drivers and by completing the model.

Selecting Activity Drivers

While the PBC team was still collecting time estimates, the subcommittee on driver assignment began work. As Srajer says, "We tried to find the optimal driver for every activity. After the first attempt, we had identified between 35 and 40 drivers, which we soon realized was too many." Wilson adds:

> After the initial run-through, we completed a separate analysis detailing how many times a driver was used: We performed a sort of cost-benefit analysis. We then gave each driver a grade—such as how easy would the driver be to collect.

Using this process, the team narrowed the original list to 25 drivers, a somewhat more manageable number.

Collecting activity driver volumes went faster than the team expected. Srajer notes, "We had been warned by other organizations who had struggled through this step. They had cautioned us that driver information often wasn't available or was difficult to find." As a result, the PBC team had already done its homework before they started the cost-benefit analysis of potential drivers. The cross-functional team also included someone from systems, which proved extremely helpful. Driver collection was completed in only one month. The PBC team was then ready to begin producing results from its new cost system.

Validation Efforts

In June 1997, the first PBC reports were distributed to operational sites, which was the start of additional validation efforts with both the operational sites and the process teams. The PBC team wanted the operational sites to review the numbers, but they also wanted feedback on enhancing the reporting specifications and presentation. As Wilson notes:

> There were some things about that first go-round that we were not comfortable with. Based on the feedback, we made several changes. We then established 1997 as the base-line year for future comparison.

Since then, the PBC information has been incorporated into the financial management reports. The financial information is updated monthly, and resource drivers are updated quarterly. Response to the project has been very positive. Wilson notes that the information is being used at all levels of the organization:

> The operational managers' bonuses are based on profitability, so they

are keenly interested in the financial management reports' results. We constantly receive calls and assist them with ways to manage their costs.

For example, one of our executive directors of operations closely analyzed his financial management report. He was evaluating the costs assigned to him and considering organizational changes in his area. He called to ask some fairly detailed questions about cost drivers, particularly one involving customer service calls. He has a staff that takes these calls, but there is also another staff at headquarters that takes some of these calls. He noticed that he was charged a premium for calls received at headquarters. He wanted to determine how he could cut costs and provide better customer service by handling more of the calls at his location. We had a 20-minute conversation, and he was able to make a more informed decision because of the information available through PBC.

Now that the information is available, people ask for additional cost studies. Lund notes:

We have made a conscious effort in recent months to get in front of people—to show them what we have and what we can provide. It has helped a great deal. The team has also made presentations at regional meetings to demonstrate what can be provided and how it was developed. If people understand how and why the system was developed, they can better understand how to use and interpret the information.

Operational managers have also used the information for internal benchmarking with different regions by comparing cost-consumption patterns. The information has helped managers focus on specific process costs that may seem out of line when compared with similar costs in other regions.

Results and Next Steps

JDHC plans to make PBC an integral part of the organization. As Parsons notes:

We do not want this critical management tool to be something that sits on the shelf and is used occasionally when you want to look at the data. The goal is for management to use the information daily. We want to continue to ask the right questions to make sure that people have the information they need to make more informed decisions.

JDHC's President recently ordered that administrative costs be reduced by 50 percent over the next five years. To do that, managers know they will have to review their processes. JDHC is also continuing to simplify key business processes. As Wilson notes:

The beauty of having this data is that we can now identify the simplification efforts and the results of continuous improvement initiatives from the data provided by PBC.

Other future plans call for electronic delivery of reports and also automated inputs and outputs. JDHC will provide ongoing education and information about PBC to enhance the model and the activity dictionary as needed and also to create Intranet reporting. Ongoing education is important in order to continue the expansion of the usage of ABM information. It is also used to train new employees on ABM as they join the company. With the increased focus on cost, a series of special cost studies will also take place.

Target Costing and Activity-Based Budgeting

Another future initiative that will be linked to PBC is target costing, which is presently in the design stage for the medical area. The Information Services group is developing the infrastructure needed to generate the reports and plans to have target costing in place by late 1999.

JDHC also plans to launch activity-based budgeting to get people to understand their drivers—and how those drivers change from one year to the next. That understanding should then be reflected in the development of budgets. Keith Wilson summed up JDHC's use of activity-based tools in the future as follows:

> We have a great start at fully ingraining PBC into decision making. We want to continue to build upon our success and imbed PBC throughout JDHC.

Lessons Learned

- *Keep it simple and set expectations at a reasonable level.* It was very important to keep the activity dictionary simple and understandable. The PBC team did its homework and did not go into the project with unrealistic expectations. No one made promises that PBC would immediately reduce overhead by 40 percent. Instead, the team created a base line and a manageable number of activity drivers. The goal was to get the project rolling and let acceptance grow within the company. By not totally disrupting everything, the team has managed to turn PBC into a tool that people are starting to use every day.
- *Get results out as quickly as possible.* You will be collecting a lot of data from people throughout the organization, which will stimulate interest in the project. It is helpful from a communications standpoint to get results back to the participants as soon as possible.

- *Be realistic with your time frame.* Plan your implementation properly. Keep the goals realistic. Consult someone who has gone through a similar project to determine how long it really takes to complete all the project steps. Also, remember that it usually takes longer than expected to roll out any kind of project for the first time.
- *Develop trust in the model's results.* You must spend time with the users of the data to explain the process and the results. If people do not trust the data, they will not use it. Validate the results every step of the way.
- *Educate your audience.* At JDHC, binders were created with educational materials for both the PBC team and managers. These materials were helpful in selling the benefits of PBC. As Lund notes, "It's not build it and they will come. It's more like build it, market it, and they will come. Accountants sometime forget that everything we do is also a marketing project."
- *Dedicated, cross-functional teams drive successful projects.* Not only did the team possess a variety of skills, but also their dedication and drive were second to none. As Wilson notes, "They were quality people. When work needed to be done and time was running out, they were always volunteering to perform work off-line, which was critical to the success of the project. We had such great people to conduct the work and take it seriously."

13

Portugal Telecom: ABM Turns a Telephone Monopoly Into a Market-Based Competitor

Written with the help of Paulo Salgado, Partner,
Margarida Bajanca, Senior Manager, and Nuno Belo, Senior Manager
Arthur Andersen, Lisbon, Portugal

Introduction

Around the globe, countries are introducing market competition into industries previously dominated by regulated or state-owned monopolies. The telecommunications industry has been a major target of these privatization efforts. Indeed, the European Union has agreed to fully liberalize telecommunications throughout Europe, which will mean the rapid introduction of competition across the continent.

But competition will bring significant challenges to all involved:

- Governments will have to ensure that high standards of customer service continue to be met.
- Telecommunications companies will have to adapt to the new environment to survive.
- Managers will have to know more about their costs to price products and create value—information that their existing cost systems simply cannot provide.

Moreover, all of these challenges will have to be met quickly.

This case study discusses how Portugal Telecom used activity-based management (ABM) to address these competitive challenges. The company which was formed by the merger of Portugal's two main telephone companies and its main broadcasting service managed to implement ABM in all parts of the business in just 20 months, which was extraordinarily fast for a company of its size. This case study explains how the company managed this feat.

Business Issues

The merger that created Portugal Telecom in 1994 was undertaken to facilitate lowering costs and obtaining higher levels of customer service. Achieving these goals was critical to the company's survival, given the new rules from the European Commission that paved the way for increased competition.

While the merger that created Portugal Telecom (PT) was necessary for the survival of the three companies involved, it raised concerns about the potential for monopolistic pricing, particularly in the interconnection business. Therefore, the Regulator–Instituto das Comunicações de Portugal (ICP) and the Directorate General of Competition and Prices (DGCP) required the company to provide cost data.

While the regulatory requirements were reason enough to implement ABM, Portugal Telecom's managers saw an even greater need—the need to understand the company's costs. Specifically, Portugal Telecom needed cost information that would help it achieve the following:

• Set appropriate prices;
• Compare its own cost data with competitive benchmarks; and
• Reduce costs to keep prices competitive.

Failure to understand costs would have left Portugal Telecom vulnerable to competition, which was becoming increasingly intense throughout Europe. Benchmark data from other countries had already indicated that Portugal Telecom would need to reduce its costs to be competitive with the prices that other companies were charging. Thus, understanding the company's costs became essential to cost reduction efforts and to the company's long-term viability.

Background

Portugal Telecom was formed in June 1994 by the merger of Telefones de Lisbon e Porto (TLP, which operated telephone service in Lisbon and Porto) and Telecom Portugal (TP, which operated telephone service in the rest of the country). The merger also included Portugal's main broadcasting service, Teledifusora de Portugal (TDP).

In 1997, Portugal Telecom's revenues were 540 billion Portuguese escudos—about U.S. $2.9 billion. The company now has nearly 18,000 employees in both fixed and mobile communications. It operates in four regional areas (recently consolidated from ten) and has branch offices throughout Portugal.

Portugal Telecom operates all public exchanges, the network of local telephone lines, and both domestic and international (through its subsidiary, Marconi) transmission facilities in Portugal. The company also provides telex, leased lines, and television broadcasting. Its subsidiaries provide mobile telephone service, paging, data communications, and cable television services.

ABM Project Rollout

In June 1995, Portugal Telecom engaged Arthur Andersen's Lisbon office to develop a conceptual design for a cost model that Portugal Telecom could use to meet both its regulatory and management accounting needs.

Exhibit 1 shows the ABM project timeline for Portugal Telecom. By October 1995, after many different approaches had been discussed and analyzed, the conceptual design for the company's ABM project was completed. Manuel Palma, the leader of the ABM project, describes the design as follows:

> The conceptual design described the steps necessary to implement ABM. It showed how resource drivers would trace resources to activities. It explained how individual activities would be grouped into network activities, customer-facing activities, and so forth. The conceptual design helped us to understand how back-office activities, general office activities, and switching activities would be treated.

The conceptual design gave management much to consider and received considerable attention. The conceptual design stimulated many discussions and was also the subject of many meetings with members of the board, other managers of the company, and Arthur Andersen to discuss the details of how costs should be treated.

By May 1996, management agreed to stop the debate and start implementing. Agreements with ICP (the Regulator) required that a system be put in place to assign costs to all products by the end of 1996. In effect, an enterprise-wide ABM implementation had to take place in Portugal Telecom within seven months. The following sections discuss the structure of the ABM team and the model design they used to achieve this objective.

By working at a furious pace, the team met its deadlines. At the end of December 1996, the team sent the Regulator the detailed ABM methodology for assigning all costs to products. It included all the resources of the organization, all the drivers, and an explanation of the treatment of network resources for all the products.

Testing With Historical Data

In January 1997, the financial results for 1995 were tested in the ABM model the team had designed. In April 1997, the team had also modeled and presented the 1996 results. After reviewing these results, the company forwarded the reports to the Regulator in June 1997. The information, which covered the costs of access lines, traffic (including international and long distance), and leased lines among others, met the initial regulatory requirements.

Exhibit 1: Portugal Telecom's ABM Project Timeline

	1994	1995	1996	1997	1998
Project Milestone					
1. Merger created Portugal Telecom.	1				
2. PT signed price convention agreement with the Regulator agreeing to define the cost of telecommunication services.		2			
3. PT engages Arthur Andersen to develop the cost model conceptual design.		3			
4. Conceptual design was completed recommending an ABM approach.		4			
5 Approach and treatment of costs discussed.		5 →			
6. Began implementation of the enterprise-wide ABM system.			6		
7. *Hyper*ABC software selected.			7		
8. Implementation completed and detailed methodologies sent to the Regulator.			8		
9. Presented the results of tests performed (using 1995 data) to the Board.				9	
10. Presented the results (using 1996 data) to the Board.				10	
11. Results sent to the Regulator showing costs of products and services including access lines, traffic, and lease lines.				11	
12. Developed model for interconnection costs to support proposals as well as other services.				12	
13. Summarized activity costs by general direction area.				13	
14. Convert budgets to activity view by general direction and implement activity-based budgets for going into 1999.					14 →

After this test of the new system, the ABM team used the model to support the interconnection proposals that Portugal Telecom used in its fee negotiations with mobile operations. Cost modeling to support interconnection pricing was completed in October 1997. Nonetheless, Portugal Telecom continues to refine its ABM model to understand and support the pricing of other services, including telex and broadcasting.

In 1997, Portugal Telecom began to obtain the ABM information needed to understand the costs associated with each business unit for example, business markets, residential markets, and infrastructures. The company will also start using the ABM system information for activity-based budgeting.

ABM Team Structure

Manuel Palma, the full-time leader of the ABM effort at Portugal Telecom, is the company's ABM "champion."

ABM was identified as a strategic project by the company's long-term strategic planning initiative called Portugal Telecom 2000 (PT 2000). As such, it received the attention of Portugal Telecom's senior management, many of whom participated on the PT 2000 steering committees.

During the conceptual design phase for the ABM project, a steering committee was created composed of three board members and some managers of the company. Later the composition of the steering committee changed. As ABM was being implemented, the project team reported instead to a steering committee that included one board member and all the general managers of the company among others.

Network Team

During the implementation, the ABM project team had two major subcommittees: a *network* team and a *customer-facing activities* team. (Exhibit 2 shows the structure of the ABM project team.)

The *network* team had responsibility for assigning the costs of the network activities (which were defined as activities developed for generic capacity) available to any product or customer. In effect, network facilities are a huge shared resource. The network team consisted mainly of engineers—three full-

Exhibit 2:
Portugal Telecom Implementation Project Team Structure

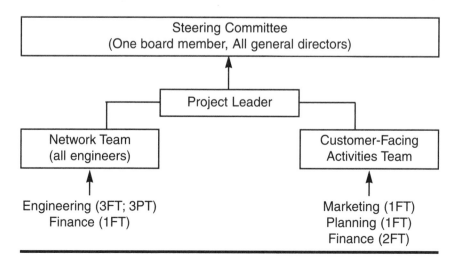

time engineers—but also one full-time member from the finance department. This team also included three part-time engineers. The challenge facing the network team was how to determine the costs of the infrastructure and related support activities. This included understanding the following:

- Where each of the network components was used;
- How the network enabled sales; and
- How individual calls consumed the network's capacity in terms of how many calls it could handle at a given time.

The network team analyzed these questions by conducting interviews, sampling, and studying traffic and switching patterns.

Customer-Facing Activities Team

Customer-facing activities are those activities performed for the benefit of customers, in response to a customer request, or for a specific product. Examples of customer-facing activities include connecting a customer phone line, handling customer repairs, or supporting a call-waiting function. The customer-facing activities team analyzed these costs and the cost of support activities. Support activities (or *business sustaining activities*) are necessary for managing the business, but they do not relate to any specific products or customers. Examples of support activities include grounds maintenance, governmental compliance, and preparing financial statements. The customer-facing activities team was also responsible for the organization and study of other resource pools, such as buildings, vehicles and information systems.

The customer-facing activities team included four full-time people—one each from marketing and planning, and two from finance. This team also used specialized consultants on a part-time basis to address specific issues.

After the initial implementation was complete, most of the members of the ABM project team returned to their previous jobs. Palma became the manager of the newly created cost system department. (See Exhibit 3 for the structure of the department.) Luis Oliveira, the leader of the network team, also remained and now manages three full-time members, two from engineering and one from finance.

The rest of the members of the customer-facing activities team became part of three teams: systems, collection and treatment of information, and reporting. These teams consist of one full-time modeler, two full-time analysts, one full-time person from marketing, and another from finance, as well as two part-time members from planning. The analysts were hired directly from the university. Consultants are also used as needed. With ABM as a component of ongoing management, a separate steering committee is no longer needed for the ABM program.

Exhibit 3: Structure of Ongoing Cost System Development

```
┌─────────────────────────────┐
│      Reports to Finance      │
└─────────────────────────────┘
                ▲
┌─────────────────────────────────────────────────┐
│         Manager, Cost System Department          │
└─────────────────────────────────────────────────┘

┌──────────────┐ ┌──────────────┐ ┌──────────────────┐ ┌──────────────┐
│ Network Team │ │ System Team  │ │ Collection and   │ │  Reporting   │
│              │ │              │ │ Treatment of     │ │              │
│              │ │              │ │ Information       │ │              │
└──────────────┘ └──────────────┘ └──────────────────┘ └──────────────┘

┌──────────────┐
│ Team Leader, │
│ (from        │
│ engineering) │
└──────────────┘

┌──────────────┐ ┌─────────────────────────────────────────────────┐
│ Engineering  │ │  System Modeler (1FT), Analysts (2FT),           │
│ (2FT)        │ │  Planning (2PT),                                 │
│ Finance (1FT)│ │  Marketing (1FT),                                │
│              │ │  Finance (1FT)                                   │
└──────────────┘ └─────────────────────────────────────────────────┘
```

Responsibilities: maintaining ABM model, data collection, modeling and reporting; and providing analysis and business support including responding to regulatory requests.

The cost system department has imbedded ABM in the permanent infrastructure of the finance function. It is primarily responsible for maintaining the ABM infrastructure (including data collection), modeling, and reporting. It also provides analysis and business support, including responses to regulatory requests. The department serves to support front-line managers in understanding their costs and in teaching people to think in terms of long-term incremental costing.

System Architecture

Portugal Telecom runs its enterprise-wide ABM system using *Hyper*ABC software. Because the centralized ABM team tightly controls the model, a single model version can be used for both management and regulatory reporting. Exhibit 4 diagrams the system architecture. The team requires that activity and driver definitions be consistent across the organization. They have tightly controlled the model to ensure consistency and comparative reporting.

The system receives data from the company's general ledger, which runs on SAP's version R-2. It also pulls data from other operating systems in Portugal Telecom. The ABM system provides outputs for both regulatory and management information needs. SAS is used to give access to departmental information and to report and analyze all information.

To provide access to the user department, Portugal Telecom is designing a data warehouse. Data for the model flows in from the company's 1,400 departments throughout Portugal. These departments are aggregated into 400 for input into the model.

The Portugal Telecom system includes 580 activities, which are assigned to

Exhibit 4: System Architecture

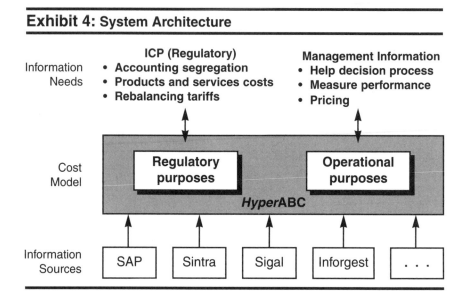

cost objects by means of 40 activity drivers. Examples of activity drivers used include the number of access lines installed, the minutes in peak hours, the number of repair requests, and the number of invoices. The model was used to produce annual results for 1995, 1996, and 1997. In 1999, the team expects to run the model quarterly for management reporting purposes and annually for regulatory purposes.

Results and Next Steps

Portugal Telecom has come a long way in a short time frame. With a mandate to meet regulatory needs, the company built an enterprise-wide ABM system in seven months. This was achieved due to the clear management mandate, the firm foundation from the conceptual design process, and the time spent aligning management prior to launching systems development.

In 1997 and 1998, this ABM information has been used not only for regulatory purposes but also to meet critical management information needs. These include price negotiations and support for cost reductions to keep these prices competitive.

Portugal Telecom plans to continue using its ABM system to support regulatory requests and to provide management information about product costs. The company also plans to enhance the existing corporate planning infrastructure to include activity-based budgeting.

Management expects the 1999 budget to be based on activities. Implementation of ABM was also completed in January 1998, at Portugal Telecom's Marconi subsidiary, which carries all the international traffic, incoming and outgoing. Also, an implementation is in process at the TMN subsidiary, which houses the company's cellular operations.

Lessons Learned

In completing its ABM system, Portugal Telecom overcame many obstacles. The ABM team had to deal with the merger of multiple cultures as several companies were brought together. The scope of the project—the entire company—was also challenging, as was the problem of completing the implementation in only seven months. Finally, much of the driver data needed for the new ABM system was unavailable.

In dealing with these issues, the implementation team learned the following lessons:

* *A sense of urgency accelerates the process.* The requirement to meet the Regulator's deadlines created a sense of urgency in the ABM team and the entire company. Any implementation team should clearly identify the reasons for a speedy implementation, whether they are new regulations, competitive threats, or management vision. Setting deadlines helps to focus ABM teams on the action that must be completed.
* *Top management leadership is crucial.* Portugal Telecom's speedy implementation occurred in large part because of top management's commitment, active leadership, and participation in the process. Because top management was interested and involved, everyone else supported the effort.
* *Communicate milestones.* Even with the commitment from top management and a sense of urgency, those on the ABM team need to publicize milestones as they are reached. This requires having a plan that lays out the milestones, the ultimate objectives, and the expected completion dates. Design a communication plan for getting this information to employees and managers alike.

- *Finance and operations departments must work together to understand the business.* Understanding cost behavior can be far more difficult than just reading financial statements. It often requires close interaction with operational managers and workers. This is especially true for complex areas such as telephone networks. Techniques such as traffic studies and switching analysis may need to be employed. Therefore, multidisciplinary teams are crucial to developing an adequate understanding of costs. A multidisciplinary approach requires:
  - Integrating information (both physical and financial measures);
  - Collecting information from nonfinancial sources; and
  - Collecting important performance information not currently captured.
- *Budgets should ultimately be determined by customer requirements.* ABM systems help everyone understand that customers and their demands are the most important factors to consider when creating a budget. Changes in customer requirements (or the standard products and services being sold to those customers) can change the activities needed to satisfy customers. The changes in activity requirements change the resources needed to be successful.

14

Shiloh Industries, Inc.: Using Activity-Based Management for Daily Decision Making

Assisted by Scott Smith, Senior Manager, Arthur Andersen, Cleveland, Ohio

Introduction

Activity-based management (ABM) has put many companies on the road to increased profitability. At Shiloh Industries, Inc., a vertically integrated steel processing company that produces automotive parts, ABM helps managers understand both customer and product profitability.

Shiloh has used ABM to guide its process improvement team to drive out costs. This case shows how Shiloh has made ABM integral to daily decision making.

Business Issues

When Shiloh Industries went public in 1993, it began the development of "Shiloh 2000"— a long-range strategic plan to improve the company's position in existing markets and also to stimulate growth in new markets.

One of the company's goals was to increase operating income as a percentage of net revenue by one percent per year compounded over the subsequent five years. The strategy required greater cost consciousness in Shiloh's production and supplier areas, while remaining competitive in its current markets.

Shiloh 2000 was launched in 1995, with the following objectives:

- Improving operating margins and revenue growth to provide favorable returns for shareholders;
- Building on Shiloh's reputation for the highest possible level of customer responsiveness and high-quality standards;
- Growing Shiloh through a strategy of selective acquisitions, plant expansions and new plant construction, always focusing on the core business of supplying parts to the automotive industry; and
- Maintaining Shiloh's commitment to management excellence.

Management recognized that improving margins and increasing revenues would be difficult in Shiloh's highly competitive market. For starters, the steel processing industry had consolidated considerably. Since 1980, the number of U.S. steel processors and service centers had decreased by nearly 50 percent. At the same time, customer sophistication had risen dramatically: Customers now required a limited number of large, well-financed, technically outstanding suppliers. Although Shiloh had the distinct advantage of being well capitalized, its success hinged on the following:

- Offering a wide range of first-rate services; and
- Responding effectively and efficiently to customer needs.

ABM was selected as the best tool for achieving a better understanding of costs and thus, better cost control. Shiloh's goal was to use ABM as a decision making tool. ABM information would be used to manage business operations for greater profitability and growth.

Background

Shiloh Tool and Die Manufacturing Company began doing business in 1950, and opened its first blanking facility in 1955. The company expanded steadily.

Expansion has accelerated over the last decade. In addition to business expansion, Shiloh has grown through acquisitions. It now operates ten plants, primarily in Ohio but also in Michigan and Georgia.

With headquarters in Mansfield, Ohio, Shiloh employs nearly 1,600 people in ten divisions. Shiloh supplies the high-quality blanks, stampings, and processed steel found in many of today's automobiles; it also provides welding and assembly services. Its customers include Chrysler, Eaton, Excel Industries, General Motors, Johnson Controls, and LTV Steel.

Over two-thirds of Shiloh's 1997 revenues came from the automotive and light truck market. Another 10 percent of revenues came from sales to the heavy truck market. The remainder of Shiloh's sales came from the heating, ventilating, and air conditioning segment and from the lawn and garden market.

ABM Project Rollout

In 1995, Shiloh launched an ABM pilot program in its main plant in Mansfield. This initial effort covered all activities and costs for that plant. The pilot took about 16 weeks to complete and included actual costs for 1994 (see Exhibit 1 for the rollout timeline).

The plant's costs were traced through individual activities, and then to all products and customers. This meant determining the costs of the plant's 600 product parts. Costs were also assigned to the plant's 60 customers.

The ABM information dramatically increased awareness of costs and profits,

Exhibit 1: Shiloh Industries Enterprise Rollout Timeline

Project Milestone	1995 Mar	Jun	Sep	Dec	1996 Mar	Jun	Sep	Dec	1997 Mar	Jun	Sep	Dec	1998 Mar	Jun	Sep	Dec	1999 Mar	Jun	Sep	Dec
1. Initiated Pilot at Shiloh Corporation Plant	1	↑																		
2. Began Medina Banking Implementation		2		↑																
3. Started Sectional Stamping			3		↑															
4. Began Valley City Steel Implementation				4		↑														
5. Began Liverpool Coil Processing Plant Implementation				5		↑														
6. Began Sectional Die Implementation										6*	↑									
7. Projected date to begin Greenfield Die and Manufacturing Project																	7*			
8. Projected date to begin C & H Die Technology Project and Shiloh of Michigan																		8		
9. Projected date to be begin Jefferson Blanking Implementation																				9

*Gap between projects due to ERP implementation.

which helped the company to remain focused, thereby achieving one of the Shiloh 2000 objectives.

The ABM Team

During the pilot, a strong ABM team was assembled. Composed mainly of departmental managers, the team included:

- The operations manager;
- The sales and marketing manager;
- The customer services manager;
- A production scheduler;
- An information systems representative; and
- An engineering representative.

Bob Pompeii served as Project Leader for the initial implementation. Thom Weber, ABM Cost Analyst (now Shiloh's ABM Manager), and Scott Wallace, the Plant Cost Accountant, were also assigned to the team. This cross-functional, senior-level ABM team was an essential factor in the smooth implementation. As Weber explains:

> If an issue came up, it was quite possible that someone had some knowledge about it. We could sit down, discuss it, and reach the right conclusion.

The ABM team had three sub-teams concerned with customer profitability, value-added revenue, and process improvements. (See Exhibits 2 and 3 for an

Exhibit 2: ABM Team and Sub-Team Structure

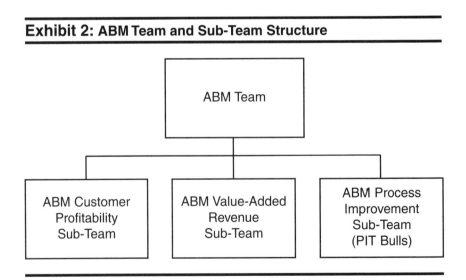

overview of the team structure and its responsibilities.)

The team's objectives for the ABM project were as follows:

- To support continuous improvement efforts;
- To monitor and reduce the cost of processing material through the plant;
- To support margin-improvement strategies through the use and improvement of ABM cost systems; and
- To supply feedback to sales for use in customer evaluations.

Training

Members of the ABM team were heavily involved in the pilot project from start to finish. At the outset, the team held a three-day training meeting. As Weber says:

Exhibit 3: ABM Team and Sub-Teams Responsibilities

ABM Team Responsibilities
- Coordination of Sub-Teams
- Overall responsibility for ABM Implementation
- Data Collection
- Analysis and Reporting

Customer Profitability Sub-Team
- Review ABM reports for minimum levels of attainment
- Review ABM reports for changes in profitability from period to period
- Analyze reasons for changes/problems
  - Similarities/differences
- Direct certain issues to Process Improvement Sub-Team and provide feedback
- Develop justification for action towards customers
- Document improvements made

Value-Added Revenue Sub-Team
- Analyze ABM model on quarterly basis to identify major activity/process costs and determine value-added status
- Feed data to other ABM teams for research and action
- Review and follow-up on the impact on cost data of activities initiated
- Document improvements made

Process Improvement Team
- Act on information/input from other ABM teams and sources
- Prioritize projects based on largest expected returns
- Document improvements made

One of the best things we did was to take this meeting off-site. That way people weren't being paged and weren't receiving telephone calls. . . . It really helped the process.

During those three days, the team also participated in a process mapping exercise that set the stage for the rest of the project. The team identified 134 plant activities, defined processes, and mapped the activities to the processes.

Management Support

It is important to note the level of support the project received from senior management. As Weber says:

Everyone, from the top down, believed in what we were doing. That belief was communicated to plant managers, who circulated correspondence that encouraged support of the project.

After the initial workshop, most members of the team devoted at least 50 percent of their time to the project, but Weber and Wallace spent all of their time on ABM.

Many companies do not win such immediate acceptance of an ABM project, but managers at Shiloh recognized early in the planning process that the ABM project had to be "sold" internally if it was to succeed. As Weber says, "We knew the things we could accomplish using ABM. We laid it out and explained the path we were taking. Everyone just kind of jumped on board."

Wallace explains the team's method for gaining management support as follows:

We used a lot of examples when explaining the process to show how the information would benefit the managers themselves. That helped immensely. For example, once managers recognized that the results of the project could help them manage their departments better, their acceptance grew. We got them involved, and when they saw what could happen, they supported the project.

Weber and Wallace both recognized the vital role senior management played throughout the ABM project. The fact that management understood and supported the project from the beginning set the stage for success. Shiloh CEO Robert Grissinger believed in ABM and had initiated the project. As he puts it, "ABM is a method to manage your business, not just a financial tool. Shiloh's goal is to use ABM to create a competitive advantage."

Software Selection

During the early stages of the project, the ABM team chose *Hyper*ABC software from Armstrong Laing. The team liked its user-friendly interface, reiterative reallocations, and exceptional validation routines.

Once the model began producing results, Shiloh started to see some startling information in regards to product and customer costs. As Weber explains:

> I think almost any person in any organization that implements ABM has some real surprises when they start seeing the data about customer profitability, product profitability, and that sort of thing. Some of the results are expected, but some are not.

Part of the implementation process involved getting people to accept the results. The project team helped by insisting on validation of results and correcting any mistakes that were found. As Weber says:

> We went back to the managers and asked them to review and validate the information. If mistakes were there, we corrected them. That helped a lot with acceptance. We refined the model to help ensure that future information was correct. As we were able to collect better drivers, we continued to enhance the model to improve its accuracy.

Reporting Results

Reporting was a challenging part of the implementation process. As Wallace explains:

> It was tough learning. We quickly learned the software and became comfortable with it, but learning how to format the reports was more difficult. It took some time to get the information formatted in a way that helped our executives and managers understand the results. You have to remember that managers were viewing data in a completely new way, so we worked with them until they thoroughly understood the information.

> We knew there was a lot of information there, but we weren't sure of the best reporting formats. We tried four or five different formats before we found the ones that would work for the whole organization. Now we use three of those formats most of the time. The process took some time because there wasn't a consensus regarding level of detail or what people wanted to learn from the information.

Data Collection

When the initial project was completed, the results were presented to Shiloh's executives. Some people questioned the accuracy and appropriateness of the drivers that had been used. In some cases the information had been based on a best guess.

So instead of moving the project forward, the ABM team decided to be more precise and make data collection a routine part of the ABM system rather than an exception. As Weber explains:

> We set up spreadsheets for data collection and incorporated them into the manufacturing system wherever possible. In a way, it created work for the managers, but it also helped them. They really needed the data, so they began to find better ways to get it for us. Not only did this help with data collection, it made the team look at the processes used to collect data. Managers interviewed their employees to find out how much time they spent on the activities, then the managers completed the grids and returned them to the ABM team.

Exhibit 4: Activity Analysis Grid

DEPARTMENT: MATERIALS MANAGEMENT
MANAGER:
INTERVIEWED BY:
PERIOD: 2ND QTR 1998

INDIVIDUAL/GROUP	Employee No. 1		Employee No. 2		Employee No. 3		TOTAL %	WEIGHTED %	PERCENT OF TOTAL RESOURCES
NO. PEOPLE	1		1		1		3		
WEIGHTING	1		1		1				
TOTAL EQUIV. EMP.	1		1		1			3	
ACTIVITY	%	WGT%	%	WGT%	%	WGT%			
ABM SHILOH	5	5.00	5	5.00		0.00	10.00%	10.00%	3.33%
ASI RELEASES		0.00		0.00		0.00	0.00%	0.00%	0.00%
BUS. PLANNING	15	15.00		0.00		0.00	15.00%	15.00%	5.00%
CORD. DISTRB.		0.00		0.00		0.00	0.00%	0.00%	0.00%
CUSTOMER SERVICE	10	10.00		0.00	55	55.00	65.00%	65.00%	21.67%
CUST. INV. REPORTS		0.00		0.00		0.00	0.00%	0.00%	0.00%
EXPEDITE		0.00		0.00		0.00	0.00%	0.00%	0.00%
EXPORT PAPERS-CUST.		0.00		0.00		0.00	0.00%	0.00%	0.00%
INPUT PRODUCTION		0.00		0.00		0.00	0.00%	0.00%	0.00%
INV. CONTROL & REPORT	30	30.00		0.00		0.00	30.00%	30.00%	10.00%
ORDER ENTRY		0.00		0.00	25	25.00	25.00%	25.00%	8.33%
PROCESS IMPROVEMENT	10	10.00	10	10.00	5	5.00	25.00%	25.00%	8.33%
PURCHASE MRO	15	15.00		0.00		0.00	15.00%	15.00%	5.00%
P.O. ENTRY		0.00		0.00		0.00	0.00%	0.00%	0.00%
SCHEDULE RUNS		0.00	85	85.00		0.00	85.00%	85.00%	28.33%
SHIP PARTS		0.00		0.00	15	15.00	15.00%	15.00%	5.00%
SPECIAL PROJECTS	5	5.00		0.00		0.00	5.00%	5.00%	1.67%
SUPERVISION-MANAGERS	10	10.00		0.00		0.00	10.00%	10.00%	3.33%
—									
EMPLOYEE/GROUP TOTAL	100	100.00	100	100.00	100	100.00	300.00%	300.00%	100.00%

See Exhibit 4 for a copy of the activity analysis grid used for recording the time spent on activities.

Shiloh discovered that although many of its reporting systems were complete, there were some gaps. People think they are doing the right thing, but sometimes they are so focused on the details of what they are doing that they don't see the big picture. At Shiloh, they were ahead of the game because in most instances they had the information they needed, but they needed to store it more effectively.

For purposes of data collection, each machine was treated as a work center. In some cases, resource accounts were summarized. In the general ledger, for example, payroll was lumped into one account instead of broken out by department. Therefore, the payroll account had to be broken down manually by department to make it more manageable. To avoid further manual analysis, the general ledger was restructured so that the data could flow directly into *Hyper*ABC.

Updates and Ongoing Activities

For modeling purposes, data used by the ABM model was originally updated only twice a year, but the team found the resulting information too old to be useful. The schedule has since been accelerated so that data is updated quarterly, including financial data, resource drivers, and activity drivers.

Communication and education continue to be keys to success at Shiloh. Wallace notes, "We developed a rapport with the teams and we kept it up. We tried to always be consistent with the terminology and with the models." They also created an activity dictionary that significantly improved the team's understanding of the model and the work performed.

Weber and Wallace are firm believers in the benefits and importance of training at all levels. People have to be made familiar with the reports and shown how to use them. Some people forget about training; they just give out reports and expect (wrongly) that people will understand them.

Rollout to Other Plants

During the initial three-day workshop, the ABM team identified and defined activities. The team also talked to the employees who actually performed the activities so that they would understand the work better and define activities and drivers more accurately.

Once the pilot was complete, new activity dictionaries were recreated for each plant rollout. As Weber explains:

> We did that on purpose. Everyone has his own way of defining things. It was important to make sure that everyone had a level playing

field. After it was all done, we matched the names to the activities and standardized them.

The rollout to the additional five plants took about two years (see Exhibit 1 for Shiloh's ABM rollout plan). Greenfield Die and Manufacturing and C&H Die Technology were acquired in 1997, and Jefferson Blanking is still under construction. Shiloh plans to implement ABM at these plants in 1999, or the year 2000 along with the Shiloh of Michigan facility. The process has also been temporarily delayed because of the implementation of Baan's Enterprise Resource Planning System. Weber has to split his time evenly between ABM and the ERP implementation.

It is important to note that in rolling out ABM, a different cross-functional team was used at each location. Weber and Wallace helped with each, but they believed that it was important for each plant to have its own ABM team. As Weber says, "They know their business better than anyone else, and having individual plant teams helped to get local buy-in when needed."

Links to Other Initiatives

Besides the original connection to Shiloh 2000, the company's initial ABM efforts continue to produce offshoots that are subteams of the core ABM team. One notable offshoot is the "process improvement team" (PIT Bulls), which uses ABM information to make improvements on the plant floor.

Capacity was one of the first areas the PIT Bulls attacked. They discovered that a handful of parts accounted for nearly 80 percent of production time spent on a specific machine. The team examined the activities required to produce these parts and discovered that scrap removal limited the productivity of the machine centers, because the machines had to be turned off whenever the scrap tub was emptied. To remedy this problem, a second scrap tub that cost only several hundred dollars was purchased for the machine. As a result, machines no longer have to be shut down whenever the first scrap tub is full, which has increased capacity by 30 percent and saves more than $400,000 a year as related to the production of the effected parts.

Another example of savings came from the packaging area, as Weber explains:

> Through ABM, we realized that we were not making expected margins on certain products, so we decided to prepare the individual packs away from the machine line. At first, we planned to do packaging and sorting off-line; ultimately, we found that it was best to send the product to a distribution center and to have it done there. We improved our service to the customer, and we saved over $200,000 per year to boot!

These examples show how Shiloh has used ABM information for process improvement. But the major outcome of the rollout is that Shiloh managers now use ABM information daily to manage the business. All financial decisions take ABM information into account. Whether it is a capital decision to lease or buy a new truck fleet, or a special request from a customer, the decision maker always reviews the ABM data. As Weber says, "With the ABM information, we now truly understand what impact these decisions have on the bottom line."

Results and Next Steps

At the initial ABM plant, a team of senior managers challenged the ABM team to find more ways to increase profits. In response, the ABM team compiled the following list of five strategic initiatives to pursue each quarter to achieve a one percent annual increase in profit margins:

1. Review the customer profitability report and take appropriate action on customers with negative contributions.
2. Analyze the customer profitability report by salesperson, customer, and part to provide feedback to sales.
3. Analyze the machine profitability reports to optimize product mix and throughput by machine.
4. Use root-cause and value-added analysis to highlight problem areas.
5. Provide feedback from all reports to other teams (such as the PIT Bulls).

In addition to these ongoing analyses, the ABM team has a short-term objective to complete the ABM rollout for the remaining four plants. Once implementation is completed throughout the company, Shiloh will start using ABM for quoting prices. The ultimate goal is to incorporate activity-based budgeting throughout the company.

Another goal is to consolidate individual ABM models into strategic business units (SBUs). The team would then be able to consolidate the models of the individual SBUs into one company-wide model.

The ABM team continues to collect data, analyze activities, review the data, and distribute reports; and, Shiloh will continue to use the ABM information to manage the business. As Weber states, "The fact that we are using the data to make decisions is what will continue to ingrain ABM in the organization."

Lessons Learned

- *Cross-functional teams are essential.* Having a highly knowledgeable, cross-functional team is critical to a project's success. It streamlines rollout of the entire project to have technically proficient team members who come from all areas of the organization. Shiloh avoided many pitfalls because it could rely on the team to brainstorm and produce the best answers.

- *Don't underestimate the problems of data collection.* Provide ample lead time to find out what data is available. But also don't get overwhelmed by collecting too much data.
- *Educate users of the information.* Don't underestimate the importance of explaining the reporting process, particularly to nonfinancial people. Also keep the reports as simple as possible, especially in the beginning. Detail can be added later, when people's comfort levels increase.
- *Remember that ABM is a management tool.* One of the most important things Shiloh learned is that ABM is a management tool. As Weber says, "It isn't the final answer: We really use ABM to direct our focus on where we should be looking to enhance our performance or improvement efforts. Whenever we begin a new ABM project, we emphasize that is isn't an accounting tool or function. Instead, it's a management tool for everyone to use."
- *Strong support from all parts of the organization is critical.* Shiloh educated the organization at all levels, which helped garner support. ABM is now integral to Shiloh's operations, enabling the company to compete like its products—by being strong, flexible, durable, and long lasting.

15

The Mutual Group: Using ABM for Shared Services' Chargebacks

Assisted by Mitch Max, Senior Manager, Arthur Andersen, Toronto, Canada

Introduction

Many organizations have reduced the cost of corporate support functions by establishing shared services organizations. In doing so, they often find that it takes more than simply consolidating service functions to truly optimize costs. If you push all support services together, how do you ensure that they are accountable to the business units they are designed to support? How do the shared services organizations justify the prices they charge?

Business units, in many companies, demand lower charges for shared services, but how can a company determine if those demands are reasonable, and also, what the services should cost? If third-party providers quote lower prices, how can the company evaluate if they offer the same service levels? For that matter, how can any company analyze service levels in relation to the costs it takes to provide the services?

To answer these questions, many companies now implementing shared services are also implementing activity-based management (ABM). Used together, the two can help reduce the cost of shared services, provide a reasonable basis for billing out service charges, and also communicate the impact of varying service levels. This case illustrates how The Mutual Group, a Canadian financial services company, successfully dealt with these issues.

Business Issues

In 1993, The Mutual Group began to implement shared services for its various business units by forming the Corporate Services (CS) Division, which was composed of five main areas:

- Information Systems;
- Finance;
- Corporate Affairs;
- Strategic Planning; and
- Shared Business Services (which included Human Resources, Administrative Services, and Legal).

At the time, CS employed 800 people and had a cost base of over $100 million dollars (Canadian), which was one-third of the company's total non-sales-related expenses.

The business units, initially, viewed CS as an overhead function that added little value, so they placed tremendous pressure on CS to cut expenses quickly. The business units also requested improved cost information to support their pricing decisions. Many of the business units believed that the cost system used by CS was inaccurate—and that, in some cases, it actually motivated the wrong behavior.

Because of these concerns, CS sought to use ABM to address the following business needs:

- To identify costs that could be eliminated or reduced;
- To provide a mechanism to accurately charge costs to business units based on their consumption of the shared services;
- To provide accurate cost information to support pricing decisions and profitability analysis;
- To communicate the service levels provided and the cost of varying levels so that users could help determine the most cost-effective level;
- To provide a means for comparing internal costs to the costs of outside service providers for evaluating outsourcing decisions; and
- To provide a better tool for facilitating budgeting by internal services and products.

This case study, therefore, illustrates how CS used ABM not only to manage expenses, but also to change the way the business units viewed them. CS soon evolved from being perceived as an overhead organization that added little value to being perceived as a business partner that was critical to the success of the business units and of the organization as a whole.

Background

The Mutual Group, which has helped Canadians secure their financial future for over 120 years, provides life insurance, healthcare insurance, corporate loans, commercial and residential mortgages, financial planning, and other related services. The company has C$39 billion of assets under management.

Tracing its roots back to 1870 as Ontario Mutual, The Mutual Group is Canada's first and oldest mutual life insurance company. With over C$280 billion of insurance in force, The Mutual Group is one of Canada's largest financial organizations and the fourth largest life insurance company in Canada. It recently acquired the Canadian Operations of Metropolitan Life. The company has more than 7,000 employees and agents to serve its customers.

Existing Systems

When the CS Division was founded, the chargeback and allocation system were fairly simplistic. Half the costs were charged back using very few drivers for large bundles of costs, while the remainder was allocated as general overhead. The largest chargeback was for Information Systems, which accounted for about 40 percent of the entire CS division.

Hourly rates across varying job classifications were established to charge the business units for internal consulting and programming services as well as for a couple of other major business processes. Other IS costs were mostly charged out based on utilization of computer time, but this created a highly inflated cost for mainframe computer time because of the other costs that were combined with the computer costs. After the ABM system had been implemented, the mainframe rate was cut by 60 percent. "Large bucket" costing methods such as these often raise concerns among the business units that receive the charges.

The allocation system at CS used various allocation bases or arbitrary drivers. Because services were bundled together for allocations, the resulting charges were rarely based on the customer's actual consumption of the services. Business units felt hampered in their efforts to influence spending because they had no influence on the allocation bases used.

Several issues arose because of CS's cost system, including:

- A critical need to understand and manage expenses because of a rapidly changing business environment;
- A belief that the cost system provided inconsistent views of expenses and inadequate tools for managing;
- Some dysfunctional behavior because of the way costs were charged back to the business units;
- Skepticism about chargebacks;
- Weakness in identifying opportunities for cost reductions; and
- An inability to link expense budgets for CS to the volume requirements of business units.

Many companies have found that simplistic cost allocations of support services create a "buffet pricing mentality." When everyone is charged the same average price, regardless of their actual usage, the incentive is for everyone to use more than the average. Think, for example, of an all-you-can-eat buffet that charges a single price: Everyone tries to get his money's worth by eating as much as possible.

This mentality creates a particularly troubling situation for managers of support departments. Top management pressures them to reduce overall costs while demand for their services is surging. Cutting back on costs is often impossible except in an arbitrary fashion, which causes general frustration and conflict between the users and providers of the service.

The key to breaking the "buffet pricing, all-you-can-eat" mentality is to use ABM to charge users only for what they consume and to clearly communicate what it costs to provide varying services. This gives consumers the ultimate choice. It also makes it possible to compare the costs and service levels of the internal provider to those of outside providers. This was the path The Mutual Group eventually took, but it took a while for the company to get there.

Preliminary Cost Reduction Initiatives

When the CS Division was formed, the business units immediately pressed to reduce expenses by 20 percent. Andrew Beacom, Manager of ABM, says that there was "intense pressure on the organization to reduce costs—and to reduce them in a rather dramatic fashion." Rather than just cutting costs across the board, CS's management decided to look closely at its business processes by costing out the activities and business processes performed.

But CS went one step further. Instead of just determining process costs at present service levels, CS's management also wanted to give the business units cost information to show what costs would be at different service levels. According to Beacom, the goal was to be able to tell the business units "this is what we perform, this is what it currently costs, and in addition, these are what the costs would be at alternative service levels."

Explaining different service levels and the related cost differences required some analysis, Beacom says:

> The persons involved in this exercise were challenged to come up with levels of service that were, say, 50 percent of the current amounts so that we would be able to say, 'This is what I can provide you for 50 percent of the current cost—and, oh, by the way, if you want current-plus service levels, I can provide you these services for 125 percent of current costs.'

The business units were asked to rank CS's processes in the order of importance. The business units were also asked to rate whether existing levels of service should stay the same, be increased, or be decreased. The units also determined which processes should be eliminated.

"We asked them to go back, look at all the bundles of services, and then rank them in terms of relative priority and contribution to their own business objectives," notes Beacom. This ranking allowed the business units to "draw an affordability line" and to identify services that they didn't see as adding value. Many of these were eliminated. For example, some public relations functions were eliminated while others like graphic services were replaced with lower levels of service combined with outsourced solutions. Additionally, service levels of certain processes were increased because the business units sought—and were willing to pay for—improved services.

This rating of CS's processes was considered successful, because it made the cost of support processes clear to the business units. It also gave the business units a mechanism for choosing the services they wanted given their affordability and value. But this exercise was a one-time initiative. Beacom explains that CS still had "no system that could track cost on an activity basis. We couldn't prove to the business units that we were actually going to deliver the savings that we promised."

As a one-time effort the project did not create a mindset of ongoing cost management. It lacked the permanence needed to change the corporate culture. It also failed to highlight how these support processes add value to The Mutual Group's customers. Yet the need for improved information and more accurate chargeback grew out of this initiative and ultimately led to the implementation of ABM.

ABM Rollout

CS focused their efforts on reviewing the expense management needs of key users in both corporate services and business units. As a result, the ABM project was launched in June 1995. The goal of the ABM project was to redesign the existing shared services cost system and thus, to provide a better framework for managing costs.

The Mutual Group needed an ongoing system that could accurately cost out CS's products and services and relate those costs to the levels of service provided. The system was to be used for:

- Charging out costs on a monthly basis;
- Monitoring overall cost reductions on both a unit cost and total cost basis; and (ultimately)
- Converting to budgeting on an activity basis.

The ABM team consisted of a six-person core team supported by another six cross-functional members from CS and three consultants from Arthur Andersen. Arthur Andersen provided training, ABM experience, help with project management, and active participation on the ABM team when needed. The ABM team had an active change management role, which focused on managing expectations, changing behaviors and accountability, training users, and providing overall support.

The ABM implementation was completed in six months and included the following steps:

- Defining the resources to be included;
- Using interviews to define activities;
- Validating the resulting activity definitions;
- Developing resource and activity drivers; and
- Mapping the costs through activities to the services provided, and then to the business units.

Exhibit 1 shows an overview of the shared services costing model.

The ABM team used a steering committee of senior managers drawn from the different functions and business units. This committee met every two weeks to update status and to resolve problems that arose.

The project also included an extra step to define the shared services products, which determined how activities were bundled. Beacom explains that this exercise focused on "how the business units wanted CS to configure activities for the bill-out purposes." Different business units might want to view chargebacks differently.

For example, the health claims operation wanted to understand all the systems costs associated with performing an on-line dental claim assessment or processing a batch of dental claims. Therefore, they wanted to know the bundled price for all the activities that supported their own business unit's products. They did not want all the detail about costs of the central processing unit or about tape storage costs in their chargebacks. They also didn't need detail about each activity included in this bundle.

As Beacom notes, "We bundled these activities up into products that were meaningful to the business units and billed them back on that basis." The business units found this to be more useful for them in their efforts to understand, control, and directly influence costs. It also speeded the rollout of ABM to areas such as group health claims processing, because part of the work had already been completed.

In addition to the original five areas, new shared services are added to the ABM model as they are identified. These include various IS areas previously contained in the business units and, more recently, a marketing area that supports part of the retail business unit.

Exhibit 1: Overview of Shared Services Costing Model

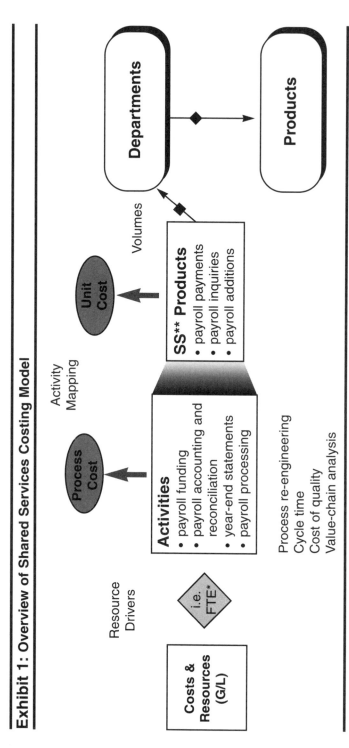

*FTE = Full-Time Equivalent
**SS = Shared Services

Ongoing ABM Responsibilities

After completion of the initial model, the ABM team became a smaller team whose purpose was to support users. This central ABM team is part of the financial management area of the Canadian Customer Business Unit (into which most of CS was merged because of a recent reorganization).

The central ABM team which has four full-time equivalent team members is responsible for maintaining the ABM model and the related reporting tools, including updating the data and producing the overall reporting. As Beacom notes, "The central team's role is to manage the infrastructure, facilitate analysis, and provide training and education." They also coordinate activity-based budgeting (ABB) and help with ABM implementations in other parts of the company.

Data used in the model belongs to the shared service area that provides the data. Each shared services activity or product has an associated product manager who is accountable for the management and analysis of the shared services product. In addition to the central team, analytical support also comes from the financial management area of the IS group and the Shared Business Services Group.

The ABM team provides ongoing training including a "training blitz" on ABB before the budgeting season, because nearly everyone needs a refresher. The team also offers refresher courses on ABM, the data collection tools used in ABB, and the reporting tool used (Cognos PowerPlay).

The team uses "drop-in sessions" to train employees. Specifically, experts in particular areas set aside time when users can drop in and ask questions, review models, or seek in-depth help about problems.

Building the User Base

Despite the support available from the central team, Beacom notes, there is "an ongoing challenge in getting people to focus on the information, getting people to use it, and getting people to incorporate it into their day-to-day living." This challenge exists even when using a user friendly visual tool like PowerPlay.

In early ABM reporting, Beacom recalls:

> We gave product managers views of the data and said, 'Okay, here—slice and dice and drill and change dimensions and so on.' We thought it was great, and they were all just sitting there with glassy eyes. To overcome this problem, we have simplified the number of reports and are moving to categorizing users into two groups—simple users and power users. Many product managers may not be adept at slicing, dicing, and drilling down, so we are giving them simplified reports that

provide a pictorial view of their results for the month. They can do the drill-downs that they need and also some rudimentary analysis. If they get stuck they've always got someone to call on for help.

Power users understand the data flow from beginning to end; they also know how to use the tools. While there may be fewer of them, the ABM team recognized that "you can't turn everyone into a cost accountant." The broader issue is to find ways to embed this information into the regular business processes and decision making frameworks.

Another advanced aspect of this implementation is that all reports are on-line—hard copies are not even distributed. The company's planned shift to Web PowerPlay for reporting will make it even easier to access data and to present the results in a user-friendly manner.

Activity-Based Budgeting

In rolling out ABB, the ABM team developed intuitive, user-friendly tools. When users go on-line to use these tools, the software lists all the products consumed last year. It also provides a completed budget projection based on current annualized consumption, as adjusted for expected volume changes. Internal customers then adjust these amounts to set their plans.

Internal customers' demands for activities are then pushed back to the shared services areas to reconcile demand with capacity and budgets for shared services resources. Most of the activity budgets for the shared services affect each other, so a reiterative process of allocation and reallocation among the shared services must occur before budgets are finalized. For example, Human Resources consumes IS activities, and IS consumes Human Resources activities.

Using this ABB process over the last two years has been made easier by the relative stability of the company's business. When the business experiences major changes (such as a major acquisition or divestiture), ABB will be much more challenging.

Results and Next Steps

The Mutual Group built an ABM model that included all shared services activities and services. The model used *Hyper*ABC software from Armstrong Laing and took only six months to build. With ABM, both CS and the business units now have a better understanding of the costs that are assigned to the internal products and services. CS can now identify and bill consumers of the products and services it provides based on actual consumption. And, because CS now understands the drivers of its costs, it can better manage those costs.

ABM has helped focus the company on the need to understand service levels. These have been captured in service-level agreements that define:

- The scope of shared services products being provided;
- The term of the agreement;
- The agreed-upon levels of service and related performance standards;
- The agreed-upon unit price and volume-commitment range; and
- The feedback mechanisms that will be used for ensuring quality service.

These service-level agreements have greatly enhanced accountability and communications.

The ABM project developed a new framework for expense management that is illustrated in Exhibit 2. The framework was designed to provide accountability for cost, time, and quality of services provided by CS, and to support the "product" volumes consumed by the business units.

This framework places accountability for volumes at the business unit level, while shared services are held accountable for rates and service levels. Monthly billings are processed on this basis. This approach also facilitates monitoring of performance measurements and the use of benchmarking to drive opportunities for process improvement.

Overall, management at The Mutual Group has been pleased with the ABM system, because it provides much better information for decision making.

Future Plans

The Mutual Group also plans to use ABM in other ways. The team is helping with the ABM implementation in the group health claims processing area. Recent acquisitions must also be considered in regards to additional ABM usage.

The ABM team has identified the need to use ABM to provide a better understanding of individual and collective customer costs. ABM may also be used to help managers better understand sales channel and product costs.

Lessons Learned

- *Customize your support to the type of user.* The ABM team identified many users who needed ABM information but had neither the time nor the interest to become power users. Making ABM reports easy to understand increased their usage.
- *Sponsorship is critical to project implementation and ongoing success.* Link the goals and objectives of operational owners to the model and involve Operations in the implementation. Also link the ABM project to other improvement initiatives and key business decisions. ABM must become integrated into the financial management framework.

Exhibit 2: Expense Management Framework

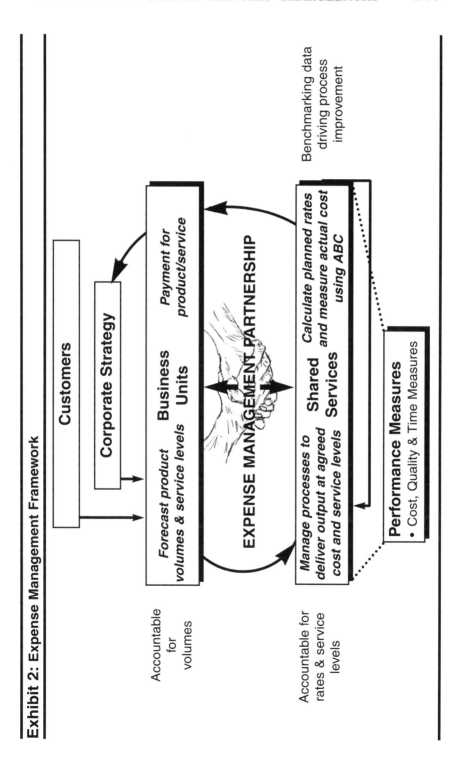

- *Provide user-friendly reports.* Develop simplified, high-level reports that address the needs of most users. Give them the information they need to manage, but don't overload them with information. Provide detailed reporting only to those power users who ask for it. Also, provide reports only as often as needed to address business needs. Switching to on-line reporting facilitates this by the elimination of monthly paper reports.
- *Review reporting and report customization needs on an ongoing basis.* Report development will probably be an evolutionary process. Continue to consult with the users to obtain their feedback and clarification of their business needs. Also, continually review technological advancements in reporting software.
- *Eliminate complexity to keep the model as simple as possible.* It is easy to define activities in too much detail, but this will cause headaches later. Keep the number of activities and cost objects to a minimum. You may lose some accuracy in the model, but it makes life a lot easier when training users about reporting and analysis of the ABM information.
- *Teach people how to use the data.* Shared services and business unit users need to be trained and educated on how to read ABM reports. Don't expect them to understand the information unless you explain it to them. Remember that you want them to use the data. You have taken a lot of time collecting and producing the information, so make sure you teach people how to use it and how it can help them in their work.
- *Consider the project a change management exercise, not an accounting exercise.* You are changing behaviors and accountabilities that are deeply ingrained. Results happen when employees change their behavior. All the accounting efforts are merely steps along the way so that these changes can occur. Behavioral changes occur faster when the ABM team continually focuses on change.

16

Transco: Answering Regulatory Questions with ABM Information

Introduction

In the early 1990s, many countries began to privatize utilities and open them to competition. In the United Kingdom, privatization had occurred in 1986 for British Gas and had brought tremendous change to the gas industry.

While legally any transporter of gas had the right to use the British Gas network, it took some time before competition gathered momentum. The Office of Gas Supply (Ofgas), the regulatory body for Great Britain's gas industry, was set up at privatization. It became heavily involved in the many changes occurring in the industry. British Gas restructured into business units in 1994, one of which was the monopoly gas transporter Transco. The break up into separate business units was followed in 1996 when British Gas demerged into two independent companies—Centrica plc and BG plc. BG plc includes Transco, Great Britain's main gas transmission and distribution business.

Business Issues

Given a changed regulatory and competitive environment, Transco had to respond to many new changes:

- The dramatic increase in the demand for information to manage the business;
- The need to understand costs, for purposes of benchmarking and setting charges; and
- The need to restructure the business to improve profitability within a regulatory regime.

Transco believed that activity-based management (ABM) would assist in addressing these challenges. ABM would give managers the information they needed to better measure the costs of their services, to benchmark against other companies, and to set prices appropriately.

Background: Transco, a Part of BG plc

Formed in March 1994, Transco manages the gas transportation system, one of the largest and most advanced in the world. In 1997, Transco had a cost base of approximately £2.1 billion (approximately US$3.5 billion). Transco delivers around 200 million cubic meters of gas every day to 20 million homes and businesses. Its network encompasses over 170,000 miles of pipeline that, if laid end to end, would stretch six and one-half times around the world. (See Exhibit 1 for an illustration of Transco's pipeline network.)

Transco does not own the gas. It transports gas on behalf of approximately 60 different shippers. Each of these shippers (who are effectively wholesalers between gas producers and suppliers) sells gas to their suppliers. In turn, a supplier sells gas to its own customers. Shippers pay Transco for shipping the gas.

Because of Transco's unique independent position at the center of the gas industry, Ofgas charged it with the creation and introduction of the business and computer systems needed to support the full deregulation of the supply industry.

Transco now performs many new activities in different areas. For example, customer service (shipper facing) activities have been added to handle the process of gas customers changing from one supplier to another.

Deregulation led to fierce competition in the gas supply industry. Consumers are constantly offered special price incentives to induce them to change suppliers. The Transco developed systems now enable the industry to keep track of consumers as they move between suppliers, and allow Transco to accurately bill for transportation charges.

ABM Project Rollout

ABM efforts at what was then British Gas began in 1992 when Steve Copley, a regional finance director, recognized the benefits of ABM. Realizing what ABM could do for the company—both from a regulatory point of view as well as from a competitive perspective—Copley championed the project and hand-picked a team to persuade top management to use ABM.

The ABM team made several presentations to Ofgas and to Shippers to show how an ABM implementation should progress and to explain the possible benefits.

Initial Efforts

In 1993, a full-time ABM implementation team was formed to begin the initial rollout. (Exhibit 2 shows Transco's ABM rollout timeline.) The ABM team began by gathering activity samples from two of the company's 12 regions. According to Ian Brown, a business finance analyst who helped lead the project from a technical standpoint, "The regional samples were then

Exhibit 1: Illustration of Transco's Pipeline Network

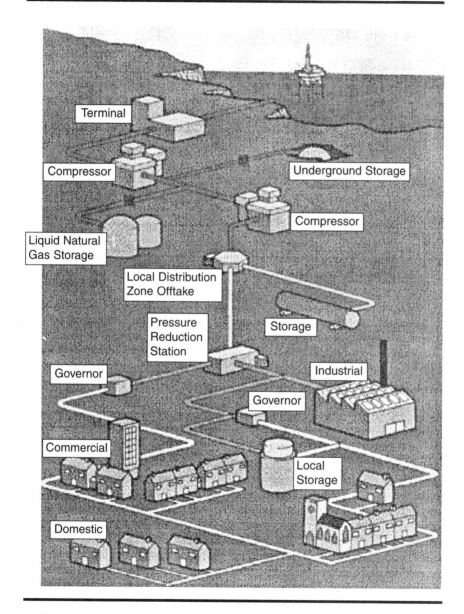

replicated throughout the remaining ten regions to build an overall company model." This approach was used for modeling the 1992 results.

ABM information for the company, including the former British Gas, was generated using nearly 1,000 activities. One ABM model covered all 12

Exhibit 2: Transco ABM Rollout Timeline

	1992	1993	1994	1995	1996	1997	1998
Project Milestone							
1. British Gas privatization begins	1						
2. Original ABC team organized		2					
3. Selected *Hyper*ABC software		3					
4. Built first strategic ABM models and ran through '92 accounts		4					
5. Worked with regulators to formulate pricing formula based on ABM results		5					
6. Analysis of ABM results		6 →					
7. Transco formed as a separate business unit			7				
8. Modeled '94 accounts			8				
9. Developed new activity dictionary				9			
10. Restructured ABM strategic model				10			
11. Developed operational models					11 →		
12. Operational ABM system is fully implemented						12	
13. Developed new suite of reports for operational models with process maps						13	
14. Used ABM results for restructuring efforts						14 →	
15. Began incorporating ABM results into performance measures and mgt. incentives							15 →

regions. A second model was built for activities of the Information Services Department.

The first challenge was to analyze the results and then, to support the development of charging methodology. Ofgas believes that cost-reflective prices support competition. Because Transco provides transportation pipeline services via an open access system, the regulatory framework requires Transco to set prices based on costs in a non-discriminatory manner. ABM information was used to ensure that prices reflect the actual costs of providing services to customers. Much of 1994 was spent analyzing information gathered over the two previous years.

At the end of 1994, the ABM team used its existing models to run through the year's results. The model structure did not change at that time. Only financial results and cost driver information were updated. As Richard Cribb, another key player involved with the technical side of the implementation, states: "Transco's early successes were greatly enabled by building a good relationship with Shippers and the Regulator, and providing the Regulator with the ABM information being requested."

A More Relevant Strategic Model

In 1995, the team began to build a model more relevant to the engineering side of the business. A series of workshops were held in which 30–40 engineers were brought in to discuss specific areas of the business, such as network development. The workshops focused on capturing activities on a day-by-day, week-by-week basis in order to develop new drivers. Using these workshops, the team was able to create a new strategic model by the end of 1995 and to begin developing monthly operational reporting models.

A new activity dictionary was created from the information the group gathered. This was closely aligned to the general ledger codes. As Brown says:

> It's almost as if we had been using ABM for many years without ever realizing it. We have general ledger codes like 'reading meters' and so forth. They were all there in the general ledger, and they actually became ABM activities.

After the new dictionary was developed, operations managers and engineers evaluated new services and products to include in the model.

Creating Operational Models

The new strategic ABM model was completed by the end of 1995. The decision was then taken to extend ABM to all levels of the company. Transco wanted *operational* information in addition to the *strategic* costing information the models already provided.

The operational ABM project began in 1996. The rollout involved training 1,500 front-line managers in the use of ABM techniques. Transco understood that providing operational information was extremely important to managing the business as well as incorporating the use of ABM information for strategic purposes.

The ABM operational team grew to over 40 temporary members, who worked with operational managers to define activities, evaluate time spent on activities, build models, and review the results. Brown continues, "In a lot of cases, the ABM information they were getting was completely different from the traditional costs which took into account only direct labor and direct wages."

The reaction was often total disbelief. Brown and the ABM team worked with the managers to validate the results by tracing the costs of services back to activities, then back to the resource costs recorded in the general ledger. In this way, the team could show the managers where every cost originated, which helped them prove that the costs were indeed correct.

As Transco made ABM operational, it began to help managers reduce costs and manage their parts of the business. The overarching goal was to drive ABM down to the lowest levels of the company.

The Activity Dictionary

The activity dictionary at Transco contained approximately 370 activities. The ABM team tightly controlled the addition of new activities into the dictionary, because they wanted to maintain consistency in the level of detail and the definitions of terms used.

Control of the activity dictionary was also necessary to facilitate internal benchmarking of activity costs. The ABM team verifies the need for an activity, before it is added to the dictionary. Once this happens, the model builders can then put it through the models on a consistent basis.

Multiple ABM Models

During the last three months of 1996, Transco built 41 separate *Hyper*ABC models—one for each area of the business. Much of the information was already available from templates. Six engineers formed a group that provided regular activity information, which led to developing a standard model complete with costs (see Exhibit 3 for the ABM system map). As Brown says:

> That's the beauty of *Hyper*ABC. Once we created one district model (we had 32 districts at the time), we could just copy the model and amend the structure slightly, and we were well on our way. By breaking the company into 41 virtual business units, then consolidating the whole thing back into one, it was possible to complete the operational rollout enterprise-wide very quickly. When EssLINK (*Hyper*ABC's semiautomatic link to Arbor Essbase) was developed, it gave us the ability to take the *Hyper*ABC models down to the very lowest level and then consolidate them back up.

In 1997, Transco's ABM system moved from a pilot project to becoming a fully operational system. By using ABM information, managers now have a different perspective regarding costs. Brown continues:

> People within the company realized it costs more than just materials and labor. It costs the support and the backup systems associated with providing that service.

Using the ABM System

During 1997, the new ABM system at Transco was implemented and became fully operational. The new system makes ABM information available to all

Exhibit 3: **ABM System Map**

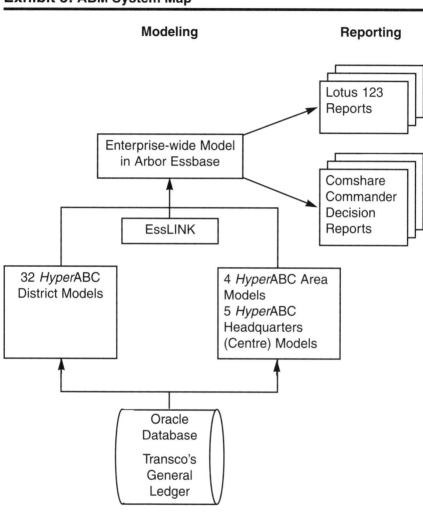

local distribution zones and corporate departments.

Throughout 1997, the ABM team produced monthly reports for Transco based on actual company costs rather than budgets or forecasts. Brown says, "It was pure actual activity reporting, used with a suite of reports, including process maps and activity rates down to the lowest levels." (See Exhibit 4 for a process map example.)

Exhibit 4: Transco Process Map

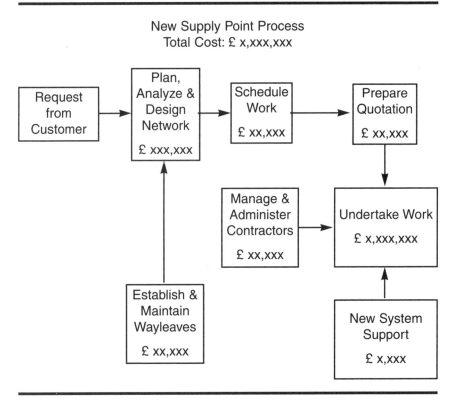

New Supply Point Process
Total Cost: £ x,xxx,xxx

Enablers of Success

Training is an important part of the Transco success. A training course that lasts one and a half days was developed quickly and proved to be quite effective.

Transco has its own trainer responsible for training staff on the ABC software and any other software introduced for providing management information. The trainer also prepares all of the documentation and helps write ABM training manuals.

Transco provides all its own training for model builders. This training is held as needed, but at least once a quarter. According to Brown, interest on the educational side of ABM is increasing throughout the company. In addition, re-education is important for those who have received training in the past about ABM but have only recently started using ABM information.

Support from Top Management

The support of top management (including Phil Nolan, the Managing Director, and his directors) was also critical to the success of the ABM project. "We have always had support for ABM from our top management team," Brown says. "Quite often they would say they believed ABM was the way to go forward. They talked about its value as a management tool and that it should be used."

Brown uses activity-based data to provide a wide range of information—everything from costs to analyses about future options.

In the future, performance management will be based around a series of performance measures, some of which will be activity driven. As Brown says, "People who, in the past, have been unwilling to learn about ABM now want the kind of information we can provide."

Results

With increasing competition, Transco continues to use ABM in all aspects of the business. Mark McGill, Manager of Management Accounting, emphasizes:

> We have ingrained ABM into Transco. ABM information is the basis for pricing gas transportation services, restructuring our business from a strategic perspective, and identifying the costs of products and services on a cost-reflective basis. ABM has proven indispensable for identifying the costs of the internal and external products and services we provide from a customer pricing perspective.

Brown concurs: "A major benefit has been the ability to provide the company's Regulator with cost information that allows for meaningful discussions based on activities. That was one of the main drivers for bringing ABM into the company."

Making ABM Both Strategic and Operational

While many organizations are struggling to implement ABM, Transco has implemented a sustainable, enterprise-wide ABM system. As McGill says, "Unlike most companies, we haven't limited ABM to just the strategic issues, we have gone much further. We have fully implemented ABM at the operational level."

Convincing operational managers to move away from traditional financial reporting toward ABM was difficult. But to illustrate the growing acceptance to ABM at an operational level, McGill shares the following statement made by an engineering manager:

> By understanding the costs and workload associated with the real business activities we undertake—and the way they can be traced to the services we provide—we are better positioned to understand where value is created or destroyed. From this information we then make

better decisions as to the management and direction of the business.

Future Plans

A new pricing formula is now in place. Transco has to reduce operating costs to keep within allowed revenues over the next five years. One of the goals is to use ABM information to help with restructuring and also with Transco's cost reduction efforts.

Transco also plans to incorporate ABM information into the performance measurement system. It is anticipated that certain management incentives will be linked to ABM measures. This change will motivate managers to use ABM to help Transco achieve substantial cost reductions.

A focus group of company employees was formed to look into performance measurement. This group concluded that for Transco to fully incorporate ABM, management incentives must be tied to ABM results.

Brown believes that the biggest change in the coming year will be the development of reports and further development of models that replicate what the performance group asked to see regularly for performance management. These measures will be directly related to ABM. Brown also foresees more of a push to get away from traditional means of managing value and budget responsibility. Brown notes, "This is the way we will be able to compete in the future. The top management team had the correct vision to push toward ABM nearly seven years ago."

Lessons Learned

- *Executive buy-in is very important to the success of your project.* When implementing ABM, change management issues consume about 85 percent of the effort, whereas technical issues account for only about 15 percent. Having buy-in from top management from the very beginning will help you work through the change management issues with relative ease.
- *A stable group of full-time resources speeds development.* Transco has had a full-time ABM team in place almost since the ABM project was conceived. These full-time workers have been able to focus on implementing ABM. This has proved critical to Transco's successful rollout.
- *Make time for analysis to understand and use the information appropriately.* Transco has spent much time analyzing the information generated by its ABM system. This analysis has enabled Transco's managers to make the best possible use of the information.
- *Financial staff may stand in the way of change.* Transco has worked closely with the financial staff to explain why ABM information should be col-

lected. They have educated the financial staff on the benefits of ABM to ensure that finance is an ally and that financial managers will use the ABM information.

- *Training is a constant requirement.* In ABM, training was essential to Transco's success. Having a dedicated trainer from within the company proved extremely helpful, because the trainer knew the company's culture, structure, systems, and business processes. Having a trainer who could prepare materials customized for Transco—thus facilitating the learning process for both managers and employees—also helped enable success.
- *Templates can speed implementation.* Using a standard template accelerated the modeling process. Transco created 41 models, so using templates helped in producing the models quickly and consistently. The models could then be used for internal benchmarking.
- *Link performance management to activity information and to management incentives.* As Transco learned, until ABM information is linked to performance measurement and management incentives, it has not become truly ingrained.

17

Warner-Lambert, S.A.: Increasing Profitability with Activity-Based Management

Introduction

Companies around the globe continue to experience shrinking margins. While competition is forcing prices down, costs are either remaining constant or increasing. For their companies to remain competitive, managers today need far more detailed information than ever before.

This has proved to be true for Warner-Lambert, South Africa (WLSA) which has faced increased competition as South Africa has emerged from its former isolation. Yet, the company has also enjoyed new business opportunities as more countries open their markets to South African exporters.

Business Issues

South Africa's apartheid policies caused not only political but also economic isolation. Since apartheid ended, WLSA has faced many issues that motivated management to seek better information. WLSA searched for ways to: improve customer service, measure profitability by products and customers, decide which products to retain, and cope with increasing governmental price restrictions in the pharmaceutical industry. (See Exhibit 1 for a complete listing of these business issues.)

WLSA prepared for the year 2000 by implementing a major change in computer systems. The company selected a new enterprise resource planning (ERP) package for implementation by 1998 year end. As part of this system effort, WLSA set out to redefine and improve its business processes. The objective was to complete this process reengineering effort before the ERP system was implemented.

Because of all these looming business issues, management was evaluating various improvement projects, including activity-based management (ABM),

---

Exhibit 1: Business Issues Facing Warner-Lambert, S.A.

---

1. End of isolation in a post apartheid era
2. Reduced tariffs and trade regulations which lead to increased competitive forces
3. Falling inflation—forcing examination of cost base
4. Legislation and the possibility of price restrictions in the pharmaceutical sector
5. Major drive for better customer service
6. Warner-Lambert's worldwide drive towards globalization
7. Product rationalization
8. Major costs in complying with FDA regulations
9. Implementation of new ERP system
10. Major new product development in the generic sector
11. The possibility of acquisitions
12. Lack of management information regarding products, customers and channels flowing from outdated legacy systems.

---

business process reengineering, customer-focused management, and systems enhancement. The alternatives made it hard to know where to begin, but ultimately the management team determined that the greatest need was for improved management information. Therefore, they turned first to ABM.

Two affiliates of WLSA in other countries had already tried to implement ABM on a small scale, but both projects had only limited success. Nevertheless, according to Wayne Elsom, WLSA's Business Planning Manager, "Warner-Lambert's world headquarters allowed WLSA to undertake an ABM project because WLSA's management believed in the concept. They were fully convinced that ABM would provide them the answers they needed."

As this case study demonstrates, ABM has proved to be a wise investment for Warner-Lambert, paying for itself many times over.

Background

Warner-Lambert, a global pharmaceutical company whose headquarters are in Morris Plains, New Jersey, generates over $10 billion in revenues through 150 subsidiaries and affiliates. Its products are produced in 78 manufacturing facilities located throughout the world.

Warner-Lambert has four major business sectors, each of which is managed separately:

- Pharmaceutical;
- Consumer Health Care;
- Shaving Products; and
- Confectionery.

In South Africa, the company operates as Warner-Lambert, S.A., which has its headquarters in Cape Town. WLSA is organized according to the same four business sectors, but all four business units share the same support departments such as finance, distribution, and human resources. Exhibit 2 shows WLSA's business unit structure.

WLSA employs 600 people and generates about U.S. $100 million of annual revenues. Two factories (pharmaceutical and confectionery) in South Africa manufacture 85 percent of the products that WLSA sells in South Africa and exports to sub-Sahara Africa. The remaining products sold in South Africa are imported from Warner-Lambert affiliates, including those in the United States, Germany, and Mexico.

Project Rollout

In late 1995, WLSA evaluated what it would take to implement ABM. The management team expected that selling ABM in South Africa might be tougher than it was to Warner-Lambert's headquarters. As Mark Macginty, leader of the Management Committee notes:

> WLSA set ambitious goals for the year 2000 and released a "Vision 2000" statement. The prime focus was to dramatically improve customer service, so it made sense to begin with the supply chain.

Exhibit 2: Business Unit Structure

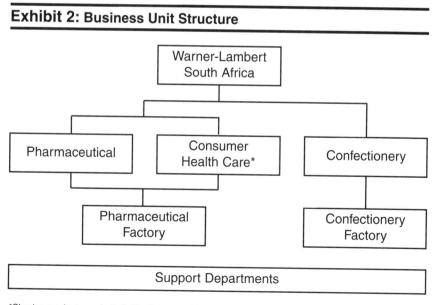

*Shaving products are included in Consumer Health Care.

The intention was to implement ABM throughout WLSA, but the pharmaceutical factory offered some major resistance. A competitive pharmaceutical company in South Africa had recently implemented ABM and major layoffs had occurred. This made WLSA's managers and employees very uneasy.

Nevertheless, in early 1996, WLSA decided to move forward with ABM in all areas except its two factories. (See Exhibit 3, which shows the timeline for WLSA's ABM project.) Elsom says:

> We were moving toward being a more customer-focused organization, so we decided we would focus on the supply chain side, then roll out ABM to the factories later in Phase 2. This strategy would give the factories time to realize that we were not on a head-cutting exercise, but rather looking for management information to help improve the business.

ABM Team Structure

Elsom, who reports directly to the Financial Director and works closely with most of the other departments, was chosen as leader of the ABM project team. The original ABM team also included three external ABM consultants and one management accountant. The team was also able to call on an expert in in-

---

Exhibit 3: Warner-Lambert ABM Project Timeline

Project Milestone	1996				1997				1998				1999			
	Mar	Jun	Sep	Dec	Mar	Jun	Sep	Dec	Mar	Jun	Sep	Dec	Mar	Jun	Sep	Dec
1. Project Launch	1															
2. Cost Base Alignment	2															
3. Process Mapping	3															
4. Interview Process	4															
5. Activity Analysis	5															
6. *Hyper*ABC Software Selected	6															
7. Building of Supply Chain Model	7 →															
8. Mgt. Presentation of Initial Results		8														
9. Critical Success Factors Identified		9														
10. Rollout to Factories		10 →														
11. Product Analysis						11 →										
12. ERP Implementation								12			→					
13. Cost Reduction			13	→												
14. Ongoing Maintenance & Reporting		14													→	
15. Development of New Performance Measurements										15	→					

formation technology on a part-time basis as needed. WLSA's managing director chaired a steering committee of top executives that proved instrumental in making the ABM project succeed. Other members included the financial director, the marketing directors from each of the three business units, the production directors from the two manufacturing plants, the human resources director, and the medical director. This steering committee served as the sponsor of the ABM Project and received regular reports about the rollout.

Elsom says:

> We also had a Management Committee (see Exhibit 4 for team structures) composed of senior managers that assisted the ABM team on a daily basis and ensured middle management's buy-in and support. They were a big help in providing prompt feedback and assistance with day-to-day decisions. We had an extremely aggressive time frame for implementing ABM, so the active participation of the Management Committee and the Steering Committee was critical in helping us to keep the project on time.

These committees also provided cross-functional representation, because

Exhibit 4: Team Structures

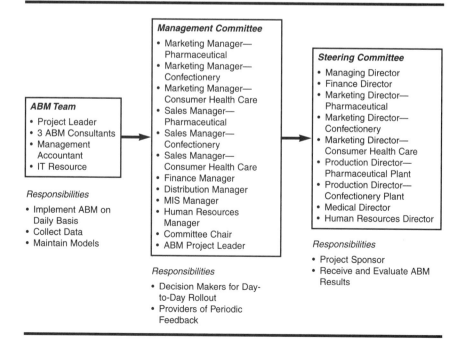

ABM Team
- Project Leader
- 3 ABM Consultants
- Management Accountant
- IT Resource

Responsibilities
- Implement ABM on Daily Basis
- Collect Data
- Maintain Models

Management Committee
- Marketing Manager—Pharmaceutical
- Marketing Manager—Confectionery
- Marketing Manager—Consumer Health Care
- Sales Manager—Pharmaceutical
- Sales Manager—Confectionery
- Sales Manager—Consumer Health Care
- Finance Manager
- Distribution Manager
- MIS Manager
- Human Resources Manager
- Committee Chair
- ABM Project Leader

Responsibilities
- Decision Makers for Day-to-Day Rollout
- Providers of Periodic Feedback

Steering Committee
- Managing Director
- Finance Director
- Marketing Director—Pharmaceutical
- Marketing Director—Confectionery
- Marketing Director—Consumer Health Care
- Production Director—Pharmaceutical Plant
- Production Director—Confectionery Plant
- Medical Director
- Human Resources Director

Responsibilities
- Project Sponsor
- Receive and Evaluate ABM Results

members of the ABM team were all consultants and accountants. The cross-functional representation was important to the project success, since the ABM team lacked cross-functional representation.

Initial Efforts

The ABM project was launched in January 1996. After members of the ABM team had been selected, they were all trained in ABM methodology and implementation techniques.

During the project launch, the ABM team traveled throughout South Africa and to the export territories to explain the goals of the project and to gain the support of WLSA's employees. As Elsom emphasizes:

> The team wanted employees to understand that people were not going to lose their jobs. It was important for them to understand how much ABM would help the organization by providing better information for management and also leading to improved systems.

Before members of the team started collecting data for an activity analysis, members of the team were thoroughly trained on the ABM concepts. As Elsom says:

> We didn't want any misconceptions. The sales representatives were still a little skeptical about what we were doing. There was concern that we were going to start outsourcing our sales force.

To prepare for the activity analysis, the ABM team spent five weeks analyzing their costs. The general ledger was in disarray; no information existed about customers or customer profitability. This scrutiny of WLSA's costs helped expose many hidden costs like customer discounts. As Macginty notes, "We were giving away 20 percent of our cost base in discounts to our customers that were not recorded and measured."

The ABM team provided all the necessary training, then spent two months collecting all the information required and conducting the activity analysis for the initial ABM model focused on the supply chain. During this time, process maps were also developed for all the business processes identified. One team member spent 100 percent of his time for the first two months dedicated to process mapping.

Process mapping highlighted the following to WLSA's management:

1. The importance of forecasting;
2. Long lead times in the supply chain that were largely caused by carrying 450 products or stock keeping units (SKUs); and

3. Growing awareness that the company was too functionally orientated versus process focused, which led to further difficulties in supply chain management.

Until this time, the project had run very smoothly. But now the ABM team began to analyze the cost objects they had identified during the planning stage. The team had originally planned to group all customers and regions together, but when they reviewed this approach, both Sales and Marketing—and also the Steering Committee—objected. They all thought that summarizing the information would render it all but useless for marketing purposes. WLSA's top management also needed specific detail about customers. Anything less would limit the usefulness of the information.

Therefore, the ABM team decided to construct a model that included significant detail—all 450 SKUs, all 4,500 customers, and all 14 regions—this decision increased the complexity of the model exponentially. Moreover, revenues were included in the model so that customer and product profitability could be analyzed.

Software Selection

The ABM team had conducted a thorough software comparison early in the project. *Hyper*ABC was selected because of its user friendliness, multidimensional cost object module, and Open Database Connectivity (ODBC) drivers. ODBC is a popular standard for sharing data files. But the decision to add extensive detail into the model was made after the software had already been chosen. According to Elsom:

> We knew that we were going to have a large model, but we got quite a surprise when we went to calculate the model, because the calculation took 34 hours to run. The problem was that the calculation routine in the software was not designed for such a large model. The cost object module alone had over 28 million possible combinations, 14 million results records, and 900,000 cost driver volumes. The size and scope of this model was more in line with a mainframe application. In all fairness to Armstrong Laing, they had never experienced such a large model (see Exhibit 5 for ABM Supply Chain Model Dimensions). At this time we also provided other software vendors with the opportunity of building the same model in their software tools. Due to the size and complexity of the model, no other venders provided us with an alternative solution.

A development team from the Armstrong Laing Group (ALG) was immediately brought in to help. An evolving series of joint efforts between WLSA and ALG—including the use of beta software, the purchase of a new

Exhibit 5:
Warner-Lambert Supply Chain ABM Model Dimensions

Departments	105
General Ledger Accounts	845
Resource Drivers	358
Activities	847
Activity Drivers	59
Activity Driver Volumes	900,000
External Cost Lines	137,780
Revenue Lines	125,000
Products (SKUs)	450
Customers	4,500
Regions	14

computer, and many rewrites of the software calculation routines—finally led to success. As Elsom explains:

> We were delayed a month, but Armstrong Laing rewrote the calculation routine in order to handle the model size. They have continued to work with us, and the calculation time is now down to two hours. Even though the project was delayed at the time, we are very pleased with the system, and the support from Armstrong Laing has been excellent.

Reporting

Because of the sheer volume of the results tables from the ABM model, PowerPlay, a reporting tool from the software vendor Cognos, is used for reporting. Information is automatically downloaded from *Hyper*ABC (see Exhibit 6 for a systems map) into PowerPlay. The PowerPlay model can then split the information into separate "cubes," multidimensional data tables, so that product managers receive only the information that pertains to them. Since the model is so large, this makes the reporting much more user friendly; the managers don't become overwhelmed with the data.

Rollout to Manufacturing

The initial ABM effort was completed in six months. The implementation in both manufacturing facilities began in August 1996 and took three months to complete. Before the rollout to the factories, standard product costs were used in the initial ABM model that was focused on the supply chain. Management

Exhibit 6: Illustration of Systems Map

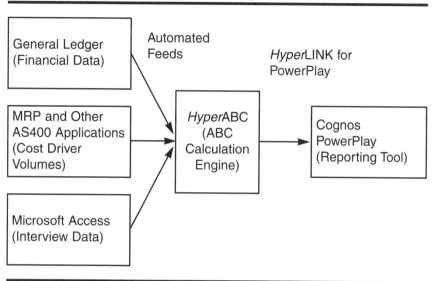

was comfortable with this for the pilot, but no attempt was made to prune the product line, until ABM had been rolled out completely.

Seeing how ABM had been applied in other areas of WLSA helped increase the factories' understanding of ABM. People in the factories also understood how the information would be used in the ABM supply chain model, which paved the way for including the factories in the ABM project.

Results and Next Steps

The first thing WLSA did with the results was to meet individually with each business sector to determine its vision for the coming few years. The sectors created critical success factors (CSFs) for themselves, and then they analyzed whether their activities contributed to the CSFs. This exercise produced a wealth of information and helped each business sector sharpen its focus.

For example, a CSF of the Consumer Health Care sector was an acquisition of another company. The problem was that the Consumer Health Care sector had no activities dedicated to reaching that goal. As Elsom says:

> After that analysis, we restructured the sector around its CSFs and added activities needed to identify acquisition targets. As a result, acquisitions have been made that have been very good for the company from a strategic point of view. It doesn't take many examples like this to prove that implementing ABM was the correct decision for WLSA.

Product Rationalization

Once implementation in the factories was complete, the next step was to iden-tify cost improvements. The product offering needed to be rationalized. Ac-cording to Elsom, "We had too many products that were unprofitable. With the ABM information, we were able to determine exactly which products were un-profitable."

An example of this was a product line that included seven SKUs. The ABM profitability report identified that five of these SKUs had healthy profits, while two were suffering massive losses. Eliminating the two losing SKUs re-sulted in increased profits. Interestingly, sales for that product line have also significantly increased.

The ABM team spent two months analyzing WLSA's product offering. Be-fore eliminating any products, they had to consider all possible effects. This ultimately led to the elimination of about 50 unprofitable SKUs across 20 brands, which—again—resulted in an increase in both sales and profits.

Because of ABM, the factories now have far more accurate costing sys-tems. Labor costs have been cut by placing employees who can do several jobs in under-utilized areas.

Other cost reductions have occurred at WLSA by sharing ABM results with customers. As Elsom notes:

> When we saw what some of our customers were costing us, we were quite surprised. We shared the information with them, and they were also surprised to see how much work went into servicing them. At this point, we negotiated with them to eliminate certain discounts they had previ-ously been receiving. Service-level agreements were also negotiated with wholesalers at about the same time. We worked with wholesalers to redesign some of the processes and to have them participate in product distribution. For certain customers, this meant that the products were delivered to a central distribution point. ABM highlighted the impor-tance of managing our supply chain all the way to the customer. It also questioned the wisdom of having seven warehouses around the country when we had enough capacity to supply from a central warehouse.

All these cost reduction efforts have reduced cost by about 6 percent exclud-ing materials. About 50 percent of this came from the elimination of dis-counts, and the other 50 percent came from changes in distribution. Most cus-tomers were cooperative after they understood the hard facts behind the changes. Furthermore, not one employee was laid off.

ABM Status

In November 1997, WLSA began implementing the ERP package from J.D. Edwards, a process that was expected to take a year. Since that time, the ABM system has shifted to a maintenance and reporting mode due to the focus on the ERP implementation. The factories' ABM models are updated monthly, and the supply chain ABM model is updated quarterly.

The ABM team now consists of the costing department, Elsom, and occasional help from the information technology department. The team spends about 30 percent of its time on ABM and the rest on other accounting, financial, and management support responsibilities.

Future Plans

WLSA's marketing department has expressed interest in expanding the ABM model. Customer costs are now traced to wholesalers in the pharmaceutical sector, since it is wholesalers that actually buy WLSA's products. Ultimately, however, the products end up in pharmacies. For the marketing department, therefore, pharmacies are the ultimate consumers, which is why marketing would like to extend the model down the supply chain to the pharmacy level. But this enhancement of the model would more than double the number of customers contained in the model — increasing from 4,500 to 10,500—a huge increase in the size and complexity of the model. Although this expansion is being examined, no decision has been made about it yet.

Performance Measurement

Additional goals being considered are to work on updating the performance measurement process and to integrate ABM with performance measurement. As a starting point, WLSA will develop performance measurements for the CSFs that each business segment identified for itself. "This action will take ABM full circle, because the CSFs were themselves generated from ABM data," Macginty notes. ABM performance measurements are being developed for the following perspectives:

- Customers;
- Profitability;
- Innovation; and
- Key business processes.

The goal is to have this performance measurement system in place by 1999.

Synergies in the Supply Chain

WLSA is also in discussions with several other large pharmaceutical companies about a joint supply chain initiative. This effort—called a "New And Synergistic Approach," or NASA for short—seeks to form a joint venture that will perform many of the vital tasks in the existing supply chain (e.g., warehousing and shipping activities).

To work, this venture will have to measure the services it provides accurately. Accurate measurement is needed for two reasons:

- First, NASA needs to prove that the cost of performing these new activities will be lower than the aggregate cost incurred by all of the individual members. In effect, there has to be proof of the assumed synergy.
- Second, NASA needs a mechanism to accurately charge member companies for the services NASA will provide.

The ABM team at WLSA has been requested to use ABM to meet these two objectives if NASA becomes operational. In the meantime, pharmaceutical distributors who feel threatened are challenging NASA.

Requests for information about WLSA's ABM implementation are now being received from many other Warner-Lambert affiliates. The success stories are quickly making their way around the company and have triggered much interest. So far, however, the Warner-Lambert affiliate in Mexico is the only other affiliate that has successfully implemented ABM. As Elsom notes, "Let our implementation be a testimony of what you can accomplish if you have a vision and are committed to the effort. Don't let initial resistance detour your goals and objectives."

Lessons Learned

- *Maintain a detailed project plan to keep the effort on track.* Project management skills are mandatory if a project is to be finished on time. Maintain a detailed project plan with appropriate milestones to monitor the progress.
- *Communicate, communicate, and communicate so that people in the organization understand the goals and objectives.* Clear, effective communication eliminates rumors and the spread of misinformation. Many people view ABM as nothing more than an excuse for layoffs, so make sure that your employees know exactly what you are doing. WLSA conducted weekly meetings, and sent out monthly progress reports and regular e-mails to keep people informed.

- *Make sure you provide an appropriate level of detail to answer questions people ask.* The marketing and sales departments at WLSA were not prepared to compromise the detail they wanted to see for customers and products. They withheld support for the project unless the detail they needed was provided. Always remember who your internal customers are, and be sure to provide them with an appropriate level of detail.
- *Don't allow your project to be viewed as a financial exercise.* Because the finance department piloted this project, it was originally viewed as nothing more than a finance project. To overcome this perception, a cross-functional team of senior managers was formed to make the daily decisions about the ABM project.
- *Top management support is critical.* At Warner-Lambert, the support of top management is needed for a project of this magnitude. Without that support, the ABM efforts would not have moved beyond the planning stage. Top management support helped keep the project on time and adequately funded.
- *Use experienced consultants.* Experienced consultants provide a wealth of knowledge from previous implementations and can dramatically speed your implementations. They can also transfer their knowledge to the company's ABM team so that the project runs smoothly after the consultants leave.

Part III

Summary

Many people have followed the developments of activity-based management (ABM) over the past 12 years. Some thought ABM was just a passing fad. But those who doubted should realize that ABM has become an enduring strategic tool for decision making.

Numerous research projects—including those conducted by the American Productivity & Quality Center (APQC) and Consortium for Advanced Manufacturing-International (CAM-I)—clearly show several important trends and best practices emerging. Perhaps most notable is the evolution of ABM from standalone pilots to fully integrated, enterprise-wide systems.

One key way to check the validity of a trend is to observe and analyze it as it occurs. These case studies provide a solid foundation in the basics of ABM, illustrations of this enterprise-wide trend, and also insights into the factors that contribute to the trend toward enterprise-wide ABM. For example, many companies now try to bypass traditional pilot projects and move directly to full enterprise-wide rollouts of ABM (see, for example, the American Seating and the John Deere Health Care, Inc. case studies).

Several factors reduce the need for a traditional pilot. These include:

- Having ABM project leaders who have successfully implemented ABM in other divisions or at other companies;
- Knowledge of best practices and literature on ABM that can be used to educate employees and managers; and
- Better software to simplify implementation tasks.

Another key way of examining trends is to predict where the trends are headed, then to look for cases where the future state of affairs has already begun.

The move from pilots to full-scale implementations, for example, is already occurring as shown by the case studies in this book about GTE Supply, Portugal Telecom, Shiloh Industries, and many others.

The new enterprise-wide ABM systems are also proving to be scalable. As the DHL case shows, the level of detail can be tailored to match the significance of the costs involved. Its approach shows how ABM can be both all inclusive of costs for global needs, yet customized for local needs, at an affordable level.

The application of ABM beyond manufacturing to service, not-for-profit, and governmental organizations is apparent from the fact that most of these case studies are non-manufacturing. These include financial markets (Dana Commercial Credit), insurance (Blue Cross Blue Shield of North Carolina and The Mutual Group), telecommunications (Portugal Telecom), government (CinCFleet), distribution (GTE Supply and Transco), utilities (Central and South West Corporation), healthcare (John Deere Health Care, Inc.) and air express transport (DHL).

Even manufacturers are expanding their uses of ABM beyond the non-manufacturing areas of their businesses by pushing into customer profitability analysis (American Seating, AscoForge Safe, Shiloh Industries, and Warner-Lambert, S.A.).

As Stephen R. Covey describes it, ABM has become an *enabler.* This has led to the trend of ABM being linked to—and leveraged from—other improvement initiatives. Examples include Blue Cross Blue Shield of North Carolina's linkage of ABM to the business process model and Dana Commercial Credit's use of ABM for continuous improvement—in a company that already had Baldrige-Award-winning quality.

As the *cornerstones of decision making,* enterprise-wide ABM systems allow organizations to approach business in new ways. Examples of this include consideration of the joint approach to distribution represented by the new and synergistic approach (NASA) concept being considered by Warner-Lambert, S.A., and the new ways of evaluating performance undertaken by Transco.

Enterprise-wide ABM is a fact-based way of understanding the work that an organization does. As such, it is a key tool for unlocking the power of any enterprise.

The key to understanding this power lies in the people who drive ABM implementations. There is tremendous power in ABM systems such as Armstrong Laing's, which make today's ABM implementers far better equipped than their predecessors. Yet it still takes individuals to pioneer implementation in each company.

In most cases, implementing ABM may not be easy. The key is to keep trying different approaches until you find ones that work. Perseverance has been a key trait of successful ABM leaders.

You should also realize that a successful ABM effort must go beyond the outputs of a single ABM manager or even an entire team. ABM leaders, including some from these case study companies, will move on to other challenges and responsibilities. As pioneers and change agents, ABM leaders are often called on to take greater responsibility in their own companies or with others. ABM projects and their leaders can be caught in the dynamic environment that seems the norm in business today. Their legacy is found in how well they have created a sustainable path for others to follow.

Other factors facing ABM efforts include:

- Changes in company ownership such as through mergers;
- Changes in leadership such as a new CEO or CFO, or some other switch in the project's champion; and
- Changes in business priorities.

All of these factors can sidetrack or stall an ABM effort.

These perils exist, just as they have always existed. Yet enterprise-wide ABM continues to advance. The success of enterprise-wide ABM rests on the soundness of its underlying principles. As Arthur E. Andersen once said:

> We cannot take a short-term view, but must take a long view in the determination of sound principles that will remain unchanged through the ages. . . . Fundamental principles will ultimately prevail.[1]

If we as authors have been successful, you will now understand the soundness of the principles of enterprise-wide ABM. You will also understand how enterprise-wide ABM systems are serving as the *cornerstones of decision making.* Moreover, you should be ready to lay those cornerstones in your own organizations. With enterprise-wide ABM, you are well on the way to building an excellent future.

---

1. Andersen, Arthur E. "Beyond the Numbers" *System, The Magazine of Business,* January 1913. Pages 1–13.

Appendices

Appendix 1: Helpful Tools

Appendix 1A: Universal Process Classification Scheme*

Operational Processes

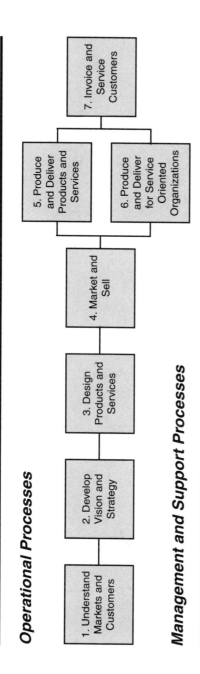

1. Understand Markets and Customers
2. Develop Vision and Strategy
3. Design Products and Services
4. Market and Sell
5. Produce and Deliver Products and Services
6. Produce and Deliver for Service Oriented Organizations
7. Invoice and Service Customers

Management and Support Processes

8. Develop and Manage Human Resources
9. Manage Information Resources and Technology
10. Manage Financial and Physical Resources
11. Execute Environmental, Health and Safety Management Program
12. Manage External Relationships
13. Manage Improvement and Change

*Developed in partnership with Arthur Andersen and the International Benchmarking Clearinghouse.

Appendix 1A: Universal Process Classification Scheme

1. Understand Markets and Customers
1.1 Determine Customer Needs and Wants
1.2 Measure Customer Satisfaction
1.3 Monitor Changes in Market or Customer Expectations

2. Develop Vision and Strategy
2.1 Monitor the External Environment
2.2 Define the Business Concept and Strategy
2.3 Design the Organizational Structure
2.4 Develop and Set Organizational Goals

3. Design Products and Services
3.1 Develop New Product/Service Concept and Plans
3.2 Design, Build, and Evaluate Prototype Products or Services
3.3 Refine Existing Products/Services
3.4 Test Effectiveness of New or Revised Products or Services
3.5 Prepare for Production
3.6 Manage the Product/Service Development Process

4. Market and Sell
4.1 Develop Sales and Marketing Strategy
4.2 Sell Products and Services
4.3 Manage Customer Orders

5. Produce and Deliver Products and Services
5.1 Plan for and Acquire Necessary Resources
5.2 Convert Resources or Inputs into Products
5.3 Transport and Deliver Materials and Products
5.4 Manage Production and Delivery Process

6. Produce and Deliver for Service Oriented Organizations
6.1 Plan for and Acquire Necessary Resources
6.2 Develop Human Resources Skills
6.3 Deliver Service to the Customer
6.4 Ensure Quality of Service

7. Invoice and Service Customers
7.1 Bill the Customer
7.2 Provide After-Sales Service
7.3 Respond to Customer Inquiries

8. Develop and Manage Human Resources
8.1 Create and Manage Human Resource Strategy
8.2 Identify Performance Competencies

8.3 Manage Deployment of Personnel
8.4 Develop and Train Employees
8.5 Manage Employee Performance, Reward, and Recognition
8.6 Ensure Employee Well-Being and Satisfaction
8.7 Ensure Employee Involvement
8.8 Manage Labor Management Relationships
8.9 Develop Human Resource Information Systems

9. Manage Information Resources and Technology
9.1 Manage Information Resources
9.2 Manage Information Technology

10. Manage Financial and Physical Resources
10.1 Manage Financial Resources
10.2 Process Finance and Accounting Transactions
10.3 Report Information
10.4 Conduct Internal Audits
10.5 Manage the Tax Function
10.6 Manage Physical Resources

11. Execute Environmental, Health and Safety Management Program
11.1 Formulate EHS Management Strategy
11.2 Formalize Environmental Management System
11.3 Manage Design for Environment Program
11.4 Manage EHS Costs and Benefits
11.5 Manage Remediation Projects
11.6 Manage Environmental Insurance Recovery Program
11.7 Measure and Report EHS Performance

12. Manage External Relationships
12.1 Communicate with Shareholders
12.2 Manage Government Relationships
12.3 Build Lender Relationships
12.4 Develop Public Relations Program
12.5 Interface with Board of Directors
12.6 Develop Community Relations
12.7 Manage Legal and Ethical Issues

13. Manage Improvement and Change
13.1 Measure Organizational Performance
13.2 Conduct Quality Assessments
13.3 Benchmark Performance
13.4 Apply Best Practices
13.5 Implement TQM

Appendix 1B: High Level Project Plan

Project Step	Week 1	Week 2	Week 3	Week 4	Week 5	Week 6	Week 7	Week 8	Week 9	Week 10	Week 11
1. Project Ramp-Up • Selling and Education • Project Planning • Training	■	■									
2. Assessment of Current Cost Environment and Data Collection			■	■	■	■	■	■	■	■	■
3. ABM Model(s) Conceptual Design					■	■	■	■			
4. Configure Prototype & Implement ABM Model(s)					■	■	■		■	■	
5. Model(s) Validation									■		■
6. Reporting and Analysis											
7. Improvement/Migration Planning											
8. Project Management	■	■	■	■	■	■	■	■	■	■	■

	Week 12	Week 13	Week 14	Week 15	Week 16	Week 17	Week 18	Week 19	Week 20	Week 21	Week 22	Week 23	Week 24
Project Step 1													
Project Step 2	▓	▓	▓	▓	▓								
Project Step 3	▓												
Project Step 4			▓	▓	▓	▓							
Project Step 5		▓	▓	▓	▓	▓	▓	▓	▓				
Project Step 6							▓	▓	▓	▓	▓	▓	▓
Project Step 7							▓	▓	▓	▓	▓	▓	▓
Project Step 8	▓	▓	▓	▓	▓	▓	▓	▓	▓	▓	▓	▓	▓

Appendix 1C: Sample Page from Activity Dictionary

9.0 CASH MANAGEMENT

Activity Number	Activity Name	Activity Definition
9.01	Summarize Current Position	All activities associated with compiling net cash position from summaries of receipts and payments
9.02	Perform Cash Reconciliation and Management	All activities associated with completing cash reconciliation (e.g., review outstanding checks, deposits in transit, examine bank statements)
9.03	Manage Short-Term Financial Requirements	All activities associated with managing short-term funding requirements with banks and other sources of credit
9.04	Prepare Cashflow Forecasts	All activities associated with preparing cashflow forecasts for short-, medium-, and long-term
9.05	Manage Debt	All activities associated with reviewing debt requirements, future capital needs, bank covenants and compliance of such
9.06	Interface with Third Parties	All activities associated with investor, bank and finance related meetings
9.07	Maintain Treasury System	All activities associated with entering data into the cash management, or accounting system
9.08	Implement & Control Cash Management Systems	All activities associated with researching and identifying cash management services, negotiating terms, bank account set-up and ongoing control of banking services
9.09	Report Treasury Information	All activities associated with creating, and producing treasury related reports for management or other review (e.g., cash flow)
9.10	Other Treasury Activities	All activities associated with Treasury activities not captured in the definitions above. Please include a brief description of the activity if you use activity number 9.10

Appendix 1D: Activity Effort Worksheet

Name: _____   Title: _____

Phone #: _____   Business Unit: _____

                                  Location: _____

Job Title Description: _____

Position Type: ____ Supervisory   ____ Non-Supervisory

                      ____ Exempt   ____ Non-Exempt

                      ____ Full-Time   ____ Part-Time

Weekly Base Hours: _____ (i.e., 40 hrs a week)

Overtime Hours worked: _____ (on average)

Using the activity dictionary provided, please complete the following section. Keep in mind, we are seeking to obtain data relating to a "typical" period of work.

Line #	Activity Number	Activity Description	Percentage of Your Time
1	_____	_____	_____
2	_____	_____	_____
3	_____	_____	_____
4	_____	_____	_____
5	_____	_____	_____
6	_____	_____	_____
7	_____	_____	_____
8	_____	_____	_____
9	_____	_____	_____
10	_____	_____	_____
11	_____	_____	_____
12	_____	_____	_____
13	_____	_____	_____
14	_____	_____	_____
15	_____	_____	_____
		TOTAL	**100%**

Activity Effort Worksheet—EXAMPLE

Name: __John Doe__   Title: __A/P Processor__
Phone #: __555-1212__   Business Unit: __CCL__
                               Location: __Long Island__

Job Title Description: __A/P Processor__

Position Type: ____Supervisory   __X__ Non-Supervisory

                  ____Exempt   __X__ Non-Exempt

                  __X__ Full-Time   ____Part-Time

Weekly Base Hours: ____40____ (i.e., 40 hrs a week)

Overtime Hours worked: ____4____ (on average)

Using the activity dictionary provided, please complete the following section. Keep in mind, we are seeking to obtain data relating to a "typical" period of work.

Line #	Activity Number	Activity Description	Percentage of Your Time
1	1.05	Training	5%
2	1.04	Meetings	5%
3	6.01	Sort Mail	5%
4	6.02	Review Invoices	8%
5	6.03	Manual Match	22%
6	6.06	Run Checks	5%
7	6.09	A/P Adjustments	13%
8	6.11	Vendor Inquiries	7%
9	6.13	Report A/P Information	12%
10	2.02	Prepare Budget Information	10%
11	2.07	Enter Budget Information	8%
12			
13			
14			
15			
		TOTAL	**100%**

Appendix 2: Glossary of Terms

Note: All terms are taken directly from the CAM-I Glossary of Terms Version 1.2 unless noted by an (*)

* ABC   See activity-based costing.

* ABM   See activity-based management.

Activity   1. Work performed within an organization. 2. An aggregation of actions performed within an organization that is useful for purposes of activity-based costing.

Activity analysis   The identification and description of activities in an organization. Activity analysis involves determining what activities are done within a department, how many people perform the activities, how much time is spent performing the activities, what resources are required to perform the activities, what operational data best reflect the performance of the activities, and what value the activity has for the organization. Activity analysis is accomplished by means of interviews, questionnaires, observation, and review of physical records of work.

Activity attributes   Characteristics of individual activities. Attributes include cost drivers, cycle time, capacity, and performance measures. For example, a measure of the elapsed time required to complete an activity is an attribute. (See *cost driver* and *performance measures.*)

* Activity-based budgeting   A process by which a company uses its understanding of its activities and driver relationships to set better budgets. This is achieved by determining estimates of volume that drive activities. Determines activity levels that drive activity costs, and gives an entity greater ability to predict spending.

Activity-based cost system   A system that maintains and processes financial and operating data on a firm's resources, activities, cost objects, cost drivers, and activity performance measures. It also assigns costs to activities and cost objects.

Activity-based costing   A methodology that measures the cost and performance of activities, resources, and cost objects. Resources are assigned to activities, then activities are assigned to cost objects based on their use. Activity-based costing recognizes the causal relationships of cost drivers to activities.

Activity-based management A discipline that focuses on the management of activities as the route to improving the value received by the customer and the profit achieved by providing this value. This discipline includes cost driver analysis, activity analysis, and performance measurement. Activity-based management draws on activity-based costing as its major source of information.

Activity cost assignment The process through which costs of activities are attached to cost objects using activity drivers. (See *cost object* and *activity driver*.)

Activity cost pool A grouping of all cost elements associated with an activity. (See *cost element*.)

* Activity dictionary A listing of standardized definitions of common activities typically used in an activity-based analysis. Activities are defined as verb/noun such as "enter orders." Activity dictionaries often have a numbering and classification scheme.

Activity driver A measure of the frequency and intensity of the demands placed on activities by cost objects. An activity driver is used to assign costs to cost objects. It represents a line item on the bill of activities for a product or customer. An example is the number of part numbers, which is used to measure the consumption of material-related activities by each product, material type, or component. The number of customer orders measures the consumption of order-entry activities by each customer. Sometimes an activity driver is used as an indicator of the output of an activity, such as the number of purchase orders prepared by the purchasing activity. (See *cost object* and *bill of activities*.)

Activity driver analysis The identification and evaluation of the activity drivers used to trace the cost of activities to cost objects.

Activity level A description of how an activity is used by a cost object or other activity. Some activity levels describe the cost object that uses the activity and the nature of this use. These levels include activities that are traceable to the product (i.e., unit-level, batch-level, and product-level costs), to the customer (customer-level costs), to a market (market-level costs), to a distribution channel (channel-level costs), and to a project, such as a research and development project (project-level costs).

Allocation 1. An apportionment or distribution. 2. A process of assigning cost to an activity or cost object when a direct measure does not exist. For example, assigning the cost of power to a machine activity by means of machine hours is an allocation because machine hours are an indirect measure of power consumption. In some cases, allocations can be converted to tracings by incurring additional measurement costs. Instead of using machine hours to allocate power consumption, for example, a company can place a power meter on machines to measure actual power consumption. (See *tracing.*)

Assignment   See *cost assignment.*

Attributes   Characteristics of activities, such as cost drivers and performance measures. (See *cost driver* and *performance measure.*)

Attribution   See *tracing.*

Benchmarking   See *best practices.*

Best practices   A methodology that identifies an activity as the standard, or benchmark, by which a similar activity will be judged. This methodology is used to assist in identifying a process or technique that can increase the effectiveness or efficiency of an activity. The source may be internal (e.g., taken from another part of the company) or external (e.g., taken from a competitor). Another term used is *competitive benchmarking.*

Bill of activities   A listing of the activities required (and, optionally, the associated costs of the resources consumed) by a product or other cost object.

* Business process reengineering (BPR)   An approach to improving the operations of a business that focuses on the horizontal process by which work is performed. This approach seeks a dramatic improvement through complete redesign (or reengineering) of the way the process is performed.

Competitive benchmarking   See *best practices.*

* Consortium for Advanced Manufacturing–International (CAM-I)
CAM-I, a not-for-profit membership organization founded in 1972, supports research and development in areas of strategic importance to the manufacturing industries. Since 1986, CAM-I's Cost Management System (CMS) Program—a coalition of members from industry, government, consulting, software companies, and academia—has been recognized internationally as the leading forum for the advancement of cost management research and practice.

Cost accounting standards   1. Rules promulgated by the Cost Accounting Standards Board (CASB) of the federal government to ensure contractor compliance in accounting for government contracts. 2. A set of rules issued by any of several authorized organizations or agencies, such as the American Institute of Certified Public Accountants (AICPA) or the Association of Chartered Accountants (ACA), dealing with the determination of costs to be allocated, inventoried, or expensed.

Cost assignment The tracing or allocation of resources to activities or cost objects. (See *allocation* and *tracing*.)

Cost center The basic unit of responsibility in an organization for which costs are accumulated.

Cost driver Any factor that causes a change in the cost of an activity. For example, the quality of parts received by an activity (e.g., the percent that are defective) is a determining factor in the work required by that activity because the quality of parts received affects the resources required to perform the activity. An activity may have multiple cost drivers associated with it.

Cost driver analysis The examination, quantification, and explanation of the effects of cost drivers. Management often uses the results of cost driver analyses in continuous improvement programs to help reduce throughput time, improve quality, and reduce cost. (See *cost driver*.)

Cost element An amount paid for a resource consumed by an activity and included in an activity cost pool. For example, power cost, engineering cost, and depreciation may be cost elements in the activity cost pool for a machine activity. (See *activity cost pool* and *bill of activities*.)

Cost object Any customer, product, service, channel, contract, project, or other work unit for which a separate cost measurement is desired.

Cost of quality All the resources expended for appraisal costs, prevention costs, and both internal and external failure costs of activities and cost objects.

Cost pool See *activity cost pool*.

Direct cost A cost that is traced directly to an activity or a cost object. For example, the material issued to a particular work order and the engineering time devoted to a specific product are direct costs to the work orders or products. (See *tracing*.)

* Drilling down The process of progressively analyzing cost detail starting at a high level and then going into the cost's respective elements and components. Each level or layer of cost is examined in more granularity allowing greater understanding but typically at an increasing level of effort (and cost) in analyzing. The process should stop when the cost of going more detailed exceeds the value of the additional detail analyzed.

* Enterprise-wide ABM A management information system that uses activity-based information to facilitate decision making across the organization.

* Financial view of costs   This is one of three primary views of cost. It represents the traditional approach to costing using the historical cost concept. It is typically used by financial controllers and tax managers to value inventory and report to shareholders, lenders, and tax authorities. This view is used in financial accounting and typically follows statutory reporting rules such as generally accepted accounting principles or tax regulations. Its focus is on the past. The measures are nearly all financial.

Fixed cost   A cost element of an activity that does not vary with changes in the volume of cost drivers or activity drivers. The depreciation of a machine, for example, may be assigned to a particular activity, but it is fixed with respect to changes in the number of units of the activity driver. The designation of a cost element as fixed or variable may vary depending on the time frame of the decision in question and the extent to which the volume of production, activity drivers, or cost drivers changes.

* Focus group   A data collection method in which a group of individuals is surveyed together. This approach allows individuals feedback and is more efficient in data collection due to the simultaneous data collection from a group.

Indirect cost   The cost that is allocated—as opposed to being traced—to an activity or a cost object. For example, the costs of supervision or heat may be allocated to an activity on the basis of direct labor hours. (See *allocation*.)

Life cycle   See *product life cycle*.

Non-value-added activity   An activity that is considered not to contribute to customer value or to the organization's needs. The designation "non-value-added" reflects a belief that the activity can be redesigned, reduced, or eliminated without reducing the quantity, responsiveness, or quality of the output required by the customer or the organization. (See *value analysis*.)

* Operational view of cost   This is one of the three primary views of cost. It represents the view of cost needed for day-to-day cost management by line managers, process improvement teams, and quality teams. This cost information is used as an indicator of performance and to determine if activities are adding value. The time focus is typically short-term with the need for immediate feedback. The measures used tend to be mostly physical.

Opportunity cost   The economic value of a benefit that is sacrificed when an alternative course of action is selected.

Performance measures   Indicators of the work performed and the results achieved in an activity, process, or organizational unit. Performance measures may be financial or nonfinancial. An example of a performance measure of an activity is the number of defective parts per million. An example of a performance measure of an organizational unit is return on sales.

Process   A series of activities that are linked to perform a specific objective. For example, the assembly of a television set or the paying of a bill or claim entails several linked activities.

Product life cycle   The period that starts with the initial product specification and ends with the withdrawal of the product from the marketplace. A product life cycle is characterized by certain defined stages, including research, development, introduction, maturity, decline, and abandonment.

Project costing   A cost system that collects information on activities and costs associated with a specific activity, project, or program.

Resource driver   A measure of the quantity of resources consumed by an activity. An example of a resource driver is the percentage of total square feet occupied by an activity. This factor is used to allocate a portion of the cost of operating the facility to the activity.

* Rollout   The steps to be taken in expanding the improvement effort from the pilot stage to full implementation.

* Rolling up   The summing up of lower level detail into higher aggregations such as in adding activity costs together to determine process costs.

* Strategic view of cost   This is one of the three primary views of cost. It represents the futuristic view of cost used by strategic planners, cost engineers and sales management to determine how to impact future costs and improve future profitability. This cost information is used to understand the cost of various cost objects such as products, customers, or channels. Its time focus is on the future, using a combination of both physical and financial measures.

Support costs   Costs of activities not directly associated with production. Examples are the costs of process engineering and purchasing.

Surrogate activity driver   An activity driver that is not descriptive of an activity, but that is closely correlated to the performance of the activity. A surrogate activity driver should reduce measurement costs without significantly increasing the costing bias. The number of production runs, for example, is not descriptive of the material-disbursing activity, but the number of production runs may be used as an activity driver if material disbursements coincide with production runs.

Target cost   A cost calculated by subtracting a desired profit margin from an estimated (or a market-based) price to arrive at a desired production, engineering, or marketing cost. The target cost need not be the expected initial production cost. Instead, it may be the cost that is expected to be achieved during the mature production stage. (See *target costing.*)

Target costing   A method used in analyzing product and process design that involves estimating a target cost and designing the product to meet that cost. (See *target cost.*)

Throughput   The rate of production of a defined process over a stated period of time. Rates may be expressed in terms of units of products, batches produced, dollar turnover, or other meaningful measurements.

* Total quality management (TQM)   Describes an approach to managing an enterprise that focuses on quality to achieve the desired results. Total quality management focuses on meeting or exceeding the needs of customers as well as other stakeholders such as employees, owners and the community as a whole. Continuous improvement is a key element of this approach.

Traceability   The ability to assign a cost directly to an activity or a cost object in an economically feasible way by means of a causal relationship. (See *tracing.*)

Tracing   The assignment of cost to an activity or a cost object using an observable measure of the consumption of resources by an activity. Tracing is generally preferred to allocation if the data exists or can be obtained at a reasonable cost. For example, if a company's cost accounting system captures the cost supplies according to which activities use the supplies, the costs may be traced—as opposed to allocated—to the appropriate activities. Tracing is also called *direct tracing.*

Unit cost   The cost associated with a single unit of a product, including direct costs, indirect costs, traced costs, and allocated costs.

Value-added activity   An activity that is judged to contribute to customer value or satisfy an organizational need. The attribute "value-added" reflects a belief that the activity cannot be eliminated without reducing the quantity, responsiveness, or quality of output required by a customer or organization.

Value analysis   A cost reduction and process improvement tool that utilizes information collected about business processes and examines various attributes of the processes (e.g., diversity, capacity, and complexity) to identify candidates for improvement efforts. (See *activity attributes* and *cost driver.*)

Variable cost   A cost element of an activity that varies with changes in volume of cost drivers and activity drivers. The cost of material handling to an activity, for example, varies according to the number of material deliveries and pick-ups to and from that activity. (See *cost element, fixed cost,* and *activity driver.*)

Waste   Resources consumed by unessential or inefficient activities.

Work center   A physical area of the plant or factory. It consists of one or more resources where a particular product or process is accomplished.

Note: Terms not indicated with an (*) were adapted with permission of the Consortium for Advanced Manufacturing-International (CAM-I) Cost Management System's Glossary of Terms. ©1991 CAM-I, Document #R-91-CMS-06, Version 1.2.

Appendix 3: Recommended Reading

Brimson, James A. and John Antos. *Activity-Based Management for Service Industries, Government Entities, and Nonprofit Organizations*, (New York: John Wiley & Sons, 1994)

Brimson, James A. and Callie Berliner. *Cost Management for Today's Advanced Manufacturing: The CAM-I Conceptual Design*, (Boston, MA: Harvard Business School Press, 1988)

Grieco, Jr., Peter L. and Mel Pilachowski. *Activity-Based Costing*, (Palm Beach Gardens, Florida: PT Publications, 1995)

Hronec, Steven M. *Vital Signs: Using Quality, Time and Cost Performance Measures to Chart Your Company's Future*, (New York: American Management Association, 1993)

Johnson, H. Thomas. *Relevance Regained: From Top-Down to Bottom-Up Empowerment*, (New York: The Free Press, 1992)

Kaplan, Robert S. and David P. Norton. *The Balanced Scorecard: Translating Strategy into Action* (Boston, MA: Harvard Business School Press, 1996)

Miller, John A. *Implementing Activity-Based Management in Daily Operations*, (New York: John Wiley & Sons, 1996)

Player, R. Steven and Roberto Lacerda. *Activity-Based Management: Arthur Andersen's Global Lessons from the ABM Battlefield*, 2nd edition (New York: John Wiley & Sons, 1999)

Player, R. Steven and James W. Gibson Jr. *Activity-Based Management in Wholesale Distribution: Winning the Profitability Battle*, (Washington, D.C: DREF, 1997)

Player, R. Steven and David E. Keys. *Activity-Based Management: Arthur Andersen's Lessons from the ABM Battlefield*, (New York: MasterMedia, 1995)

Shank, John K. and Vijay Govindarajan. *Strategic Cost Management: The New Tool for Competitive Advantage*, (New York: The Free Press, 1993)

White, Timothy S. *The 60 Minute ABC Book: Activity-Based Costing for Operations Management*, (Bedford, Texas: CAM-I, 1997)

Index

C

H

I

J